PRAISE FOR *RESCUERS*

"The tales of courage that Ms. Drucker and Ms. Block uncovered among 'ordinary people' defy the stereotypical image of heroism."
—*The New York Times*

"A timely reminder of the enormous goodness of the human spirit."
—*The Washington Post*

"Awe-inspiring testaments to bravery and goodness."
—*Publishers Weekly*

"A subject of such acutely observed truth…a record of the possibilities of mankind for transcendence."
—*The Houston Post*

"A welcome addition to Holocaust literature."   —*Library Journal*

"*Rescuers* is both a record of good deeds performed under the most trying circumstances imaginable and a guide and inspiration for generations to come. The oppressive yoke of the Holocaust legacy is somewhat lightened through the edifying message of these knights of the spirit."

—Mordecai Paldiel
Director, Department of the Righteous,
Yad Vashem

"An extraordinarily edifying and compelling book that tells us about the human capacity for decency and goodness, even under the most adverse and forbidding of circumstances. A major contribution to the literature of altruism."

—Robert Coles
Professor of Psychiatry and Medical Humanities,
Harvard University

"Gay Block's portraits describe with remarkable psychological insight men and women who risked their lives to hide, protect, and save Jews during World War II. Her color photographs describe a special kind of aristocrat, one with innate dignity and nobility. As a visual document, they are a contemporary link with a moment in history and a reminder that as individuals we bear responsibility for shaping our history. This moving body of work is an affirmation that ordinary people can be heroes."

—Susan Kismaric
Curator of Photography,
Museum of Modern Art

RESCUERS

PORTRAITS OF MORAL COURAGE IN THE HOLOCAUST

RESCUERS

Portraits of Moral Courage
in the Holocaust

Gay Block and Malka Drucker

Prologue by
Cynthia Ozick

Afterword by
Rabbi Harold M. Schulweis

New York

This book benefited from the involvement of the Jewish Foundation for Christian Rescuers, a project of the Anti-Defamation League. Founded in 1987 by Rabbi Harold M. Schulweis, the foundation is dedicated to honoring and supporting Christians who rescued Jews during the Holocaust era. Programs sponsored by the foundation include providing monthly grants, companionship, and understanding to rescuers in need, and teaching through conferences and publications the values of altruism and moral courage as exemplified by the rescuers. For more information, write the Jewish Foundation for Christian Rescuers/ADL, 823 United Nations Plaza, New York, NY 10018.

First published by Holmes & Meier Publishers Inc.

Cataloguing-in-Publication Data
Block, Gay.
    Rescuers: portraits of moral courage in the Holocaust / Gay Block and Malka Drucker; prologue by Cynthia Ozick; afterword by Rabbi Harold M. Schulweis. — 3rd ed.
    p. cm.
    Includes bibliographical references.

    1. Righteous Gentiles in the Holocaust—Biography. 2. World War, 1939–1945—Jews—Rescue. I. Drucker, Malka. II. Title.

D804.65.B56 1988   940.5'18'0922
                                                       QBI98–277

ISBN: 1-57500-062-8
Revised Edition

TV Books, L.L.C.
Publishers serving the television industry.
1619 Broadway, Ninth Floor
New York, NY 10019

Text design and production by Joe Gannon.
Manufactured in the United States by Royal Book Manufacturing.

For Barry and Alison, Ivan and Max

And so we understand that ordinary people are messengers of the Most High. They go about their tasks in holy anonymity. Often, even unknown to themselves. Yet, if they had not been there, if they had not said what they said or did what they did, it would not be the way it is now. We would not be the way we are now. Never forget that you too yourself may be a messenger. Perhaps even one whose errand extends over several lifetimes.

—LAWRENCE KUSHNER
Honey from the Rock

CONTENTS

ACKNOWLEDGMENTS

The story of how this book took shape and became a reality is a book in itself, with patience and persistence among the chief lessons we learned. What often kept us going were the following people who believed in the project and encouraged us. The rescuers themselves begin the list, who by their example of bravery, intelligence, and compassion not only gave us our story but our inspiration.

Rabbi Harold M. Schulweis, founder of the Jewish Foundation for Christian Rescuers, a project of the Anti-Defamation League (ADL), and Dr. Eva Fogelman, its first director, provided the initial direction for the project. E. Robert Goodkind, first chairman of the foundation, assured the foundation's support for the book. Peter Cundill and Associates, particularly Ursula Kummel, also generously helped in the funding of the project.

Translators in every country served as navigators and companions during our long days of interviews. Thanks go to Mimi Gilboa Yarden, Lusia Schimmel, Debbie Klein, and Ivan Vranetic (Israel); Maria Morgens (United States); Sarah Perry (France); Achsah Vissel (the Netherlands); Erna Seykorova (Czechoslovakia); Gunther Schroeter and Frauke Neumaier (Germany); and Stephane Gerson (Belgium). Bob Pann and Maya Stepvan helped translate videotapes. In addition, Danny Rogovsky, Denise Siekierski, Miroslav Karny, Dr. Jindrich Flusser, Christian and Martine Gilain, David and Jacqueline Inowlocki, Nico Vissel, Ute Klingeman, Gitta Bauer, Robert Goldmann at the ADL in Paris, and the Israeli Embassy in Bonn all enriched and eased our travels with their help in arranging appointments, accompanying us on interviews, or simply providing a good idea at the right time. Special thanks go to Dr. Mordecai Paldiel, director of the Righteous Among the Nations at Yad Vashem, Alan Bayer of the ADL in New York, and David Szonyi and Diana Stein of the Jewish Foundation for Christian Rescuers.

We are grateful for the scholars we met who helped to deepen our understanding of rescue, particularly Dr. Henry Mason, professor at Tulane University; Pierre Sauvage, filmmaker of *Weapons of the Spirit*; Myriam Abramowicz, filmmaker of *As If It Were Yesterday*; and Doctors Samuel and Pearl Oliner, authors of *The Altruistic Personality*. We appreciate Adaire Klein and the Simon Wiesenthal Center Library for research assistance in the preparation of the maps.

We are grateful for the expertise and support of darkroom assistants Cathy Opie, Sherri Zuckerman, Craig Skinner, and Karen Ritvo, and for Kim Kahn's sensitive transcribing of the videotapes. Thanks also to Andrew Roth for rephotographing rescuers' wartime material in Israel.

Publishing colleagues Ed Marquand, Liz Van Doren, Willa Perlman, Barbara Karlin, and Andrea Brown generously gave suggestions and advice. Special mention goes to the late Donald Hutter, who was among the first to believe in this book. Others who offered support and services include Magdalena Salazar, Joe Natterson, Gus Block, Steve Silverstein, Ed Klagsbrun, Laurence Miller, Howard Greenberg, Anne W. Tucker, Cynthia Macdonald, and Susan Kismaric.

For the original edition, we were fortunate to have the excellent design and packaging services of Curatorial Assistance. Special thanks to Wendell Eckholm for his enthusiasm and editorial expertise, to Graham Howe for his original belief in the project, and to Karen Bowers for her creative design. The partnership became complete when Miriam Holmes, at Holmes & Meier, acquired the original book and provided the astute, sensitive, and challenging services of editor Sheila Friedling, who has our profound gratitude for helping us to create the book we hoped it would become.

Francine Chermak, Bonnie Strull, Barry Block, Max Drucker, Alison Block, Ivan Drucker, Pam Treiber, and Sidney Shlenker, all family members, became part of this book by contributing intellectual, emotional, and financial assistance. To our families and friends we offer thanks for listening to our stories, sympathizing with our struggles, and remaining steadfast in your certainty that we would make good our promise to the rescuers—that their lives and deeds would be remembered.

The following is a partial list of the institutions exhibiting Rescuers:
Museum of Modern Art, New York
Museum of Fine Arts, Houston, Texas
Corcoran Gallery of Art, Washington, D.C.
Santa Monica College Photography Gallery, California
Jewish Community Center of Cleveland, Ohio
Cincinnati Public Library, Ohio
Lawton Gallery, University of Wisconsin, Green Bay
Presentation House, Vancouver, British Columbia
Occidental College, Los Angeles, California

Michener Art Museum, Doylestown, Pennsylvania
Tufts University, Medford, Massachusetts
Virginia Beach Center for the Arts, Virginia
Des Moines Fine Art Center, Iowa
Charach-Epstein Museum Gallery, West Bloomfield, Michigan
Levis Jewish Community Center, Boca Raton, Florida
Hollywood Art and Culture Center, Hollywood, Florida
Photography Hall of Fame, Kirkpatrick Center, Oklahoma City
Texas A & M University, College Station, Texas
Judah L. Magnes Museum, Berkeley, California
Witte Museum, San Antonio, Texas
Mead Museum, Amherst, Massachusetts
Goethe Institute/Schatten Gallery, Emory University, Atlanta, Georgia
Museum at Stony Brook, New York
Mahn-und Gedenkstätte, Düsseldorf, Germany
Volkshochschule Dorsten, Recklinghausen, Germany
KZ Gedenkstätte Mittelbau-Dora, Nordhausen, Germany
Gallery F15, Moss, Norway
KZ Gedenkstätte Buchenwald, Weimar-Buchenwald, Germany
Melanchthon Akademie, Köln, Germany

PROLOGUE

Cynthia Ozick

There is a story about Clare Boothe Luce complaining that she was bored with hearing about the Holocaust. A Jewish friend of hers said he perfectly understood her sensitivity to the matter; in fact, he had the same sense of repetitiousness and fatigue, hearing so often about the crucifixion.
— Herbert Gold, *Selfish Like Me*

Of the great European murder of six million Jews, and the murderers themselves, there is little left to say. The barbaric years when Jews were hunted down for sport in the middle of the twentieth century have their hellish immortality, their ineradicable infamy, and will inflame the nightmares—and (perhaps) harrow the conscience—of the human race until the sun burns out and takes our poor earth-speck with it. Of the murder and the murderers everything is known: how it was done, who did it, who helped, where it was done, and when and why. Especially why: the hatred of a civilization that teaches us to say *No* to hatred.

Three "participant" categories of the Holocaust are commonly named: murderers, victims, bystanders. Imagination demands a choosing. Which, of this entangled trio, are we? Which are we most likely to have become? Probably it is hardest of all to imagine ourselves victims. After all, we were here and not there. Or we were Gentiles and not Jews or Gypsies. Or we were not yet born. But if we had already been born, if we were there and not here, if we were Jews and not Gentiles . . .

"If" is the travail of historians and philosophers, not of the ordinary human article. What we can be sure of without contradiction—we can be sure of it because we *are* the ordinary human article—is that, difficult as it might be to imagine ourselves among the victims, it is not in us even to begin to think of ourselves as likely murderers. The "banality of evil" is a catchword of our generation; but no, it is an unusual, an exceptional, thing to volunteer for the SS; to force aged Jews to their knees to scrub the gutter with their beards; to empty Zyklon B canisters into the hole in the roof of the gas chamber; to enact those thousand thousand atrocities that lead to the obliteration of a people and a culture.

The victims take our pity and our horror, and whatever else we can, in our shame, cede to their memory. But they do not puzzle us. It does not puzzle us that the blood of the innocent cries up from the ground—how could it be otherwise? Even if humanity refuses to go on remembering, the voices crushed in the woods and under the fresh pavements of Europe press upward. The new plants that cover the places where corpses were buried in mass pits carry blood in their dew. Basement-whispers trouble the new blocks of flats that cover the streets where the flaming Warsaw Ghetto fell. The heavy old sideboards of the thirties that once stood in Jewish dining rooms in certain neighborhoods of Berlin and Vienna are in Catholic and Protestant dining rooms now, in neighborhoods where there are no longer any Jews; the great carved legs of these increasingly valued antiques groan and remember the looting. The books that were thrown onto bonfires in the central squares of every German city still send up their flocks of quivering phantom letters.

All that—the looting, the shooting, the herding, the forced marches, the gassing, the torching of synagogues, the cynicism, the mendacity, the shamelessness, the truncheons, the bloodthirstiness, the fanaticism, the opportunism, the Jews of Europe as prey, their dehumanization, the death factories, the obliteration of a civilization, the annihilation of a people—all that it is possible to study, if not to assimilate. Pious Jews, poor Jews, secular Jews, universalist Jews, baptized Jews, Jews who were storekeepers, or doctors, or carpenters, or professors, or teamsters, Jewish infants and children—all annihilated. Thousands upon thousands of Jewish libraries and schools looted and destroyed. Atrocity spawns an aftermath—perhaps an afterlife. In the last four decades the documents and the testimonies have been heaped higher and higher—yet a gash has been cut in the world's brain that cannot be healed by memorial conferences, or monuments, or even books like this one. Lamentation for the martyred belongs now to the history of cruelty and to the earth. There is no paucity of the means to remember; there may be a paucity of the will to remember. Still, we know what we think of the murders and the murderers. We are not at a loss to know how to regard them.

But what of the bystanders? They were not the criminals, after all. For the bystanders we should feel at least the pale warmth of recognition—call it self-recognition. And nowadays it is the bystanders whom we most notice, though at the time, while the crimes were in progress, they seemed the least noticeable. We notice them now because they are the ones we can most readily identify with. They are the ones imagination can most readily accommodate. A bystander is like you and me, the ordinary human article—what normal man or woman or adolescent runs to commit public atrocities? The luck of the draw (the odds of finding oneself in the majority) saves the bystander from direct victimhood: the Nuremberg "racial" laws, let us say, are what exempt the bystander from deportation. The bystander is, by definition, not a Jew or a Gypsy. The bystander stays home, safe enough if compliant enough. The bystander cannot be charged with taking part in any evil act; the bystander only watches as the evil proceeds. One by one, and suddenly all at once, the Jewish families disappear from their apartments in building after building, in city after city. The neighbors watch them go. One by one, and suddenly all at once, the Jewish children disappear from school. Their classmates resume doing their sums.

The neighbors are decent people—decent enough for ordinary purposes. They cannot be blamed for not being heroes. A hero—like a murderer—is an exception and (to be coarsely direct) an abnormality, a kind of social freak. No one ought to be expected to become a hero. Not that bystanders are, taken collectively, altogether blameless. In the Germany of the thirties it was they—because there were so many of them—who created the norm. The conduct of the bystanders—again because there were so many of them—defined what was common and what was uncommon, what was exceptional and what was unexceptional, what was heroic and what was quotidian. If the bystanders in all their numbers had not been so docile, if they had not been so conciliatory, or, contrariwise, if they had not been so "inspired" (by slogans and rabble-rousers and uniforms and promises of national glory), if they had not acquiesced both through the ballot box and alongside the parades—if, in short, they had not been *so many*—the subject of heroism would never have had to arise.

When a whole population takes on the status of bystander, the victims are without allies; the criminals, unchecked, are strengthened; and only then do we need to speak of heroes. When a field is filled from end to end with sheep, a stag stands out. When a continent is filled from end to end with the compliant, we learn what heroism is. And alas for the society that requires heroes.

Most of us, looking back, and identifying as we mainly do with the bystanders— because it is the most numerous category, into which simple demographic likelihood thrusts us; or because surely it is the

---

easiest category, the most recognizably human, if not the most humane—will admit to some perplexity, a perplexity brought on by hindsight. Taken collectively, as I dared to do a moment ago, the bystanders are culpable. But taking human beings "collectively" is precisely what we are obliged not to do. Then consider the bystanders not as a group, not as a stereotype, but one by one. If the bystander is the ordinary human article, as we have agreed, what can there be to puzzle us? This one, let us say, is a good and zealous hater (no one can deny that hating belongs to the ordinary human article), encouraged by epaulets, posters, flashy rhetoric, and pervasive demagoguery. And this one is an envious malcontent, lustful for a change of leadership. And this one is a simple patriot. And this one, unemployed, is a dupe of the speechmakers. Such portraits, both credible and problematical, are common enough. But let us concede that most of the bystanders were quiet citizens who wanted nothing more than to get on with their private lives: a portrait entirely palatable to you and me. The ordinary human article seeks nothing more complex than the comforts of indifference to public clamor of any kind. Indifference is a way of sheltering oneself from evil; who would interpret such unaggressive sheltering as a contribution to evil? The ordinary human article hardly looks to get mixed up in active and wholesale butchery of populations; what rational person would want to accuse the bystander—who has done no more than avert her eyes—of a hardness of heart in any way approaching that of the criminals? That would be a serious lie—a distortion both of fact and of psychological understanding.

Yet it is the nature of indifference itself that bewilders. How is it that indifference, which on its own does no apparent or immediate positive harm, ends by washing itself in the very horrors it means to have nothing to do with? Hoping to confer no hurt, indifference finally grows lethal; why is that? Can it be that indifference, ostensibly passive, harbors an unsuspected robustness? The act of turning toward—while carrying a club—is an act of brutality; but the act of turning away, however empty-handed and harmlessly, remains nevertheless an *act*. The whole truth may be that the idea of human passivity is nothing but the illusion of wistful mortals; and that waking into the exigencies of our own time—whichever way we turn, toward or away—implies action. To be born is to be compelled to act.

One of the most curious (and mephitic) powers of indifference is its retroactive capacity: it is possible to be indifferent *nunc pro tunc.* I am thinking of a few sentences I happened to be shown the other day: they were from the pen of a celebrated author who was commenting on a piece of so-called Holocaust writing. "These old events," she complained, "can rake you over only so much, and then you long for a bit of satire on it all. Like so many others of my generation"—she was a young adult during the forties—"who had nothing to do with any of it, I've swallowed all the guilt I can bear, and if I'm going to be lashed, I intend to save my skin for more recent troubles in the world."

Never mind the odd protestation of innocence where nothing has been charged—what secret unquiet lies within this fraying conscience? What is odder still is that a statement of retroactive indifference is represented as a commitment to present compassion. As for present compassion, does anyone doubt that there is enough contemporary suffering to merit one's full notice? Besides, a current indifference to "these old events" seems harmless enough now; the chimneys of Dachau and Birkenau and Belsen have been cold for the last forty-five years. But does this distinguished figure—a voice of liberalism as well as noteworthy eloquence—suppose that indifference to "old events" frees one for attention to new ones? In fact, indifference to past suffering is a sure sign that there will be indifference to present suffering. Jaded feelings have little to do with the staleness of any event. To be "jaded" is to decline to feel at all.

And that is perhaps the central point about indifference, whether retroactive or current. Indifference is not so much a gesture of looking away—of choosing to be passive—as it is an active disinclination to feel. Indifference shuts down the humane, and does it deliberately, with all the strength deliberateness demands. Indifference is as determined—and as forcefully muscular—as any blow. For the victims on their way to the chimneys, there is scarcely anything to choose between a thug with an uplifted truncheon and the decent citizen who will not lift up his eyes.

We have spoken of three categories: criminal, victim, bystander. There is a fourth category—so minuscule that statistically it vanishes. Fortunately it is not a category that can be measured by number—its measure is metaphysical, and belongs to the sublime. "Whoever saves a single life," says the Talmud, "is as one who has saved an entire world." This is the category of those astounding souls who refused to stand by as their neighbors were being hauled away to the killing sites. They were willing to see, to judge, to decide. Not only did they not avert their eyes—they set out to rescue. They are the heroes of Nazified Europe. They are Polish, Italian, Romanian, Russian, Hungarian, French, Yugoslavian, Swiss, Swedish, Dutch, Spanish, German. They are Catholic and Protestant. They are urban and rural; educated and uneducated; sophisticated and simple; they include nuns and Socialists. And whatever they did, they did at the risk of their lives.

It is typical of all of them to deny any heroism. "It was only decent," they say. But no: most people are decent; the bystanders were decent. The rescuers are somehow raised above the merely decent. When the rescuers declare that heroism is beside the point, it is hard to agree with them.

There is, however, another view, one that takes the side of the rescuers. Under the steady Jerusalem sun stands a low and somber building known as Yad Vashem: a memorial to the Six Million, a place of mourning, a substitute for the missing headstones of the victims; there are no graveyards for human beings ground into bone meal and flown into evanescent smoke. But Yad Vashem is also a grove of celebration and honor: a grand row of trees, one for each savior, marks the valor of the Christian rescuers of Europe, called the Righteous Among the Nations. Mordecai Paldiel, the director of the Department for the Righteous at Yad Vashem, writing in the *Jerusalem Post* not long ago, offered some arresting reflections on the "normality" of goodness:

> We are somehow determined to view these benefactors as heroes: hence the search for underlying motives. The Righteous persons, however, consider themselves as anything but heroes, and regard their behavior during the Holocaust as quite normal. How to resolve this enigma?
>
> For centuries we have undergone a brain-washing process by philosophers who emphasized man's despicable character, highlighting his egoistic and evil disposition at the expense of other attributes. Wittingly or not, together with Hobbes and Freud, we accept the proposition that man is essentially an aggressive being, bent on destruction, involved principally with himself, and only marginally interested in the needs of others....
>
> Goodness leaves us gasping, for we refuse to recognize it as a natural human attribute. So off we go on a long search for some

hidden motivation, some extraordinary explanation, for such peculiar behavior.

Evil is, by contrast, less painfully assimilated. There is no comparable search for the reasons for its constant manifestation (although in earlier centuries theologians pondered this issue).

We have come to terms with evil. Television, movies, and the printed word have made evil, aggression, and egotism household terms and unconsciously acceptable to the extent of making us immune to displays of evil. There is a danger that the evil of the Holocaust will be absorbed in a similar manner, that is, explained away as further confirmation of man's inherent disposition to wrongdoing. It confirms our visceral feeling that man is an irredeemable beast, who needs to be constrained for his own good.

In searching for an explanation of the motivations of the Righteous Among the Nations, are we not really saying: what was wrong with them? Are we not, in a deeper sense, implying that their behavior was something other than normal?. . . Is acting benevolently and altruistically such an outlandish and unusual type of behavior, supposedly at odds with man's inherent character, as to justify a meticulous search for explanations? Or is it conceivable that such behavior is as natural to our psychological constitution as the egoistic one we accept so matter-of-factly?

It is Mr. Paldiel's own goodness that leaves me gasping. How I want to assent to his thesis! How alluring it is! His thesis asserts that it is the rescuers who are in possession of the reality of human nature, not the bystanders; it is the rescuers who are the ordinary human article. "In a place where there are no human beings, *be* one"—it is apparent that the rescuers were born to embody this rabbinic text. It is not, they say, that they are exceptions; it is that they are human. They are not to be considered "extraordinary," "above the merely decent."

Yet their conduct emphasizes—exemplifies—the exceptional.

For instance:

Giorgio Perlasca, an Italian from Padua, had a job in the Spanish Embassy in Budapest. When the Spanish envoy fled before the invading Russians, Perlasca substituted the Spanish "Jorge" for the Italian "Giorgio" and passed himself off as the Spanish *chargé d'affaires*. He carried food and powdered milk to safe houses under the Spanish flag, where several hundred Jews at a time found a haven. He issued protective documents that facilitated the escape of Jews with Spanish passes. "I began to feel like a fish in water," he said of his life as an impostor: the sole purpose of his masquerade was to save Jews. And he saved thousands.

Bert Bochove was a Dutch upholsterer who lived with his wife and two children in a large apartment over his shop, in a town not far from Amsterdam. At first he intended to help only his wife's best friend, who was Jewish; her parents had already been deported. Bochove constructed a hiding place in the attic, behind a false wall. Eventually thirty-seven Jews were hidden there.

In a Dominican convent near Vilna, seven nuns and their mother superior sheltered a number of Jews who had escaped from the ghetto, including some poets and writers. The fugitives were disguised in nuns' habits. The sisters did not stop at hiding Jews: they scoured the countryside for weapons to smuggle into the ghetto.

Who will say that the nuns, the upholsterer, and the impostor are not extraordinary in their altruism, their courage, the electrifying boldness of their imaginations? How many nuns have we met who would think of dressing Jewish poets in wimples? How many upholsterers do we know who would actually design and build a false wall? Who among us would dream of fabricating a fake diplomatic identity in order to save Jewish lives? Compassion, it is clear, sharpens intuition and augments imagination.

For me, the rescuers are not the ordinary human article. Nothing would have been easier than for each and every one of them to have remained a bystander, like all those millions of their countrymen in the nations of Europe. It goes without saying that the bystanders, especially in the occupied lands, had troubles enough of their own, and hardly needed to go out of their way to acquire new burdens and frights. I do not—cannot—believe that human beings are, without explicit teaching, naturally or intrinsically altruistic. I do not believe, either, that they are naturally vicious, though they can be trained to be. The truth (as with most truths) seems to be somewhere in the middle: most people are born bystanders. The ordinary human article does not want to be disturbed by extremes of any kind—not by risks, or adventures, or unusual responsibility.

And those who undertook the risks, those whose bravery steeped them in perilous contingencies, those whose moral strength urged them into heart-stopping responsibility—what (despite their demurrals) are they really if not the heroes of our battered world? What other name can they possibly merit? In the Europe of the most savage decade of the twentieth century, not to be a bystander was the choice of an infinitesimal few. These few are more substantial than the multitudes from whom they distinguished themselves; and it is from these undeniably heroic and principled few that we can learn the full resonance of civilization.

RESCUERS

PORTRAITS OF MORAL COURAGE IN THE HOLOCAUST

INTRODUCTION

Malka Drucker

Whoever sheltered or even simply assisted a Jew risked terrifying punishment. In this regard it is only right to remember that a few thousand Jews survived through the entire Hitlerian period, hidden in Germany and Poland in convents, cellars, and attics by citizens who were courageous, compassionate, and above all sufficiently intelligent to observe for years the strictest discretion.

—Primo Levi, *The Drowned and the Saved* *

I first became aware of Holocaust rescuers during a visit in 1979 to Yad Vashem, the Holocaust memorial in Jerusalem. Carob trees flanked a path called the Avenue of the Righteous, and on a small marker beside each tree was the name of a person who had rescued Jews. I assumed these people were dead and the trees were their memorial. Ten years later, when my rabbi and mentor, Harold Schulweis, created the Jewish Foundation for Christian Rescuers, I discovered that the rescuers were still alive. Because I write books for young people, Rabbi Schulweis suggested that I write a children's book about these special people and their remarkable stories.

The idea appealed to me, but at first I didn't know why. Many who study the rescuers are personally connected to the subject. Some are survivors who were given help, others are children of survivors, yet I was born at the end of the war and nobody in my family knew anyone who was killed in Europe. When I discussed the project with my friend, portrait photographer Gay Block, she responded with the same interest in the subject, wanting to meet and photograph the rescuers. As Jews we felt a responsibility to know about the history of our people, but after our first two interviews, one with Zofia Baniecka, whose empathic spirit spoke to us even though we had no common language, and one with the kind and gentle Bert Bochove, we knew that our reason for meeting the rescuers was not simply to learn history. We wanted to meet more people like them, people who had risked their lives to save strangers, and we hoped that they could teach us about courage and compassion.

The original idea grew into an extensive, impressionistic study of

---

*All works cited in this book are listed in the Select Bibliography in the back of the book.

Holocaust rescuers that has resulted in this book, a film, and a traveling exhibit of the portraits. We traveled through eight countries, including the United States, to interview 105 rescuers from eleven different countries.

We felt compelled to meet these people while it was still possible. First-hand accounts would help us to understand an incomprehensible time, to give us a sense of what it felt like to live under a brutal regime or occupation. Lawrence Langer, in his book *Holocaust Testimonies: The Ruins of Memory*, describes levels of memory reflected in testimonies from survivors. "Common memory" is chronological, ordered, and detached from feeling, but "deep memory" makes possible the intense reliving of past events that only a participant or witness can experience; it is the direct engagement with the terrible past to which "the sympathetic power of the imagination" responds, and which gives us an important understanding not only of that inexplicable time but of its impact on the personalities of the rescuers. Because the rescuer often remembers that time more vividly than any other in his or her life, each interview offers a personal, emotional picture of the Holocaust. When Ivan Vranetic described how he, at seventeen, carried a little girl on his shoulders for ten kilometers in Yugoslavia to protect her from waist-deep snow, youthful strength shone in sixty-year-old eyes even as he cried, remembering her frostbitten toes.

Dr. Eva Fogelman, the first director of the Jewish Foundation for Christian Rescuers, gave us the names of rescuers she had interviewed as part of her doctoral research. Since several were in Southern California, where we live, we began our work there. This sampling would prove to be representative of the range of rescue we would encounter: John Weidner formed a rescue network that saved more than eight hundred; Margot Lawson was active in the Dutch underground; Bert Bochove hid thirty-six in his house; Irene Opdyke saved eighteen in Poland under the nose of a German major; and Jacob Oversloot kept his business partner and his wife in his home for two years. "I told them to take off their stars and we'd go for walks together," he said.

A conference in 1984 sponsored by the U.S. Holocaust Memorial Council found a fresh group of rescuers in the United States and Canada. Not all of them had been acknowledged by Yad Vashem, but the survivors they had saved, learning of the conference, submitted their names, and we had access to this list. We also depended upon Yad Vashem's lists, but because it keeps records only of the date the rescuer received his or her medal, not whether the rescuer is still alive, we needed help in updating the information.

The following summer we went to Israel where Dr. Fogelman had furnished us with the names of some thirty Yad Vashem recipients living all over the country. Our prearranged translator and navigator set up appointments for us, sometimes three interviews a day, and we needed at least one translator at each interview to translate from Hebrew or Polish. With Mihael Michaelov, his friend Ivan Vranetic translated from Bulgarian to Hebrew as he spoke, and then someone translated to English. It was the same procedure with Amfian Gerasimov, who spoke Russian.

Denise Siekierski, a French Jew who had worked in the Resistance, spent half the year in Israel as a volunteer at Yad Vashem. Her mission was to make current the file on French rescuers, while finding and honoring new ones. She led us to most of the rescuers we met in France, most notably Emilie Guth and Ermine Orsi, with whom she worked during the war.

The Netherlands holds the record for the most Yad Vashem recipients, but our translator and navigator in Holland, a young Jewish woman, wanted to find undiscovered rescuers for us. So she put an announcement in the weekly Jewish paper asking survivors to supply the names of their rescuers. This single ad produced over thirty-five rescuers, most of whom were unknown by Yad Vashem.

We went to Czechoslovakia because we wanted to visit a friend who was working there. With the help of Miroslav Karny, a Czech historian and survivor, we met two rescuers in Prague, Libuse Fries and Antonin Kalina. Fries had offered significant help to our translator and her brother, and Kalina had saved 1,300 children in Buchenwald. Neither had been honored by Yad Vashem because Czechoslovakia does not have diplomatic relations with Israel. On the other hand, Yad Vashem provided us with most of our interviews in Germany, because the Israeli Embassy in Bonn had recently honored a large number of rescuers, although at least half of the awards were posthumous. Myriam Abramowicz, the creator of *As If It Were Yesterday*, a documentary film recounting the efforts to save Belgian Jews, gave us her list of Belgian rescuers, and David Inowlocki, himself a hidden Jewish child, set up our appointments and accompanied us on many interviews.

The rescuers welcomed us warmly, offered us food and drink, and tried to help us carry the heavy photographic equipment. It felt like visiting doting relatives. Their easy generosity cheered us, and after each interview we felt we had made a new friend. Living in cities requires being wary of the stranger; meanness prevails more often than goodness. The Torah calls it "causeless hatred." The rescuers, with causeless goodness, balanced the scale.

Each interview took a minimum of two hours, longer if it had to be translated, and we videotaped each one. The rescuers were gracious hosts, tolerated our filling their rooms with tripods and cameras, and were patient with our questions, but sometimes they shook their heads and said, "You don't understand. How can people of your generation understand?" In a letter to us six months after we interviewed him, Dutch rescuer Arnold Douwes wrote:

> I cannot push aside the thought that two American ladies cannot possibly have any idea of what happened in the Netherlands between spring 1940 and spring 1945. The time of the Nazi boots. How I hated those boots! We heard them everywhere, together with those despised songs with which those creatures, whose legs were stuck into those boots, contaminated the cities, towns, villages, and countryside.

We did our best to understand an incomprehensible time; at least we tried to share their pain. Some told us they had stayed awake the night before, thinking about the war, in preparation for the interview. We worried about leaving a rescuer who lived alone, close to evening, with memories of the Holocaust freshly stirred. At the end of the interviews, Gay would ask them, almost apologetically, to pose for a portrait. To us, it felt superfluous, even frivolous, compared to what they had been talking about. To them, they couldn't understand why someone would want their photograph.

Rescuers ranged from those who saved a single life to well-known heroes such as Raoul Wallenberg, who saved as many as 100,000; Père Marie Benoît, who issued false papers to 4,000 in France; and Pastor André Trocmé, who led his village of Le Chambon to shelter 5,000 Jews. We interviewed Sebastian Mendés, son of Aristides de Sousa Mendés, Portuguese ambassador to France during the war. He wept as he told us how his father, after being forbidden by the Portuguese government to issue visas to Jews, had issued 10,000 visas in Bordeaux before being recalled back to Portugal. There he was stripped of his rank and ostracized; in 1954 he died in a pauper's hospital.

These rescuers demonstrated extraordinary daring and brilliant leadership, and are famous because of the great numbers they saved. However, we regard people such as Alex and Mela Roslan, who, by hiding three Jewish boys from the Warsaw Ghetto in their apartment, risked instantaneous death for themselves and their children, as no less worthy of honor. All accounts of rescue, regardless of the number of people actually saved, provide the only light in the darkness of the war that claimed 6 million Jews, over two-thirds of world Jewry.

Who were these people who did not say, "That's not my problem"? Why were they different from others? Were they afraid? Why did they take such great risks? What has life been like for them since the war? Did they remain altruists? Have they been changed by their wartime experience? What did their deeds mean to them and to their children? The rescuers' moving narratives reveal the complexity of the answers to these questions.

Rescuers do not easily yield the answer to why they had the strength to act righteously in a time of savagery. It remains a mystery, perhaps a miracle. Many helped strangers, some saved friends and lovers. Some had humane upbringings, others did not. Some were educated, others were barely literate. They weren't all religious, they weren't all brave. What they did share, however, was compassion, empathy, an intolerance of injustice, and an ability to endure risk beyond what one wants to imagine.

Louisa Steenstra watched as her husband's ear was torn off by a Nazi's German shepherd and then helplessly witnessed his murder. Emilie Guth was carrying the child of her Jewish lover, whom she was unable to marry during the war, when he was killed by French collaborators. As Claudine Gilain said, "At such times it is normal to be afraid." They are people who lived in the world and allowed themselves to be connected to those around them. They did not distinguish between "us" and "them"; instead they identified with the victim. When so many looked the other way, the rescuers kept their eyes open, and this character trait still distinguishes their lives in old age. Countess von Maltzan rails against Israel's current politics, and Andrée Herscovici decries South Africa.

Samuel and Pearl Oliner, in their five-year study of the altruistic personality, examined the personalities of the rescuers in a "social psychological orientation, which assumes that behavior is best explained as the result of an interaction between personal and external social, or situational, factors. We view an altruistic behavior as the outcome of a decision-making process in which the internal characteristics of actors as well as the external environments in which they find themselves influence each other." The "internal characteristics" that many rescuers possessed began at home, where, for example, Emilie Guth remembered seeing her mother slide money under the tablecloth of a poor family. Or Marion Pritchard's upbringing in a family that respected its children and taught them that we are all responsible for one another. When those women were confronted by the "external environment" of Nazi oppression, they made the "decision" to help.

Nehama Tec, a professor of sociology who has researched compassion and altruism, explained at a conference held to examine the experience of children hidden during the war that rescuers come from "all walks of life, all religious and political affiliations, and all family configurations."* Although she has found no pattern here, she sees "a set of interdependent characteristics and conditions" that Holocaust rescuers share:

1. They don't blend into their communities. This makes them less controlled by their environments and more inclined to act on their own principles.
2. They are independent people and they know it. They do what they feel they must do, what is right, and the right thing is to help others.
3. They have a long history of doing good deeds. (Tec has interviewed child survivors, whose rescuers were usually mature people. Our rescuers were much younger, most not over twenty-five during the war, so they had little chance earlier to demonstrate this characteristic.)
4. Because they have done the right thing for a long time, it doesn't seem extraordinary to them. If you consider something your duty, you do it automatically.
5. They choose to help without rational consideration.
6. They have universalistic perceptions that transcend race and ethnicity. They can respond to the needy and helpless because they identify with victims of injustice.

Unlike social scientists, however, we weren't looking for patterns or

---

*The Conference on the Hidden Child, sponsored by the Anti-Defamation League, was held in New York on 12-14 May, 1991.

categories—we wanted to understand the individual rescuer. Categorizing the rescuer can be misleading; it separates us from reality. We may prefer to believe that these people, examined collectively, possess incomprehensible heroism or goodness, because then we don't have to speculate how we would behave in similar circumstances. Perhaps it is easier to acknowledge evil because we do not want to know that we have the same capacity for goodness.

To understand these people as no different from us, possessing the same doubts, fears, and prejudices, raises the uncomfortable question, "Would I do what they did?" Can any of us imagine having a guest in our home for two days, two weeks, two years? It might be difficult if the guest were a friend, much less a stranger, or perhaps someone we didn't like. And these were no ordinary guests. Keeping them required ingenious strategies of deception on the part of the rescuers as well as months or years of unrelenting physical hardship, danger, and stress. If their "hospitality" were discovered or betrayed, the rescuers faced torture, imprisonment, and death. Took Heroma and her husband hid for a year a woman that neither of them found stimulating, but they felt it only right to have dinner with her every night. When asked to take in another Jew, a well-known intellectual, they decided, since they had space for only one person, that they had no right to choose one life over another, so they kept the woman throughout the war.

Although our sample of rescuers was random in that we usually knew little about them before our meeting, we believe this book conveys the major issues of Holocaust rescue not by means of objective analysis but through personal narratives, lived experiences as remembered and recounted by the rescuers. Told in the rescuers' words, the stories reveal the interaction of social and psychological factors that led these people to intervene on behalf of Jews.

When asked why they risked their lives to save others, the rescuers gave few clues. Christine Hilsum-Beuckens laughed and said, "I'm just a compulsive helper. How could I not?" Yet for her and others we interviewed, close association with Jews was a key motivation. One-fourth of the people we interviewed were either married to Jews, were friends of the Jews they rescued, or worked with them. Wilhelm Tarnawski was a Polish Catholic who eloped with Maria, a Jew, when they were teenagers. He saved not only her, but together they successfully hid eighteen members of her family in their homes in Gawja. He told us that if the Germans were going to kill him for hiding Maria, he might as well try to save her whole family.

Marion Pritchard was a student in the school of social work in Amsterdam when her analyst, a Jew, went into hiding. She helped form a network of students to provide him and other Jews with food and shelter. Bert Bochove's wife, Annie, had made a Jewish friend when she was in a sanatorium recovering from tuberculosis. Years later her friend, Henny Juliard, asked to stay with them, and that was the beginning of the Bochoves' hiding thirty-six Jews for three years.

Alex Roslan sold textiles and many of his customers were Jews. When the Nazis created the Warsaw Ghetto, Alex lost much of his business and was curious about what happened to the Jews. So he asked someone to take him through the Warsaw Ghetto, where he saw so much suffering that he came home to tell his wife, Mela, that they had to do something. Irena Landau's father worked for a wealthy Jewish factory owner when the Nazis confiscated his business, and he came to her for help.

Another 25 percent of the rescuers we met did not necessarily know Jews personally, but they felt protective of them because of religious dogma. John Weidner, a Seventh-Day Adventist in the Netherlands and son of a minister, knew the Jews as the Chosen People. Pieter Miedema and Marc Donadille were both Protestant ministers who felt it their Christian responsibility to save Jews. Marie-Rose Gineste worked with the Catholic underground to encourage priests to resist the deportations and to promote resistance in their church. Gustav Collet worked in Belgium with Abbé André, who saved hundreds of Jewish children.

Although not all of the families were religious (only 15 percent believed that family background was their primary reason for helping Jews), the great majority of rescuers we interviewed described their families positively as having a tradition of tolerance and altruism. Andrée Herscovici told of her liberal, bourgeois parents helping refugees during the Spanish Civil War. Gertruda Babilinska cried when she remembered her mother teaching her to love others as herself. Since most of the people we met were in their teens or early twenties during the war, many still lived at home. Tina Strobos, along with her parents and grandmother, hid Jews in the house they shared, and Helena Orchon and Marguerite Mulder also helped their parents in rescue efforts.

In some cases, the motivation to rescue was more political, especially in Western European countries where Germany had been mistrusted for generations. Claudine Gilain, from a French Socialist family, spoke bitterly of seeing German cruelty in the Alsace region during World War I. Gilain also was motivated because she was a Huguenot in a primarily Catholic country. Zofia Baniecka, the daughter of a Polish sculptor who was part of Warsaw's intelligentsia, remembers hearing in her home early concern about Nazism. Tina Strobos, Fritz Heine, and Antonín Kalina came from families with a long tradition of anti-Fascist, pro-Socialist affiliations. Liberal Germans also despised Nazism from its inception. Reared in an intellectual home in Frankfurt and educated in political science, Gertrud Luckner traveled all over her country to enlist young Germans, especially college students, to fight against Hitler.

Unlike the bystanders who chose to accept life's unfairness, the rescuers adopted an activist, aggressive stance when confronted by Nazi oppression of Jews. Whether his or her opposition stemmed from religious belief, a political ideology, a family tradition of social activism, or personal experience, almost every rescuer was unusually intolerant of human injustice. A few rescuers were awakened to injustice because of their dysfunctional families. Ala Sztajnert's father, a vicious anti-Semite, beat her. She sought revenge by saving Jews. Countess von Maltzan, whose mother was anti-Semitic, suffered as a child from her mother's irrational hostility toward her. She believes that this experience awakened early in her a sense of justice and a sympathy for the oppressed.

The rescuers supported the findings of Nehama Tec's personality profile, with the great majority of them demonstrating empathy and compassion for others. Joe and Janke DeVries were hiding a Jewish boy in their home when they found out that he had an eighteen-month-old sister. Joe looked for her and brought her home: "You should have seen Bobby's face when I walked in with her." Most spoke of having learned kindness at home and having been taught to regard all people as equals. Marion Pritchard remembered being shocked when as a four-year-old child she observed another child being hit by a parent: it was something she had never imagined.

Even among the rescuers who had been taught that the Jews had killed Jesus and thus bore an unconscious anti-Semitism absorbed from their societies, a universalistic empathy prevailed. Stefan Raczynski shrugged and said he would have done the same for a hungry cat: "When the Jews came out of the forest and they were hungry, you had to feed them."

Although they were aware of their empathy, the rescuers weren't impressed by it. "It is the normal thing to do," Arie van Mansum asserted. Dutch rescuer Semmy Riekerk said, "I'm not all good. I had the opportunity and I happened to have made the right choice. A human being is like a piano. Circumstances play the keys. The war brought out the highest and lowest in people." Perhaps, as Dr. Tec says about people who have a long history of doing good deeds, it doesn't seem extraordinary to them.

The rescuers test our definition of what we regard as ordinary behavior. Are they ordinary people who did extraordinary things? This assumption implies that acts of compassion, empathy, and responsibility for one another are typically viewed as exceptional and that indifference is perceived as the normal response. On the other hand, if we regard the rescuers as extraordinary people, we separate ourselves from them. In the Prologue, Cynthia Ozick wrestles with this question: who, she asks, is the "ordinary human article," the rescuer or the bystander? Although she would like to regard the rescuers and their altruism as unexceptional, she concludes that the rescuers are heroic precisely because there were so few of them: "When a continent is filled from end to end with the compliant, we learn what heroism is." Unfortunately, bystanders create heroes.

In addition to possessing an open heart, the rescuers, we found, were independent people, some with a streak of rebelliousness and nonconformity, others with an adventurous spirit. Arnold Douwes was arrested in 1936 in Chicago for attempting to get a black man served in a restaurant. Agnieszka Budna-Widerschal amazed herself with her daring and inventive lies when confronted by Nazis. Margot Lawson took obvious pleasure in outwitting them. A German working with the Dutch underground in Amsterdam, Lawson worked as a double agent; ingratiating herself with the Nazis was sport for her. Rescuers who had intermarried, such as the Yakiras, Eliases, and Tarnawskis, as well as Budna-Widerschal, had already demonstrated unusual independence in not blending into their communities of origin.

This is not to say that the rescuers were fearless, but as Andrée Herscovici explained, "When you feel you're doing something important, fear is in the background." Johtje Vos said she was never afraid of the Germans, but always of the bombs. Joe DeVries described the time as so tense, "I could have slit a throat." Even the most visibly daring types such as Jan Karski, Arie van Mansum, and Arnold Douwes carried an extra burden of fear after they were arrested. Perhaps what made the fear, or tolerance of risk, as Dr. Fogelman calls it, bearable was a self-confidence that described the majority of rescuers. They believed in themselves and felt that things would turn out all right. Aart and Johtje Vos described themselves as "up" people. The religious rescuers said their faith in God gave them courage. Stefania Burzminski recalled hearing God speak to her in the house where she hid thirteen Jews.

One of the reasons that we study the rescuers is that they represent the highest form of moral achievement. Just as we study the eating and exercise habits of great athletes in the hope we will improve our own performance, so we examine the rescuers closely to find a way to teach altruism. Many rescuers came from caring, empathic, supportive families that sensitized them to another person's suffering and gave them confidence to act, but not all rescuers had the benefit of a benign childhood. Several had alcoholic parents who beat them; Robert Gachet grew up in a cruel orphanage; Ermine Orsi married at sixteen to get away from an abusive stepmother; and Arie Verduijn's mother hated him.

Family may provide the deepest education, but it is not the only means through which we learn goodness. Social scientists suggest that we can learn altruistic behavior by studying the rescuers, and that the lessons can be taught in other ways, through religious institutions, schools, television, film, and books. We hope they are right. That was part of our intention in writing this book.

The book is organized geographically because of the uniqueness of each country's experience under Nazi rule. The roles of government and church, national character, culture, politics, geography, and the prevailing attitude toward Jews all affected rescue activities. In general, resistance was better organized in Western European countries, although collaborators existed in high numbers in those countries, too. In the Netherlands, the NSB, once a mildly anti-Semitic political party, became, at Nazi urging, the chief organization of Dutch collaboration. Although Belgium had a well-developed underground, it didn't make saving Jews a priority, so the Jews themselves organized their own network, the Committee for the Defense of the Jews (CDJ). With few resistance networks and risk of death if caught, a Polish or Ukrainian rescuer almost always worked alone, fearful of native anti-Semitism as well as of the Gestapo, whereas the underground in Belgium and the

Netherlands offered protection to its members. Rescuers from every country said, "You didn't tell anyone anything if you didn't have to." Aart Vos remembers refusing money offered by Vincent van Gogh's nephew for "the work I hear you're doing to save the Jews." Vos told him he had the wrong Vos, and refused the check.

Religion as a motivation for helping the Jews transcended geographic boundaries, but the churches in general, as with most institutions, did not act with compassion. There were exceptions in certain countries. The strongest resistance to the Nazis in France came from Protestant groups, many of whom identified with the Jews because they were an oppressed minority in a predominantly Catholic country. The French mountain village of Le Chambon, led by its courageous Huguenot minister, André Trocmé, and his wife, Magda, saved 5,000 Jews. Bulgaria saved most of its Jewish population because of church intervention.

Although we recognize the limitations of defining people by their nation-state, there is such a thing as national character. For example, the Dutch like to think of themselves as independent-minded, and therefore, as a matter of principle, did not want the Nazis to tell them what to do with part of their population. What worked against this independent spirit, however, was the high value the Dutch put on doing a job right, so when the Nazis gave the Dutch various tasks designed to eliminate Jews, they did their work well, without caring about its purpose. On the other hand, people in Poland, an independent country only for a short time, were conditioned to follow an invading country's orders. The rescuer in Germany was put to the unique test of being a traitor to the Fatherland, an especially grave sin in a country that placed the highest value on obedience to the state.

The terrain of a country also influenced the possibility of rescue. A flat country without forests, such as Holland, made hiding extremely difficult, while the mountains in France, and its proximity to safe countries such as Switzerland and Spain, provided havens for thousands of Jews. Finally, the more isolated the Jew was from the national majority, the more he or she was at risk. Generally, Jews in Western Europe, with the exception of Belgium, belonged to long-standing communities that were fairly assimilated into society. Eastern Europe, with the exception of Bulgaria, provided the opposite experience. In Poland, which had the largest Jewish population, with 3 million, many Jews lived separately, spoke their own language, and dressed in a way that immediately identified them as the other.

The scope of rescue took many forms, depending upon the country and upon the individual; yet every rescuer made the commitment to do whatever was necessary to save lives. In all but a few places, rescue required confiding in nobody, sometimes not even a spouse. Rescuers carried wastepots down from attics, lived with unrelenting tension for years, lied, stole, and sometimes killed to protect those for whom they felt responsible. Some worked alone, others in underground networks, but few could have saved Jews without help. At least ten others, Marion Pritchard said, were necessary. It wasn't only the person who risked his or her own life, but the milkman who never asked why the family needed an extra liter of milk, or the postman who didn't ask about the dark-haired child peering around the open door, who also helped to save Jewish lives.

We interviewed a rescuer who did no more than provide a back room for an hour to Jews who happened to be on the street during a raid in the Ukraine. We met others who devoted all their time during the war to saving Jews. Père Benoît, Marc Donadille, Marion Pritchard, and Gilbert Lesage saved incalculable numbers of Jews by working in the Resistance to provide false papers. One of the founders of the Polish underground, Stefan Korbonski, printed false papers and contraband leaflets warning Jews of raids and created a telegraph system between Warsaw and the free world.

Of the eleven Belgians we interviewed, all but one worked with the same underground network, the Committee for the Defense of the Jews, and their stories, like chapters in a book, are linked to one another. Paul Pensis told us of rescuing Jewish children from a convent, and later Esta Heiber described her own and her husband's arrest as having been caused by someone discovering that they had ordered the rescue in that particular convent. Yvonne Jospa was Andrée Herscovici's director. Because the CDJ had been created by Jews, it wasn't surprising that three of our interviews were with Jewish rescuers—Fela Herman, Esta Heiber, and Yvonne Jospa. Our young translator, a Belgian Jew, while listening to Andrée Herscovici, discovered that his great-uncle had been the financial director of the CDJ.

Ermine Orsi, Countess von Maltzan, and John Weidner escorted hundreds of Jews to safe havens. Marie Taquet, Henriette Ceulemans, Simone Monnier, and Mireille Gardere hid children in boarding schools. Amfian Gerasimov and Paul Kerner sneaked food into the ghetto, while others such as Alex Roslan, Piotr Budnik, and Agnieszka Budna-Widerschal smuggled Jews out of the ghetto and into their homes. Pieter Miedema, Jan de Haan, and Arnold Douwes found hiding places for Jews; Seine Otten, Zofia Baniecka, and Bert Bochove hid large and revolving numbers of Jews in their houses throughout the war. Of these, de Haan, Douwes, and Baniecka were also actively involved in the organized resistance of their countries.

The Stenekes and Streekstra families kept another family or a few people in their homes for years. Jean Kowalyk Berger endured arguments among those she hid, and Christine Hilsum-Beuckens had to retrieve a man she was hiding who had gone mad and had escaped naked into the streets. Alex and Mela Roslan had to dispose of the body of one of the three children he was hiding. Marion Pritchard had to shoot a Dutch collaborator about to denounce her and the family she was hiding. From a radical and determined act of altruism to a brief moment of compassion, they all did God's work.

For some the war was their moment of glory: never had right and wrong been so obvious, their reason for living so clear, and never again would they have such an important task before them. For Bert Bochove, the war years were the best years: he had the opportunity to do good, and he loved having a house full of people. Semmy Riekerk says her bonds with other Resistance workers are more substantial than any other personal connection, "even stronger than the mother to the child." For others, the war was devastating. Some had to give up a career or interrupt an education. Louisa Steenstra lost her husband because they tried to save Jews. Many rescuers such as Gitta Bauer and Marion Pritchard expressed regret that they did not do more. Still, most of those we interviewed possessed an enviable peace with themselves. Even if they never acted selflessly or heroically again, they did not question the rightness of their acts: they knew, without any doubt, that they had once helped to save a life.

Although the rescuers suffered during the war, many spoke of enjoying occasional good times. Of course, the people they helped may not remember things quite the same way because despite the shared experience, their roles were so different. Regardless of the hardships endured by the rescuers, they at least possessed some control over their lives: they had chosen to put themselves at risk, while the hunted Jew was entirely dependent upon others for survival. As powerless as everyone felt in a country occupied by the Germans, nobody was as powerless as the Jew. Andrée Herscovici said, "When I was taking the children away from their parents I was only twenty years old. When I became a mother myself, I couldn't even imagine the torture those parents must have felt." And yet, Herscovici could also add, "Everything I am today I owe to that period of my life." Rescuers often spoke with deep compassion and understanding for the survivor's experience. Arnold Douwes observed that the task of hiding Jews was easier than to be a Jew, saying, "Imagine sitting in a hole for two years! I don't know if I could have done that."

The experience of those who were rescued is not the focus of this work, but we must at least mention that many paid a price for survival, especially the children robbed of their childhoods. Although the rescuers saved lives, they couldn't revive spirits crushed by losing a family or living in fear for one's life for years. While David Inowlocki describes his time as a hidden child in Belgium as happy and carefree, Andrée Herscovici says, "For forty years the children I placed wouldn't talk about that time at all. Now they want to talk about it all the time, and they describe such anguish." Many children who were hidden grew up confused and lost, unsure of their identities. Children in Poland witnessed daily deportations of friends and family, and living in hiding there was much more treacherous than in other countries. For many who were rescued, the wounding memories that have kept the war an aching presence could fill another book.

The postwar years gave the rescuers the opportunity to rebuild their lives, but many experienced disillusionment and disappointment. John Weidner thought that everything would be "paradise" after the important lessons learned by the war. He, like many who fought tyranny, despaired afterward that the lesson of the war was that there is no justice. In the Netherlands, the war resisters did not get to rebuild the country; instead of punishment, many NSBers gained positions of authority and the country returned to its traditional schisms.

In Poland, not only did the rescuers not get acknowledgment for their good deeds, but they found themselves to be social pariahs for helping Jews. Many could not find jobs or housing, and some were even killed. A number of people who still remain in Poland keep their rescue of Jews a secret. At least fifty rescuers emigrated to Israel. Some, such as Wilhelm Tarnawski, Irena Yakira, and Agnieszka Budna–Widerschal, gained entry because of their Jewish spouses. Governesses Gertruda Babilinska and

Veronica Parocai came to Israel with the children they cared for in Poland and Hungary, respectively.

Until 1985, the rescuers in Israel, nearly all Polish, were largely ignored, and because they weren't Jews, were denied full government benefits and pensions. Many lived in poverty, and, ironically, some of them had encountered crude racism. In 1985 "Kolbotek," an Israeli television program the equivalent of "60 Minutes," called attention to the plight of the rescuers in Israel, and after forty years the government corrected the injustice; with a special stipend, rescuers are finally living with dignity and comfort. Soon after, Shoshana Raczynski, whom Stefan saved and later married, created a social support group among the forty rescuers in Israel.

Even rescuers who adjusted successfully after the war revealed emotional wounds caused by the risks they undertook. John Weidner, who led hundreds of Jews out of Holland into the free zone, said, "We all expected to be finished by the time we were seventy—tension and danger took years from our lives." Some had nervous breakdowns, others suffer from chronic diseases, many relive the war through nightmares. Only a few can bear to see films of the period.

For some, the memory of war has intensified as they have advanced in age. After 1945, Christine Hilsum-Beuckens busied herself with raising a family and working as a translator of German and English books; she rarely thought about the war. Fifteen years ago, while watching on TV the trial of a collaborator, she began to have nightmares. She laments, "Yes, my dears, the war is growing on us fast now that we are old." Many rescuers never talked about their wartime deeds until recently; it was too painful and no one was interested. Marion Pritchard found that Americans didn't want to hear about the war, so she stopped talking about it. In some families, however, the war years provided adventure stories for the children of rescuers. Those who spoke proudly of their parents as role models were usually born after the war or were too young to remember it, but for the children who remember, the story is often different. Some are angry that their parents put their lives in jeopardy and remember the war with bitterness, but for children who were old enough to help, such as Greta DeVries, Liliane Gaffney, and Paul Kerner, such feelings are outweighed by their pride in having helped save lives.

Despite the satisfaction that rescuers derived from their deeds, a few, such as Stefania Burzminski and Irene Opdyke, felt that the Jewish community had not done enough to acknowledge the rescuers. Jean Kowalyk Berger, a Ukrainian who lost her house to the Russians after the war, arrived in the United States needing help. She went to a Jewish agency (HIAS, the Hebrew Immigrant Aid Society) for assistance in finding an apartment and a job, but they turned her away, explaining that they helped only Jews. Ermine Orsi wondered if Jews would do the same for her as had she done for them. A number of rescuers never hear from the people they saved. Claudine Gilain would be happy to receive a yearly greeting from the boy she hid for three years.

Whether anything is owed to the rescuers is a difficult question to answer. Indeed, are they owed anything, or is the good deed itself the reward? If something is owed, what is its nature and who owes it? The ones who were rescued? All Jews? Or perhaps all people: the rescuers redeemed our faith in humanity by demonstrating that goodness does exist.

Few of those we interviewed possessed more than simple comfort and many are poorer than the people they saved. For the rescuers who left their homelands, the struggle with learning a new language and new customs made financial success more difficult. It is also possible that the qualities that make an altruistic personality are not the same ones necessary to be a successful businessperson. Despite their own needs after the war, at least one-fourth of the rescuers continued to perform altruistic deeds. Tina Strobos volunteered time to improve conditions in Harlem, Bert Bochove helps anyone he can, and Germaine Belinne, in her eighties, still volunteers at a home for the aged.

Although no one acted for the sake of recognition or for medals, most rescuers appreciate the medal awarded them by Yad Vashem. Since 1962, the institution has honored over 9,000 rescuers, called in Hebrew *Hasidei Umot Ha-olam*, the Righteous Among the Nations, with most of the medals having been presented since 1980. In many of the homes we visited, the memorial's bronze medal on which is inscribed, "Whoever saves a single life is as one who has saved an entire world," held a place of honor. Even rescuers who have been frequently acknowledged said that the Yad Vashem medal comes first, all others second.

Anne Frank gave the victims of the Holocaust a face and a voice. To empathize with that child is to know her as ourselves. As Rabbi Harold Schulweis observes in the Afterword, the faces in this book give us another picture of the Holocaust with which we can identify. The pho-

---

tographs serve to give a different face to the word "hero" than the one to which we are accustomed. They challenge our ideas about what we think heroes look like: they aren't all square-jawed, broad-shouldered, handsome men with unwavering eyes, nor do these faces necessarily project conventional images of serenity and wisdom. These people look like us, like ordinary people. We learn from the photographs that heroism and goodness are not represented by stereotypical physiognomy but rather are expressed by a person's deeds, mind, and heart.

Photographs cannot reveal what is special about these women and men. A rescuer walking down the street today would go unnoticed, just another "old person"; yet these people are the aristocrats of the world. Successful people in our society usually stand out: their clothes, dwellings, cars, and important titles tell us to notice them. One can distinguish their power and position by what they own or control. No external symbol, however, marks those who continue to give us a reason to hope for the redemption of the world.

For years books about the Holocaust rarely mentioned the few who were brave and intelligent enough to shelter Jews, but recently books and films are chronicling Holocaust rescue. After forty-five years, why? It could be that it has taken this long for the Jewish community to look past the darkness and see a bit of light, but perhaps the reason is more universal. All of us hunger to know about these people because we need to believe that kindness, compassion, and courage exist in all kinds of human beings, and because we want to teach these values to future generations. The world is fragile and its resources finite; human technology has made life easier but more dangerous. This generation has important choices to make that will affect the world we leave to our children. When Europe was a torture chamber and almost everyone cried, "But what can *I* do?," a few people knew what to do. History gives no promises, but the people in this book offer us hope, revealing that goodness is, indeed, part of the human spirit.

The Netherlands

While Dutch identification with the Jews has been exaggerated and the part played by Nazi sympathizers underrated, it is nonetheless true that the Dutch population, especially the intellectual, political and religious, by and large opposed the Nazi policies, including those against the Jews, with determination.

—Yehuda Bauer, *The Holocaust in Historical Perspective*

As of January 1, 1991, Yad Vashem, the Holocaust memorial in Jerusalem, had honored 9,295 Christians who rescued Jews during the Holocaust. With 3,372 rescuers, Holland claimed more rescuers than any other country. Yet no other country in Western Europe, including Germany, lost so much of its Jewish population. Eighty to ninety percent of Holland's Jews, over 100,000, were killed. How can it be that a country with so many rescuers lost so much of its population?

First, Holland was a geographically difficult place to save Jews. It is flat and without forests, a land with few hiding places. Its borders are Germany, Belgium (which was occupied), and the North Sea: there were no easy escape routes. Yet landscape was not the major obstacle to protecting the Jews of Holland. Despite Holland's relative lack of anti-Semitism and its tradition of tolerance, the country's leadership allowed Dutch Jews to be deported. Queen Wilhelmina and her government fled to England soon after the Nazi invasion, and the secretaries-general were left to follow Nazi orders.

Without the compliance of Holland's civil employees, the Germans never could have been so successful in their deportation of Jews in Holland. A Dutch official in charge of designing identity cards created a pattern so intricate that it was more difficult to forge than the German identity card. The designer's feelings about Jews were irrelevant; he was a man who was proud of his work.

Besides the capitulation of the government, 80,000 people belonged to the NSB.* Others sought the generous bounty given for every Jew turned in. Of the 25,000 Jews hidden in Holland, only one-third to one-half of them survived because most were denounced by neighbors. Even those people who hated the Nazis and sympathized with the Jews did nothing because they feared the possible consequences, although these consequences were infinitely less serious than in Eastern Europe, especially Poland. In Holland, only a few had the temperament to tolerate risk, and the empathy and compassion that made their acts almost involuntary; these attributes allowed only 20,000 out of 143,000 Dutch Jews to survive the war.

The National Socialist Party was mildly anti-Semitic before thewar, but in 1938 it began excluding Jews and later began to follow the anti-Semitic policies of the German forces.

The Germans assured the Dutch that they would never occupy their country, but cynics and realists prepared for an invasion; others remembered that Holland had stayed neutral in World War I and thought that it could avoid war again. Shocking all but a few, the Germans marched into the Netherlands on May 10, 1940, and in five days had dominated the country. They would occupy Holland longer than any other Western European country except Norway.

At first the Germans sought to ingratiate themselves among the Dutch, whom they saw as cousins. They did not want to be seen as barbarians, but they had to convince the Dutch that it was necessary to get rid of their Jews. Propaganda movies showing Jews as less than human drove home the message. Marion Pritchard, seeing *The Eternal Jew* in Amsterdam, heard fellow students say that even though they knew the film was absurd, it had affected how they saw Jews. Liberal intellectuals such as Took Heroma and Tina Strobos were not fooled, however, and began resistance work early in the occupation. Gradually, Jews became the "other," a group of villains or victims to be shunned, and step by step their rights were taken from them. The Germans moved slowly so as not to provoke public protest. One of the most serious steps was to require all Jews to live in Amsterdam, making the task of rounding them up that much easier. Within two years the Jewish population was penniless and isolated from the non-Jewish population.

In 1942, the deportations began. Jews were ripped from their houses at night, after curfew, or grabbed off the streets during the day. Some went into hiding, others threw away the "Jude" stars they were forced to wear and tried to pass as Aryan. Few were successful. By 1943, 100,000 Jews had been sent to Westerbork, the internment camp set up by the Dutch in 1939 to prevent German refugees from gaining asylum. Weekly trains took Jews from Westerbork to Auschwitz. Louisa Steenstra was one of the few Dutch citizens who entered Westerbork and was able to leave. She had gone to bring clothing to friends.

When the Germans began in 1943 deporting Dutch boys sixteen and older to work in Germany, Holland finally organized an effective network to find hiding places. Although it was far easier for the underground to place the Dutch boys, it did help Jews to hide. Jan de Haan, who worked to place Jews, provided papers, and later was a secret agent in the Resistance, remembered, "In the neighborhoods where I placed my Jews, I couldn't press too hard. When I would ask someone to hide some Jews, if they said, 'But we have children of our own, and it would endanger them, and there are NSBers living all around me. . . ,' well, I just couldn't press too hard." By then, however, only 20 percent of the Jews remained. The northern part of Holland, Friesland, was the best hiding place, because farms were isolated and the families were strong Christians. Most of the Canadian rescuers who now live in the province of Ontario came from this region. Although some believed that the Jews had killed Jesus, they still felt that their duty was to help those in need.

Some Dutch rescuers, like Arnold Douwes and Seine Otten, did resistance work as well as hiding Jews. One of their major problems was raising money to help feed the people in hiding. Two Jewish men, Peter and Herman, worked with them by selling drawings they had made. They asked buyers to pay "as much as they could afford" to support "the divers" (people in hiding).

The last winter of the war, when most of Europe was already liberated, was especially brutal for the Dutch. The temperature was so cold and fuel so short that people burned doors and furniture to stay warm. The Nazis shut down all forms of transportation and shipped whatever food Holland produced to Germany. People walked for hours to find a few potatoes or an onion. In May 1945 the Nazis finally surrendered. Holland's cities were decimated, and it would take years to rebuild the country.

Despite the relief at the war's end, people remembered who had collaborated, who had been "good" and who had been "wrong." Many of the rescuers and Resistance members, such as Arie van Mansum, left the country in bitter disappointment, immigrating to Canada or the United States for a fresh start. Others tried to put the war behind them and build families and careers. Many were troubled with nightmares. The war had left its mark not only in exposing the evil of the Third Reich, but in revealing, as Semmy Riekerk observed, the best and the worst in human beings.

One of the cards created to raise money for people in hiding. The quotation, from the New Testament, is a plea for more people to take Jews into their homes: "Never forget to be hospitable, for by hospitality some have entertained angels un-awares."

In this card, made just after D-Day on June 6, 1944, the ax identifies the Allied soldier, and the message on the bottom reads "Assault!"

JOHANNES DEVRIES

Johannes and Janke DeVries, 1939.

Joe DeVries greets us with an outstretched hand and a big smile. "I'm Joe!" he says as he walks us past a touch of Holland in his Dutton, Ontario, home, a tidy row of shoes lined up by the front door. Joe's daughter, Greta, and her husband, Cyril, have traveled from Toronto to help her father with the interview, but Joe needs no one to stir his memory. Warm and relaxed, he remembers vividly and fondly how he and his recently deceased wife, Janke, hid two Jewish children in his home in southern Holland for the duration of the war.

A few years ago my wife and I were sitting in the kitchen having a cup of coffee and then we came to talking about that time. I said, "I still can't understand how we'd be so crazy to risk our lives for those strange people." And my wife said, "Yeah, we'd never do it again, would we?" "No," I said, and she looked at me and we laughed. She said, "You know just as well as I do we would do the same thing over!"

I was born in 1911, in Opperkooten, a village in Friesland, the farming country in Holland. I was the second youngest of nine children. My father worked hard on his small farm to make ends meet. I was closer to my mother, but she was also strict and hardworking. We went to Sunday school but I sneaked out to go swim in the canal. The rules in our family were that we couldn't lie, steal, or kill, and we had to help the elderly and children. Otherwise, we grew up free; you know, those days were different, and we were in the country.

I was only seventeen when I married Janke. I couldn't find work in Friesland, so we moved south to Hoensbroek, in Limburg, and I started mining coal. Greta was born in 1929, and our son came two years later. We knew during the thirties that Jews were beginning to come from Germany to cities in Holland. Then, in 1940, Rotterdam was bombed and many children who had no homes were sent out to people all over Holland. We took one of these children. He stayed a year, and after he left a woman came to the house to talk with Janke. She knew we had had the boy from Rotterdam, and she asked if we would take another child. Janke said "yes" right away, but then the woman said, "It's a Jewish child." Janke said, "Oh, I'll have to talk it over with my husband."

We talked for some time, but we decided, "When you would close the door on someone like that and you heard later that he was destroyed, how would you feel the rest of your life? I think I would be destroyed myself." So in 1942, Salomon Haringman came to live with us. Of course, that name sounded too Jewish so we called him Bobby. His father was killed in Sobibor, along with his parents and all his brothers and sisters. Their mother asked the underground to help her find a place for her children to hide, and then she went into hiding herself.

Bobby was three and a half years old. He was scared like a little bird because he had been moved around too much. The first night we found out he was asthmatic, and was still wetting the bed. We were glad they brought him to us and not to someone else who might have turned him back. We all loved him; he was so sensitive and intelligent. Greta was fourteen, and used to take him outside at night in back of the house where there were no houses, so he could walk around outside. He would cry for his mother, and Greta would cry, too.

Bobby had a little sister, one and a half years old. I snooped around and found that she was with a woman who wanted to give her up because she was too scared. So I talked it over with my wife, and we decided to take her. We thought, "If they shoot us for keeping one, they'll shoot us for keeping two." I didn't tell Bobby I was going to get his sister, and when I came in with her he was in the front room playing. I thought they'd break the house down, they were so excited to see each other. Her name was Eva, but we called her Eef. And they were our children. There was nothing like our children and the Jewish children. They were all our children. But daily life was difficult. I was so tense during those years, I felt like a fiddle string. I could have slit a throat.

All the neighbors thought Bobby and Eef were children from Rotterdam. It may have been safer if we would have taken the kids to Sunday school, but I didn't believe that was right. Some people did try to make their Jewish children into Christians, but we never did it.

Limburg was an area known for keeping Jewish children. Sometimes the underground would need a place for a Jew to stay for a couple of days, or a couple of weeks, and we would always take them. We kept about fifteen other Jews for short periods of time. The underground promised to provide food stamps, but they didn't always get to us. Sometimes I had to go up to Friesland to get food from the farmers, and it was dangerous traveling back with the food because the Nazis always patrolled the roads.

We always had to be careful. The Dutch Nazis were the worst because it was hard to know who they were. I saw one little girl being taken from the home where she was hiding, and I vowed then never to let my kids be taken. We were lucky to have a good friend in the police department. He would let us know if there was going to be a raid. We'd clear out of our house and leave it empty for a few days, maybe even two weeks. Once he even hid my wife and kids in the jail for two nights.

We did have some funny times. We took all the kids to the village photographer during the war, and Eef was so adorable that he put her photograph in the window of his studio. My wife ran down there real fast and bought both the picture and the negative.

The war ended in the south of Holland in the fall of 1944, but Mrs. Haringman wasn't free until the spring of 1945. She knew what village we lived in, but she didn't know our name. The underground had rules about things like that. We sent her pictures of them all during the war, but they said it wasn't safe for the parents to know where their children were. So when she came to Hoensbroek to find them, she gave their pictures to the local priest and he brought her to our house. He was surprised, because he never knew these kids were Jewish. The thing was, the children didn't want to go to their mother. When she asked Eef, "Do you recognize me?" Eef answered her, "You're my mother but you left us and now we have new parents." She could see that they had been taken care of pretty well because they wanted to stay with us. But they had to go back to Amsterdam and we visited back and forth all the time.

In 1947, Mrs. Haringman got cancer, and Greta went to Amsterdam to stay for a time to help take care of the kids. We knew we were going to move to Canada, so we went to her and asked if we could adopt Bobby and Eef and take them to Canada with us. But never try that with Jews, because it was the mother's wish that they have a Jewish education, which we couldn't give them, and that they go to Israel.

When we moved to Canada, it was like taking a heavy weight off. The wartime was still hanging on you in Holland. We were never homesick a minute, and that was forty years ago. The children went to Israel according to their mother's will, in 1949. We lost touch with them until we finally got a letter from Bobby in about 1951 or '52. He had written to the police department in Hoensbroek, and found our address. Now they had taken Israeli names, Shlomo and Chava. In 1977, Janke, Greta, and I all went to

Israel to get our medal and plant the tree at Yad Vashem. We spent about three weeks with Shlomo and Chava. They've visited us here, too. They're coming again this summer. It will be their first trip since my wife died.

When I was in Yad Vashem, I felt very proud of what we did. I still do. Right after we got back from Israel, some friends came over for a visit. We showed them the big medal and certificate we'd gotten, and this fella said, "You people think you did a very good deed. Well, you committed a big sin. Those Jews, they killed Jesus." I said, "You haven't read your Sunday school lessons very well, because it was the Romans who killed Jesus, since Jesus was a Jew himself." But I went to the closet and took out his and his wife's coats and I told him, "Here's your coat, you better go and never come back." My wife cried when they left. I could have killed him.

The way I see it, there are a lot of people who have no faith in human kind and they're only afraid for their own skin and not for yours or his or hers. They're selfish. I was scared in that time but never for myself. I was scared they'd get the kids, or my own kids, or my wife, but I was never scared for myself.

There were people who couldn't have hidden Jews but they'd cover and protect those who did. No one could imagine what it was to go through a war like that. I hope if there comes another war, that the very first bomb would hit us. What it must have been like for that mother to give up her children to someone she didn't know.

Bobby and Eef (Salomon and Eva Haringman), 1944.

Greta DeVries, age thirteen, just
before the war.

Eva and Salomon (Eef and Bobby) with their
Aunt Shelley, in Amsterdam, 1948.

Shlomo and Chava (Salomon and Eva's Hebrew names) in Israel, 1955.

ARIE VAN MANSUM

Arie van Mansum, 1940.

Arie van Mansum risked his life dozens of times; he is every inch a hero, but no one would ever guess this by meeting him. An insurance broker in the agency he founded when he moved to Ottawa after the war, he lives in a pretty and neat home on a quiet street. It requires imagination to understand the passionate character of this man who gives a diffident, laconic, and occasionally mumbled account of his wartime deeds. Yet once we see past the lack of facial and verbal expression, we notice him clench his fists in anger as he talks about the Dutch collaborators, especially of those who were not punished after the war. And when he tells us how he felt after the war, when he saw Jews once again walking down the streets of Maastricht, he smiles with tears in his eyes.

Well, the Holocaust didn't start with the Germans picking up Jews and sending them to concentration camps and putting them in gas chambers. The Holocaust started in the hearts of the people. As soon as you go and say, "That Jew!" or whatever, that's where it starts, you know. That was the beginning. As soon as you put one race higher than another one, you get that.

I was born in 1920 in Utrecht, but we moved to Maastricht in the south of Holland when I was six years old. I was the second child, one sister was older and one brother and sister were younger. We were simple people with not much education. My father was a laborer with the Dutch railroad, and I was very close to my mother, who stayed home with the children.

We were members of the Reform Church of the Netherlands, which is more strict than the Dutch Reformed. When we moved to Maastricht we were in the minority because the city was 90 percent Catholic. There were about seventy or eighty Jewish families but we didn't know them. We had no contact because we were a laborer's family and the Jews were businesspeople; we went to the Protestant school and they went to public school. In 1939, I was active in the young people's group of our church, and we went to a meeting at City Hall to discuss what to do about refugees coming in from Germany. I was the representative from the church, to try to decide how to help them. You couldn't tell the difference between Jews in Holland and others, anyway. But we had no chance to make any decisions before the war broke out.

In 1940, I was working as a traveling salesman for a wholesale wallpaper company. A man from my church who was an accountant for some Jewish people asked me to become the representative for distributing the underground newspaper, *Free Netherlands*. I agreed, and every month I took 500 to 1,000 newspapers and distributed them on my trips. I came in contact with an elder in the Reformed Church, Van Assen, who told me a Jewish family needed help, and asked if I would accompany them to the hiding place he had found for them. I did it. Then, after I had done more of this, he approached me to find a hiding place for a Jewish family. I contacted Mrs. Freilich and found a place for her and her daughter in Heerlen. But her son, Fritz, looked too Jewish, so I took him home myself. He was my age and my parents liked him. He had to stay in the house all the time, since he looked so Jewish, but it was through him that I came into contact with more families who needed help. Then I needed to get food stamps for all these people. I figured out a way to forge the food-stamp cards, and every week I went from one food-stamp office to another to get them because I needed so many. Soon I was getting 150 ration cards, and I finally met a man in the food-stamp office who was willing to get them all for me. When I needed 250 cards to deal with he got scared, so then a man who was the head of the police department in Haarlem did it for me.

One day some students in Amsterdam contacted me. The Germans were putting all the Jewish children together in the nursery, and the overflow in a converted theater across the street. Each day when the Germans took them out for a walk, the students would kidnap some of them and take them to hiding places in other parts of Holland. I began finding places for them, mostly in the south of Holland because there people had come from Poland and were darker skinned, so it was easier for a Jewish child to live among them. One day I was told of a Jewish boy in the hospital who would be shipped to Westerbork if we didn't get him out. I had a friend who was a nurse and she rescued him. I placed him with a Catholic family where he stayed till the end of the war.

Another time I needed to find a place for a baby fast because the family had already been summoned to Westerbork. My mother said she would take this eleven-day-old baby, and my girl friend and I went to pick her up. People thought we were a married couple with a newborn child. My mother really loved that baby. Later I placed another baby someplace else. I could go on telling these stories. Every day a new problem came up that I had to figure out a way to solve.

I quit my job and did this resistance work full-time. Every month I visited the people I had placed to take them food stamps and mail with news from their families. Many were very depressed, and I had the opportunity to lift them up a little and they appreciated that.

I was still living at home with my parents, and my sister, Margaretha, helped me as well. When I was arrested in October 1943, she took over all the work I had been doing. I ended up in Haeren in prison, for six months of solitary confinement. Then I was sent to Amersfoort concentration camp until September 1944. I was mistreated during interrogation, and was scared to death like anyone else. According to me, the Germans were stupid. When they arrested me, I had some addresses on me of families in hiding, but they never checked them out. I was taking care of about a hundred people, but they never found them. Only one family I had placed, the Weslys, was found and arrested, and the son was killed. A three-year-old boy. But this wasn't because of the list.

I was released from prison in Utrecht, which was in an area already liberated by the Allies. I couldn't go home because Maastricht was still occupied, so I stayed in Utrecht with an aunt and began underground work again. I was delivering *Free Netherlands* when I was again arrested in February 1945, and sent back to the concentration camp. I stayed there until the end of the war. All this time my sister did the work with the food stamps and the families in hiding that I had been doing. She died last year of a stroke at sixty-five, in Holland.

The baby stayed with my mother until June 1945, when the parents picked her up. It was hard on my mother; she was very attached. But the parents said, "We don't have family anymore. Can we adopt you as grandparents?" So we all remained like family until they emigrated to Israel.

I'll tell you, the best years of my life were when I could help Jews in the wartime. That was one of the best time periods of my life because it gave such satisfaction. I mean, the moment that I came back from prison in May 1945, I walked through the streets of Maastricht, and I saw Jews walking there, Jews I helped in the wartime, I started to cry. That was the satisfaction, you know. You saw those people walking through the street! And then it was a double satisfaction when I saw them in Israel, in their own country. It was fabulous!

Fritz lives in Belgium now. He is the secretary of the Jewish community. I moved to Canada because I was very disappointed in Holland. Many people who did no resistance work took the most prominent positions after the war. I'll give you an example. I had a friend I worked with, he was a Socialist, a teacher in the public high school. And one day he approached me. He said, "There's a Jewish family, the Schmidt family, and the chances are that they're gonna pick them up, either today or tomorrow. We need a place for them quick! Please help."

So I found a temporary place for the family, a family with four children. They were a poor family, he had a used furniture store. So that night we went over to get the people from their house and when we were sitting and they were packing, all of a sudden two Dutch policemen came in and told them that a Gestapo van would come in an hour or so to pick them up. And they asked us what we were doing there. We said, "Well, we were just buying some furniture." And he said, "You'll have to discuss that with the trustees because you'll have to leave now." So we walked outside and waited, walked up and down in front of the house for over an hour. One policeman came out to call the Germans because it was taking so long for the van to come to pick up these people. I asked that policeman, "Please, stay away for half an hour—give us a chance." He said, "I'm sorry, sir, I'm just doing my duty." This family was picked up and never returned. But this same man, after the war, got a promotion in the regular police force. That made me so furious. And besides, this policeman was assigned to the police force responsible for punishing NSBers. We registered a complaint when we saw him but nothing was done. They said he was just doing his duty. And those people were all picked up, the six people, and none of them came back. That makes you furious!

But I still say there was nothing special about what I did. I did what *everyone* should have done. Those people who did nothing on either side were scared and only looked after themselves. But I had feelings during wartime, and after the wartime even more, that I could have done more. I remember one day when I was walking through a rail station and a train came in loaded with Jewish people in those, you know, those livestock wagons. I, I stood there, you know, and I could do nothing, you know.

All of my Jewish friends are in Israel now, and we're like one big family. They called a few days ago to ask when I will come again. I went to Israel for the first time in 1981, with a tourist group, and when they met me at the hotel, they were mad. They said, "You shouldn't go with a tour; you should have stayed with us." I had received my medal from Yad Vashem in 1970; my sister was one of the first to be honored. When I went to Yad Vashem to look for my tree, it wasn't there. They said, "No, we have been waiting for you to come to plant it yourself." So I said, "Okay, give me a shovel." But they said "No, it's a celebration and a ceremony." So my friends said, "You come next year and we'll pay for the trip, and you'll stay with us." But I said,

"I'll pay for it." So we went back the next year. I think people don't understand what goes on in Israel. Maybe the Palestinians have a better PR department than the Israelis.

My children never knew what I did until recently. They asked, "Dad, why didn't you tell us?" But first, I'm afraid people will think I'm bragging, and I'd hate that. It's nothing to brag about. My sister went to Israel four times, and I keep in close contact, but otherwise I don't want to brag. Now, lately, some people in the Jewish community convinced me to share my story for the next generation. So I talked to kids, to churches, to memorial gatherings of Jews. And my children think it's enormous. My six-year-old grandson called and said, "Hey, Grandpa, I heard you were in jail!" So my daughter has started to tell them.

I guess I have helping in my blood. After the war a large group of people came from Indonesia, and my sister and I helped them. And here in Canada I work for a rescue mission. But, you know, not everyone had the opportunity to help during the war. I wouldn't say I had courage. If you'd have asked me before if I could have done it, I'd have said, "Oh, no, not me!" But if the moment's there and there's somebody in need, you go help, that's all.

Arie with Fritz (standing) Arie's parents on his left, and his sister, Margaretha, on his right.

Award ceremony for Arie van Mansum, 1945. His Jewish friends present him with a portrait and a certificate listing the names of those he saved.

Van Mansum (center) in Jerusalem with some of the Jews he saved, 1983.

RESCUERS

MARION P. VAN BINSBERGEN PRITCHARD

**Marion van Binsbergen
Pritchard in her UNRRA
uniform, 1946.**

*At an age when many migrate south, Marion Pritchard lives in a curtainless
farmhouse on 125 snow-covered acres deep in the woods of Vermont. The sunny
house she shares with her husband, Tony, the daffodils on the coffee table, and
her equanimity are misleading: the terror and mystery of the war remain close
to Marion. Through a variety of efforts, Marion estimates that she managed to
save approximately 150 Jews, but still she expresses regret for not having done
more. Now a practicing psychoanalyst, Marion's recent interest has been to
study altruistic behavior, which she believes originates in the family.*

I was born in 1920. My father was a liberal judge in Amsterdam, and a member of the board of regents of the prisons there. I learned tolerance from him.
He was more accepting of all people and their differences than my mother, who
was tiny, tough, cheerful, critical, self-confident, very British and class-conscious. She wasn't the intellectual my father was, but he wasn't brazen the way
she was. When they returned from a trip abroad, she would hide her cigarettes
and he would declare every one of his 150 cigars. Being a judge, he did the
right thing while she played her illegal radio with the windows open.

I think it was my parents' unusual way of child-rearing that provided
the motivation for me to behave the way I did during the war. I was never
punished and always encouraged to express my feelings, both the negative
and positive ones, in words. And when I asked questions I got answers. I was
never told I was too young or anything like that. I was treated with respect
and consideration from the time I was born.

I went to a private school where there were Jews in every class. In Holland, the Jews were considered Dutch like everyone else. I wanted to become a therapist so, at nineteen, I entered the school of social work in Amsterdam, and was there when the Nazis occupied Holland in 1940.

The Germans didn't start attacking Jews immediately. It is much easier to segregate a part of the population when the rest is with you. So they began mildly, with propaganda. One example is a film we were required to see in school called *The Eternal Jew*. We sat through it, laughed aloud, and thought it was ridiculous, but what impressed me in retrospect is that one of the students said to me the next day, "You know, that was an awful movie, scurrilous, and I don't believe a word of it, but what it has done is divided us into 'them' and 'us.' I wish it didn't, but now I look at people and say, 'Huh, you're Jewish.'" And this was a person who was determined to help Jews, but the split had been made. Then there was the Aryan attestation. If you were Jewish you filled out one form and if you were Aryan, as they call it, you filled out another. My father refused to sign the form, as did I. He had read *Mein Kampf* and believed Hitler would do what he said. But when I spoke that way to my friends, especially my Jewish friends, they didn't want to accept it. Some even became angry. But I'm action-oriented like my mother.

Even my twelve-year-old brother wanted to take action. He and his friends put on the yellow star. My mother told him to take it off, but my father supported my brother. The question is: when is a child old enough to take a stand? Anyway, my brother had a terrible experience which demonstrates the randomness of the German response. He was coming home from school and he and his friends were talking about the Germans and called them "lousy Krauts." The officers overheard them and took them to headquarters. They let my brother go after about forty-five minutes, but called the other boy's mother and gave her a choice. They told her that her son had been disrespectful to the occupying forces and asked if she wanted them to give him a beating or if she wanted her husband arrested. She was fixing lunch for the other kids, right? So she told them to give the boy the beating and they told her when to come pick up her son. Well, when she went to pick him up, he was dead. Twelve years old.

I was at a friend's apartment studying one night in 1941. Because of the curfew, if you went out you had to spend the night. The students who lived in this apartment listened to the Allied broadcasts on the radio and made copies and distributed them. I didn't even know they were doing this. You didn't tell anyone what you were doing if they didn't absolutely need to know. It seems that someone betrayed them and the Germans came the night I was there and arrested everyone in the house. So I was in prison for seven months. I always thought I had my mother's ability to ignore fear until I spent some time in jail and that was very frightening. And it's funny how you remember fear on an unconscious level. The Germans always picked up people at night after curfew. They were the only ones who had motorized vehicles, so if you heard a truck at night, you knew what it was. When we moved up here to the Vermont woods—we live on a dead-end road—for the first several years we lived here, if a truck came up here at night, I got up and looked out the window. I was scared.

In 1942 I was doing some social work in a rehabilitation center. The woman in charge was afraid a particular Jewish family was about to be taken, and she asked me to take the two-year-old son home. I did it, but I never told my parents he was Jewish. They weren't suspicious; it was the kind of thing I was apt to do. He stayed several months until I found him a safer place outside Amsterdam. His name was Jantje Herben, and I don't know what happened to him after that.

I had gone into analysis by 1942, because I wanted to become an analyst. At about the time the Frank family decided to go into hiding, my analyst asked if I could help him find a place to hide. He knew I was already involved in trying to help people avoid being sent to Westerbork, so I and two other of his analysands found him a place to hide and took him food, clothes, and news from the outside. His wife was in another place. You know, people would take one person but not two, a child but not an adult, or an adult but no children. But he was discovered and didn't survive.

Just about this time, I witnessed a terrible thing. One morning on my way to school I passed a small Jewish children's home. I saw the Nazis loading children, from babies to about eight years old, onto trucks. They were all crying, and when they didn't move fast enough, a Nazi would pick them up by an arm or leg, or even hair, and throw them onto the trucks. I was so shocked by this treatment that I found myself in tears. Then I saw two women coming down the street try to stop them, and the Germans threw them into the trucks, too. I stood frozen on my bicycle. Before this I had known of the threats but I hadn't actually seen the Germans in action. When I saw that, I knew that my rescue work was more important that anything else I might be doing.

A friend of mine was hiding with her husband and was pregnant. The people keeping them couldn't have a baby in their apartment so I asked another couple, also friends of mine, to take the baby when it was born. They said they were already giving money to save Jews, and were paying for Jews to have plastic surgery, but they felt that taking a child was a bit much. But the next morning they had changed their mind. She pretended to be pregnant and fixed a nursery and hired a nurse. They had a nanny for their four other children, but decided to have nothing to do with the baby so they wouldn't get attached. The baby was premature and the nurse wasn't available, so I stayed for a week, taking care of him. Well, the baby was fine but the parents didn't survive. I heard at the end of the war that he had been totally accepted as a member of their household, and they were trying to decide whether to tell him about his parents. I thought it was wonderful, whether or not they told him, but the Zionists later informed me otherwise.

The nursery where the Germans placed all Jewish children who were on their way to Westerbork was next door to a teachers' college. The workers in the nursery along with the student teachers smuggled out more than 1,000 Jewish children in laundry hampers, knapsacks, and the like. These were average people you might never think would do this. So one can't know what one would do.

One day I was given a little girl to place in a home in northeast Holland. I was told this was a sure thing, that if I took her there they would take her. When I arrived after a long train ride, the man at the station told me that the address was not available. I was tired, so he invited me to his house to rest before returning to Amsterdam. They were people of modest means, and in his house were his wife and four or five children. I fell asleep and when I woke up the woman was changing and feeding the baby and this was how these people made up their minds. We talk about moral decisions. These people just knew that this was the thing God would have wanted them to do. When the man walked me back to the station he apologetically explained that they had told the other children that this was my illegitimate baby and that my punishment would be that I could never see it again. It was a safe story so the villagers wouldn't be suspicious. And this is just one day.

In 1942 I was asked by friends in the resistance to find a place for a man, Freddie Pollak, and his three small children, aged four years, two years, and two weeks. I decided to move them into a large house in the country which belonged to an older woman whose son-in-law was a friend of Freddie's. In that year, I only came to live with them on weekends, but by 1943, I moved in full-time to take care of the children while Freddie worked on his thesis. Of course, I became very attached to the children, especially Erica, who was just a baby when we started. I maintained the fiction for the people in the neighborhood that they were my children, but some people knew, I'm sure. I didn't teach them prayers, but they had Christian names.

We had some floorboards removed under a rug, and built a hiding place in the basement in case of raids, which we had at times. One night four Germans and a Dutch Nazi policeman came to search the house. Everyone was in the hiding place, and they didn't find it. But a short time later the Dutch Nazi returned alone. He had learned that Jews were often in hiding places, and that if you returned just after a raid you might catch them in the house. That's exactly what had happened. Erica had started to cry, so I let the children come up. When the Dutch policeman came back, I had to kill him with a revolver a friend had given me but I had never expected to use. I know I had no choice, but I still wish there had been some other way. An undertaker in town helped me dispose of the body by putting it in a coffin with another body. I hope the dead man's family would have approved.

There was no such thing as a routine day, even after I was hiding the Pollak family. In the village of Huizen, near where we were living, was a house called "Het Hooge Nest." The people living there were Lientje Brilleslijper, the daughter of a Jewish family of circus artists and musicians, her Aryan, common-law German husband, Piet, and their daughter, Kathinka. Lientje and Piet had decided early that not only were they going to survive personally, but they would assist as many others as they could in the process. They invited all Lientje's Jewish relatives to join them. They also concentrated on keeping Jewish culture and tradition alive through their work as artists. Lientje was a dancer and singer, Piet was a musician. Another fifteen to twenty-five Jews were living in the house at various times. They were warned repeatedly that they were taking too many chances, but their response was always the same: "How can we refuse anyone who comes to us for shelter?"

On the twelfth of July, 1944, they were having breakfast when the house was surrounded by police and SS. They searched the house for the other inhabitants while an officer named Punt guarded Lientje, Piet, her sister, Jannie, and the three toddlers. While he questioned them, Lientje whispered to Kathinka not to be scared, and then threw a very convincing fit. Her whole body bounced up and down on the floor, she rolled her eyes and screamed, "Just do not take the children to prison, do not take the children." Clearly taken aback, Punt asked, "What should we do with them?" Jannie answered, "Take them to the physicians in the village." While Punt thought this over, Lientje threw another even more convincing fit, and Punt hastily agreed. Two policemen took the children to the homes of the doctors, who had to swear they would release them only to the Nazi authorities. The adults were taken to Gestapo Headquarters in Amsterdam where they spent the night, and where, the next day, they were questioned. When Lientje refused to provide information, the SS officer hit her in the face and said, "I know how to make you sing, little bird. I am going to order your child to be brought here, and confronted with you."

That night was the last night Piet and Lientje shared a cell in the prison. Piet was taken back for more interrogation in a van, with his sister-in-law, Jannie. At one point the van stopped and one of the two guards disappeared, saying he would be right back. Jannie gave Piet a meaningful look, then began to flirt with the remaining guard. Piet took advantage of the distraction and jumped out of the van and managed to reach the house of Gentile friends.

Now, in the garden house of the villa next door to me lived a Jewish ballet dancer, Karel Poons. He had not been able to tolerate the confinement of being in hiding for more than a few months, so he had dyed his hair, wore country clothes, and carried an identity card without the mandatory black "J" for Jew. He was passing as a Gentile, which was a risky business at best. He frequently rescued Jews, and on Thursday night, July 13, someone, I think his name was Jan Hemelrÿk, came and asked Karel and me if we would try to kidnap Kathinka the next morning. He and some other friends had tried to rescue her, but failed. The only result had been that a police guard had been assigned to the house. I didn't want Karel to come with me. If we failed, I would probably be in some kind of trouble, but there was no doubt about what Karel's fate would be. He insisted, however, and at eight-thirty the next morning we went to the village. Since I was quite familiar with the layout of the house, we agreed that I would go in through the back door and try to find Kathinka while Karel would distract whoever answered the front door.

I found the doctor's wife and all the children upstairs in the bathroom. Fortunately Kathinka was already dressed. I grabbed her, ran down the stairs, put her on the back of my bike, and pedaled off. It seemed as though she knew how high the stakes were. She was so small, so brave, and so scared, but she didn't utter a sound. In the meanwhile, Karel at the front door had encountered the doctor and the guard. He kept them occupied for as long as I needed to get away. Without his courage and ingenuity, Kathinka would have been arrested half an hour later when the Gestapo appeared. They were enraged that their hostage had escaped, and arrested the doctor. They also put up FBI-like posters all over the village, offering a reward for information leading to the capture of Kathinka Anita Bosch, born August 1941.

I wanted to tell you this story because it is about a Jewish rescuer. I believe that if it is important to ascertain the factors that lead to altruistic behavior, why not study all rescuers? Why discriminate against Jews? Does it not lead to a distortion of history to remember the Jews only as victims? There were many Jews who found a way to save their own lives for whom it would have been much safer to maintain a low profile, and yet that is not what they chose to do. Many Jews were courageous rescuers, and many did not survive just because they decided to try to save others Jews. I believe they should be honored the same as a non-Jew who tried to rescue Jews. In all, it had taken about thirty people to rescue little Kathinka. In addition, and not incidentally, I want you to know that after Auschwitz and Bergen Belsen, Lientje, Piet—his real name was Eberhard—and Kathinka were reunited. They had another daughter, and Lientje carried out her plan to perform Yiddish songs of celebration, defiance, and remembrance for the next fifty years. She involved her husband and both daughters in a three-week tour of the northeastern United States in 1986. She had changed her name to Lin Yaldati. She died last year. Her husband is still alive and lives in East Berlin, as does Kathinka, who has become a cellist.

Toward the end of the war there was no point in even going to pick up ration cards because there was no food to buy. Thousands of people, mostly women and children, traveled to the farms in Friesland to buy, barter, or beg for food. My bike had no tires by then, but I rode it this great distance and traded some family silver and my flute for what seemed like a wonderful amount of food. On my way home I had to cross a river near Zwolle where the Germans were known to patrol. As I approached this point, I, along with about forty others, was arrested and taken to be questioned. When we were told that our food was confiscated but that we would be allowed to leave the next morning, I became enraged. Probably it was all the years of the war pent up inside me, but I began to scream at the Germans about their war and their cruelty. The others tried to stop me, but they couldn't. The Germans didn't answer me at all, but the next morning I was taken across the bridge on a truck, and my food and bicycle were returned with no comment. I don't know what made them do it, but I do know that these Germans had some decency left.

When you bring up a baby, as I did Erica, since she was a few weeks old and suddenly you have to give her up, it isn't easy. So when I saw the ad from UNRRA, the United Nations Relief and Rehabilitation Administration, I went to work in the Displaced Persons [DP] camps for two reasons: it was a job and I needed a job, but most important, I thought I might find out quicker than if I stayed in Holland what had happened to a lot of my Jewish friends.

In the DP camp, I was in the office which processed the papers for placing people. There was an orphaned fourteen-year-old Jewish boy who wanted to go to his aunt and uncle in Brooklyn. I began to process the papers, and the Zionists came to me and said, "No, we've lost millions of Jews, and the ones who are left are going to Eretz Yisrael to start a Jewish state." I argued with them, because I thought this boy should be able to go to his family. That night they ran-sacked my office. Later, at another DP camp, I became friends with some Zionists and I came to understand what they were doing, and why.

Tony and I met in a DP camp. He had been an officer in the United States Army, and had seen the DP camps and decided he wanted to come back to Europe to work in them. He was running the one I was working in. After we worked in camps for two years, we married and came to the United States in 1947. We were full of stories and memories of what we'd done, but people soon said, "Hey, enough already. We're tired of hearing about Jews and DP camps." So we stopped and never talked about it again. And I never wanted to talk about the war, perhaps because I had some guilt that I didn't do enough. There were times that I had to choose the safety of Freddie and the children over going to help someone else, and maybe that was just rationale. We just got busy with our lives, Tony entered Harvard on the G.I. bill, and I looked for a job in social work. I called the Jewish Family and Child Service in Boston because they were helping Jewish refugees put their lives back together, and I knew I had experience with this. I had an interview, but they told me they were sorry but the philosophy was not to hire Gentiles. I thought this was too bad, and went to work with the New England Medical Center instead. Then they called me a year later to see if I was still interested. I asked what had happened to their philosophy, and they said they were having trouble dealing with these people through interpreters, so I was hired on the basis of my fluent Yiddish.

We had three sons, and I never even told them about the war. I had always had a photograph of Erica on my desk, but they just thought it was of me as a baby. When our oldest son applied for the conscientious-objector status during the Vietnam War, he had a conversation with his father about his army career and our attitudes about war and peace, and I told him I had been involved in objecting to the German presence, but I didn't tell him specifically what I'd done. We didn't talk about that until the letter came from the Israeli Embassy in 1983 saying they wanted to give me a medal. I have come to agree with Elie Wiesel who believes in remembering and telling. But it's difficult; I still find myself weepy when I retell a story.

All of our sons are incredibly good fathers. Our oldest has a Ph.D. in history and works for the office on aging in Connecticut. One has a Ph.D. in philosophy and taught for a while, but now is a member of Mr. Bennett's think tank. The third went to Dartmouth and works on the commission for aging in Vermont.

I have some basic notions about raising children. I never thought it was important whether or not my children knew what I did during the war. This wouldn't be what made them altruistic. I'll try to explain to you what I mean.

There are certain periods in a child's development in which learning comes naturally and effortlessly, whereas if the timing is off, learning the same things requires a much larger expenditure of time and effort. For instance, between one and two years old we all learn to talk. I was brought up quadrilingually: my mother was British and spoke English to me, my father was Dutch, I had a French governess, and we had German maids. So by two years old I was fluent in four languages, as were about two hundred other children in Amsterdam who were brought up under the same set of circumstances. I believe this can also be true for learning to care about others.

There is a controversial psychoanalyst, Alice Miller, who said, "Morality and ethics are prostheses which are necessary when something essential and basic is missing, when development of a real sense of self has been thwarted." The flip side of that gives evidence to my point about the importance of early child-rearing. Why did hundreds of thousands of Germans, good Germans from their very cultured country, follow Adolf Hitler, seemingly without question? The Dr. Spock of Germany during the nineteenth century, Dr. Schraeber, preached obedience, and so did his followers. They said if you break a child's will, by whatever method, before they're two years old, they'll do what you tell them to do. If this happens under a benevolent government there are no terrible consequences. But when overnight the government changes to Fascist or Communist, the people will still follow orders. And all the concentration camp directors said the same thing: "I wasn't responsible. I just did what I was told. I had a good Christian upbringing and I was taught to be obedient." That kind of obedience is a disaster. Children must be helped to develop their own sense of what is right by questioning.

It worries me that people have such disregard for children, that they put them in day care so easily. If you want to raise an altruistic generation, a generation of people who will care about one another and be willing to make some sacrifices—to use that dirty word—for one another, then the first people who should make sacrifices are the parents. The mother or father may have to sacrifice one of their careers for a few years and stay home with the child to demonstrate that the child is important enough to stay home for. If the parents don't think so, why should anyone else?

And I think it will make a difference if a child sees their parents behave in a caring way about larger issues, too. They'll see if their parents are racist, if they're anti-Semitic, if they support war and things like aid for the Contras, they'll probably grow up to do the same.

I don't know if the war changed me exactly. I think I've become more cynical and less optimistic. I thought naively that things would be different after the war. But I think it's very difficult for people to change, even a little bit. Now I'm asked all the time to give interviews and lectures. I do a lot of it, but I still have an analytic practice, and it's important to keep my life as private as possible. CBS has asked me to be on "60 Minutes," on a segment about rescuers. I'm very hesitant about it, but it's tempting because if I do it they want Erica to be interviewed with me, and I'd like that very much. She is a psychologist in Amsterdam, the mother of two daughters. I see her about once every two or three years, but I'd welcome the chance for an extra visit.

In 1991 Marion attended the Conference on the Hidden Child in New York, where she was reunited with Kathinka, whom she hadn't seen since the war. Erica was unable to attend because, at the age of forty-eight, she had just given birth to another child.

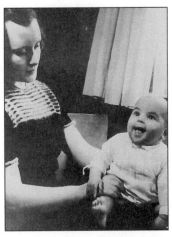

Marion Pritchard with
Erica, sitting on the
bench that was the
entrance to the basement
hiding place.

Freddie Pollak with
his daughter, Erica,
1944.

Lex and Tom Pollak before the war.

Lientje and
Kathinka, 1942.

Kathinka, East Berlin, 1987.

Marion and Tony Pritchard at
their wedding, 1947.

Marion and Tony Pritchard,
1988.

BERT BOCHOVE
WITH HIS FAMILY

Bert Bochove, 1946.

Bert and Betty Bochove live in a three-bedroom, two-bath home in Lomita, California, where they raised six children and two foster children. Bert's furniture upholstery shop occupies the garage. During the interview neighbors call and drop by for a variety of reasons. Bert insists on making us lunch, which consists of cold meats, Edam cheese, bread spread with butter, and fresh strawberries.

Betty, whom he married in 1953, has had a debilitating illness since 1968, and the family is as thoughtful and caring with her as she is with them. After interviewing Bert, we return a second time to meet the children, asking them to share their thoughts and impressions. Bert's oldest children, Eric and Marise, who were born in Holland during the war to him and his first wife, Annie, now live in other cities and could not be present.

BERT: I was born in 1910, in a small town in the Netherlands. Our house was on a canal, my father had a store, and there were eight of us kids, so we had a fine time. In our community many people were narrow-minded and very religious, but I was very lucky that my parents were, in a way, modern-thinking. My father and mother had a good marriage, I think, and they were religious, but in a different way from the other people. We always went to church in the winter, but in the summer we went sailing on Sundays. So I didn't grow up with the idea that you needed Christ to make it.

When I was three I got polio and I was in the hospital a long time. I had to do exercises and get my leg strong again; I was really spoiled by my mother and a wonderful nurse, and I managed to get my leg back to almost normal. One day when I was about eleven I did something that got me a medal from the Queen! It was autumn, and we were playing football on the waterfront when I heard someone fall into the water from their rowboat. It was a boy about a year younger than I was. I saw him go down two times, and it was obvious he couldn't swim, so I threw my shoes off and I dived after him. By the time I brought him the ten yards or so back to the wall, there were about thirty-five people standing there. I wondered later why somebody else didn't jump in the water.

I met my first wife in 1935. We married in 1941, and since she was a pharmacist we bought a drugstore in Huizen, about twenty minutes from Amsterdam. We lived above the drugstore, and the first months were pretty quiet. But in 1942 things started getting bad for the Jews. The way it started was, my wife's girl friend, her name is Henny, came to us. She was Jewish and she needed help. We didn't ever talk about it. It was something you had to do, and it was easy to do because it was your duty. And that was the beginning because when her husband came, that was all right, too. And when the sister came, well, why not? And that was the way it went till there were thirty-seven people.

As the people started coming I knew I had to build a hiding place because I had people working for me in the drugstore and you never knew if you could trust them. In fact, that was one of our biggest troubles. Anyway, the hiding place was between my house and the house next door where there was a fire wall. I made it so that the door shut automatically behind you, and no one ever discovered it. Really, it was impossible to find. And we added a balcony onto the front of the house so the Jews could go out for a little fresh air. We aired our blankets on that balcony, and if they crawled out onto it and stayed down, the blankets would hide them.

One person we had working in the store came from an ad we had in the newspaper. She was from a town close to the border, and later we found out she had German relatives. Then, we found out too late that she had a German soldier boy friend. I think she was more dumb than meaning harm, but she told him things that she shouldn't have. Once when she was on vacation, one of the Jewish fellows in the house found a letter addressed to her and we all decided to open it. It said, "Dear Yopie, when you are on vacation, we will get the people out of the house." You see, she had been living in our house and had become friends with the Jewish people. But she still betrayed them. She didn't really know they were Jewish because they all had false names, but she guessed. Anyway, we sent the people who were staying with us to another place, so when the Gestapo came they didn't find anyone.

There were many people hiding in Huizen, and most of the people hiding them got money from the underground. I was making enough money from the drugstore, mostly from selling paraffin and soap, two precious items during the war, that I didn't need that money, so I stood a little bit more free of everything. And because I grew up near farms, I knew where I could go to get food. I would borrow the town garbage truck and go to the country and pick up three or four thousand kilos of potatoes at a time and divide it between all the people in town. On one of these trips, the fellow driving the truck was pretty funny. Our truck was so heavy and we didn't have enough gas, so we got to this bridge and our truck wouldn't go all the way across. Water was running over the bridge, but he told me not to worry. All of a sudden we hear footsteps and he said to me, "That's what we wanted." It was a regiment of German soldiers, and he told them, "Well, you see, we have here potatoes for the Wermacht in Amsterdam, and if we don't get them there we're in trouble." They could understand that, so they gave us gasoline and we drove off. Before daylight we had them safely in the community!

The Rodriguez family was brought to our house by friends of ours in the middle of the night because they had been betrayed. The next day we went to their house and saved all their furniture, just in time. We found a house for their two children in my birthplace, and we sent them to Utrecht. When they were walking up the stairs to the place they were to be hidden, they passed some other people walking down. Mr. Rodriguez saw that the man was wearing black boots, which meant he was an NSBer, so he spit on the stairs in front of the man. That was not very smart. The next day they were picked up. They were the only people we lost. But their two children survived.

You know, I always knew that it was dangerous, that the risk was there, of course. And I knew every day that something could happen. But I was never really afraid. My worry was more for the family, for Eric and his mother—because you know our first child was born during the war. But personally, no, I wasn't afraid. I could sleep at night.

The moment I found out about liberation there was nobody in the house, which was the first time I had that experience in over three years. They had all gone outside and it was night before they came back! That day, the weather was the most beautiful you could imagine, but then the day the war started, the day was also beautiful.

Our second child, Marise, was born in 1945, just after the war. But my wife, Annie, had tuberculosis. I think it was because of the tension from the war, and the last year, the hunger winter, had been so terrible. She spent a lot of time in Switzerland, but she died in 1949. In 1951 I sold the store and rented a room with my two children in Betty's mother's house. I didn't know them before. Betty and I met in 1952, when she came to take care of the boarders while her mother was away.

BETTY: I saw Bert sitting on our couch with Marise standing in front of him. When he put his hand on her head in such a loving way, well, I think I fell in love with that hand. You know, Bert is not a hugging person. He may not touch you for two weeks, but then he will come by and put his hand on my face or something like that, and I know his love from that, just the care he takes.

BERT: We married in 1953, and we moved to America in 1956, and we had four more children. We also took care of other children who needed a place to live sometimes. You know, I like having a lot of people around to take care of. The war was terrible, but in some ways it was the best time of my life. There were always so many people around, and I got such satisfaction from helping out, from keeping people safe and comfortable.

BETTY: The kids grew up with all the stories from the war.

LIDY: I remember in elementary school, my first-grade teacher found out from someone else what my father had done. I had heard it before, but that was when I started realizing that my dad was a hero in people's eyes.

ANNA-MARIE: I think my dad has a good self-image. And he's a doer. He doesn't think about things, he just does them right away. He's got so much self-confidence, and I think he must have been born with it, and he does what's necessary without thinking about it.

BETTY: And now I see our children saying "yes" when anybody needs help, before they have time to think about it. You know, people always ask Bert how he was able to do what he did during the war, and I think I've just found the answer after thirty-five years of marriage. Recently, in the middle of the night, I dropped something on the floor which I needed. I absolutely couldn't find it. So finally I poked Bert and asked him to help me. He tried, but he couldn't find it either, so, out of desperation, he went from the bed onto the floor. I looked at him, with his bad knees, and I said, "Now how are you going to get up?" He said, "We'll worry about that when we get there." And that's the same attitude he had when taking care of those people. By the way, it took him quite a lot of effort and time to get back onto the bed that night!

ANNA-MARIE: I think our whole family is, maybe I shouldn't say it, but maybe a little bit more aware of people's feelings than most people are. If someone has a flat tire or something, we stop to help. I don't know if I would have done what he did. I've thought about it. I probably would.

LIDY: My parents were always patient and nonjudgmental of my friends. I think I've got a good judge of character from my parents simply by how they treat each other and how they treat their friends.

JILL: As long as I can remember there have been small crises in our family and things just had to be done, and everyone just got together and did it.

LIDY: They took in two foster kids for years, and they continue to help them.

JILL: They've taken in quite a few strays.

LIDY: But Dad never took in anybody that he didn't think would appreciate it.

BETTY: Recently, we were watching "The Cosby Show" and there was a knock on the door and there is a very dirty young man, about thirty-five years old. He said, "Do you have any work for me?" So Bert said, "No," and I see Bert grabbing for his wallet so I said, "Ask him if he has had a meal." The moment the man said, "No," the door goes open and Bert has him in the house. Now I would have said, "Here, have a seat out on the porch and I'll bring you some food," but not Bert. He has him out in the kitchen; it was hilarious! Because then he said, "Please, I'll eat my food while watching television!" And when Bert brings him the spaghetti, "Is there any cheese?"!

KO: I'm proud to death to talk about what my dad did whenever the subject comes up. People don't believe it, as a rule. You know, people are more inclined to believe somebody's shortcomings than somebody's strengths, especially ones with the consequences as great as the acts that my father did then. People are more inclined to believe your failures than your successes.

LIDY: The thing about him is that he's quiet and you're never sure what he's thinking. But he never had to say it because you could tell he loved you by looking at his hands and his eyes.

ANNA-MARIE: He's expressive; it's just not in your standard way.

Bert Bochove died on August 13, 1991. Betty told us: "Bert always wanted to be buried in a pine box. So we went to pick out a casket and we saw the fancy ones with velvet lining. We said, 'No, he just wanted the pine box.' "

"The man there said, 'But you don't want that. Those are the Jewish ones.' Then we saw the pine box and that's what we chose. At the cemetery, when the casket was lowered a little, we saw that there was a Jewish star on top. And we thought, 'That's just the way it should be.' "

Bert Bochove with his first wife, Annie, and their two children, Eric and Marise, 1944.

This is the balcony adjacent to the attic where Bert hid thirty-seven Jews. This photo was taken after the war.

The drugstore before the balcony was added, 1941.

Bert and Betty Bochove with their children and grandchildren, 1987. Left to right: (back row) Anna-Marie with her husband and child; (middle row) Lidy, Bert, Jill, Ko's wife, their children, and Ko; (front row) Betty with another of Anna-Marie's children.

RESCUERS

MARGUERITE MULDER

**Marguerite (on right) with
her youngest sister, 1944.**

*In spite of the multiple sclerosis that has confined her to a wheelchair, Mar-
guerite Mulder comes to the door and welcomes us into her apartment in
Oegstgeest, an Amsterdam suburb. It has been painstakingly designed and
modified to make it possible for her to live alone. During the war she was part
of a large Dutch Reformed (evangelical) family that held stereotypical views
about Jews. The Mulders nevertheless viewed Hitler as a murderer, and
believed in helping persecuted people. Marguerite worked with her parents to
hide Jews in their home in Groningen.*

Generally, you didn't have Jewish friends. I was born in 1921 in Groningen,
a farming town in northern Holland. My parents had seven girls and four
boys, and I was the ninth one. Mother was the daughter of a farmer and,
though it was unusual in those days, she became a teacher. Father taught English in high schools and universities. I liked my father but I was a little afraid
of him. My father would say, "Always pay your taxes and give money to the
poor." I went to a Christian school, and I remember seeing Jewish boys and
girls coming home from their school.

I once went to a synagogue and saw the men and women separated and
always talking—it was very different from our church. My older sisters
would go to the home of a Jewish family on our street on the Jewish Sabbath
to turn lights off and on. Just before the war, a Jewish family moved in next
door. You just didn't say anything to Jews, but their son's name was Max and
we said hello to each other. They were all killed.

The first of the Jews came to our house in 1941. He was a Roman

Catholic Jew, a friend of a friend of my brother. He stayed for a few days, and then Father said to my brother-in-law, "Ask Dite [Marguerite's sister] if he can stay at your house for a few days." Dite's husband answered, "I don't want to die for a Jew." They were very afraid. Being courageous is not inherited. You either are or you aren't. We sent this first Jew to an uncle in the north, and then he survived by hiding in Amsterdam.

In 1942 someone asked if we'd take a girl, and I went to pick her up on my bike. She was six years old. She said to me, "My name was Slager"—that's a very Jewish name which means "butcher"—"but now my name is Baker." Then I understood what it meant to be a Jew in the Netherlands. It made me angry. I got off my bike and said to her, "I'm going to do everything I can for you." Her ten-year-old sister came to us later. She stayed with us and then with one of my sisters and then with a sister of one of my sisters-in-law. She stayed there until after the war. Her parents were taken, her father was killed, and her mother was put in the gas chamber but the door wasn't well closed, and she escaped with two other women. She survived, and so did all three of her children.

The Jews betrayed themselves by registering as Jews. They should never have put it on their cards. We knew a family who didn't look Jewish and didn't register and left Amsterdam and were fine throughout the war. But they should have known not to identify themselves for the Nazis. Hitler said in *Mein Kampf* that he would kill all the Jews. But no one believed it.

In 1942 we moved to a house that was a little distance from other houses. A Jewish woman came for two weeks, another Jewish girl came for two or three weeks, and another for a few days. Then an older woman, about seventy-two, came at Christmas in 1943. Two of my sisters who came to visit that Christmas said, "Why do we always have to do it? Why we and nobody else?" I said, "There isn't anyone else." This woman was supposed to stay for only a few days but they couldn't find another place for her. What she did was mend all the socks and all the underwear, chores my mother didn't like to do. And she was extremely intelligent. She had interesting discussions with my father.

Later, in March 1944, Flory Asscher came to us. She was just like a sister to me. My father gave her the same pocket money he gave us. Her husband, Eli, was in a P.O.W. camp. My father used to say of Eli, "He is a Jew who doesn't cheat." This is something Jesus said, you know. Not that all Jews cheat. Eli was a nice man, and Flory is a beautiful woman. We promoted them to our brother and sister. They live in Beersheva, in Israel, and I have visited them twice. We're still friends, after forty-three years.

In October, one of my brothers was killed by the Germans because he was mentally retarded and didn't respond fast enough to a German command. Flory had to leave us for a few days during the time of his funeral, and we sent her to another family. The man of that family tried to seduce her. She had been with twenty-three families before us and she said, "Father was the first man who didn't try to touch me. He was just a father to me."

In all, about sixteen Jews stayed in our house at one time or another. I told my parents to be very careful because I was sure the SS would come to our house. I told them I was leaving, and Flory went to another house, too, so we weren't there when they came. My parents went to prison, and my father started having heart failure. He told them, "I always knew when the U.S. entered the war you would lose." They brought them back home, but all the furniture was gone except for one couch and four chairs. Later we got furniture from the houses of Nazi collaborators [NSBers].

Then we heard my youngest brother was killed. In 1940 he had said, "The Germans are like fleas—they're everywhere." So he left to fight and ended up in England with British Intelligence. He was dropped into the Netherlands and captured in April 1945. He was found dead in his cell. They said it was a heart attack but we all thought he was tortured. Then in October 1945, my father died, so in one year my mother lost two sons and her husband.

People ask why were my parents and I able to do these things for the Jews. I think it's in one's character, and besides that, of course, we prayed the Lord would help us. And I think it's because of my character that I'm still alive today. It's because I'm able to neglect my M.S. I'm able to put it aside and try to live with the rest of me. And I think my parents did this, too.

After the war I was ex-tremely tired. I kept going to doctors who couldn't find anything. They said it was psychological, probably the result of the stress of the war. But in 1961 I went to America as a visitor's exchange worker. I was a dietician in a hospital, and I thought the change of scenery would help me. Multiple sclerosis was finally diagnosed in 1964. If it had been found earlier, I probably never would have gone to the United States. It was such a relief to find out it was a real illness and not psychological. But I wasn't able to accept it until 1967. I said, "I'll commit suicide." Then I started to understand what it means to believe in God. I was fighting with God at first, and then I thought about Jacob wrestling with the Lord. I won, but I was left crippled.

They always said the Jews crucified Jesus and they have to convert themselves to Christianity. In 1940 the mother of my best friend said that the Jews were responsible for the fix they were in because they crucified Jesus. I began to read because I wanted to know what was true. The first thing Jesus said was, "Father, forgive them, they know not what they do." And then the Jews said, "Blood will come over us and our children for twenty-five generations." So I read more. Saint Peter said, "You Jews, who crucified him. . . . " But that wasn't true; it was the Romans. But the Jews did it, too, of course.

Well, everyone is anti-Semitic, and Christians hate God because he said they must do this and that, and also because God gave first to the Jews and later to the Christians. And now with all the problems in Israel, people think it is good they can hate Jews again. Nobody says the Arab countries have a responsibility to the Palestinians. They say the Israelis should help them and give them a homeland.

My mother died in 1973, just a few weeks before she was going to receive the medal from Yad Vashem. But she knew she was going to get it, and she said, "Now I won't have my medal." But I have it, and in 1985, I went to Israel and planted our tree along the Avenue of the Righteous. I stayed with Flory and Eli. We'll keep in touch with one another until death. It was a terrible time, but a wonderfully human time, too. I have no regrets. I would do it again, just the same.

Marguerite's father and mother, at the wedding of one of their daughters, 1944.

Sonja Slager with her older sister, Vreesje, in the Mulders' garden, 1943.

The wedding of Eli and Flory Asscher, 1942. Her Star of David is hidden by her flowers.

Marguerite's brother, Dirk, who was shot and killed by a German soldier in 1944 because he was mentally retarded and didn't understand a command to halt.

THE NETHERLANDS

JOHN WEIDNER

John Weidner..

Because John Weidner, at seventy-six, still puts in a full day's work, we met him in his office at American Dietary Laboratories in Pasadena, California, the health-food supplement business he started in 1957, when he emigrated from Holland to America. A Seventh-Day Adventist, he believes that people have a moral responsibility to take care of their bodies. Although he no longer needs to work, he continues to do so because he wants to be able to give money to worthy causes. He has not only received a medal from Yad Vashem for saving hundreds of Jews but has been honored by the Dutch government and by the United States for rescuing fliers who had been shot down. Despite a speech impediment caused by Nazi torture, he is often asked to speak at Holocaust remembrances. He talks about his frustration with the world's inhumanity since World War II, but his faith never wavers.

I am Dutch, but my father was a minister in the Seventh-Day Adventist Church, and he was in Brussels for his ministry when I was born in 1912. My mother read me stories from the Bible. My favorite was about Daniel and how the bad people were punished. I used to ask her to read it to me over and over again. The Jewish people brought us the Bible, and I was raised to love and respect them. My father spent time in prison in Switzerland because he refused to send his children to public school on Saturday, which is our Sabbath. Later he spent the war in jail because he protested what was happening to the Jewish people.

The basis of the Ten Commandments is to love God and your neighbor. When the war started I thought I had to do something. But what could I do? I could maybe help one or two Jewish people. Then, because I had gone to school for ten years on the border of France and Switzerland, I realized that I could use my knowledge of the border to get many Jews into Switzerland.

I was in the textile business in Lyon in the south of France. In 1940 southern France, known as the "free zone" because it was not yet occupied by the Nazis, became a haven for Jews fleeing the Nazis. But once the Jews reached the south, the French put them in detention camps. Pétain's Vichy government cooperated with the Nazis by regularly handing Jews over to them for deportation and death. I began by taking mostly Dutch Jews out of these camps and escorting them to safety in Switzerland. As our organization grew, it was given the name "Dutch-Paris." We finally saved more than 800 Jews, more than 100 Allied airmen, and many others who needed refuge from the Nazis.

In the beginning it was difficult to get Jews into Switzerland because the Swiss were overly careful. They were concerned that Germany would take them over. Then, when America showed some interest in the defeat of Germany, Switzerland became more liberal.

Hitler's ideology was totally against my concept of love and compassion, so totally against my ideals of love and family that I had to try to help. I slowly got friends and family to join me, and our organization grew very large. I was busy going to Switzerland to get the registration papers we needed before any Jew would be accepted into Switzerland. My college was right on the border, and just behind the college were the mountains. In order to avoid the guards and the dogs, I would bring refugees down into Switzerland that way. All my friends at the school would watch the guards during the night and tell us when to go, then they'd cut the barbed wire, and we'd be in Switzerland.

As we grew larger, we got the help of some organizations. The World Council of Churches in Geneva, representing big Protestant organizations, provided us with funds. At first I used all my own money and then my friends'. When you start an organization with all these people, you have to travel, to eat, to find hotels, and it costs money. The World Council and the Dutch government gave us money to help the Dutch people.

Our organization was made up of all kinds of people. Catholics, Protestants, Jews, agnostics, everything. I was the head, but my right and left hands were two Jews. I had great admiration for them because they were in danger as Jews and as members of the underground. These men could have stayed in Switzerland and been safe, but they took this double risk instead.

I had to change my name three times, because John Weidner was the most wanted man on the Gestapo's list. We helped many people; we never looked only for important or rich ones. A Jew was a Jew to us. But I did have people who paid. For example, one man I escorted personally was a Jew from Belgium, but of Dutch ancestry. I took him, his wife, his mother and father, and his four children to Switzerland. [After the war, the man became one of the founders of Club Med.] Then a very important man of the Dutch underground had to go to London. I took him to Spain, and from there, he got to London. Later he became the minister of justice in the Dutch government-in-exile. Another man was French, but not Jewish. After I got him to England, he became the minister of justice of the French government in England. Sometimes an Allied airman would be shot down over Holland, and we would pick him up, usually from some Dutch person's house, and take him to Spain and then to England. Anyone we took to Switzerland had to stay there, but if someone wanted to get to England, or anywhere else, we took him to Spain. It was more difficult to get to Spain, so nearly all the Jews were taken to Switzerland.

Most of them had no money. I remember one day we had a woman and her husband, and she said, "We have nothing, we are poor." So, okay, we took them. And then we came over the border, and they have a loaf of bread, and the Swiss say, "What is that?" And they say it's bread, so the Swiss took the bread and he cut it in half, and there was a gold bar inside. So they confiscated it. She was just human. Not nice, maybe, but human.

So we had to deal with that kind of thing. But I always said that when people say they have no money, maybe they have, maybe not, but you help everyone. I have never refused anyone penniless.

The most terrible thing for me, and something I can never forget, is that my sister was arrested and killed. I brought her into the organization, and one day one of our agents was arrested. The Nazis found a little book on her with all the names and addresses of our group, so in one or two days, they arrested half of our people, about 150 agents. My sister was among them. Forty of those arrested never returned. My sister died in Ravensbruck. I think of that every day. We had to decide whether to punish the agent for carrying the list. This was strictly against the rules. And besides, she talked when she was tortured. But I know how hard that is, because I also was tortured. I didn't talk, but I can't really blame her for not being able to withstand the torture. It's possible that I may have been born with some special quality which made it easier for me not to give in. As for the woman, we decided not to punish her.

Another thing that I can never forget: one day I was in the train station in Lyon, and there were a lot of Jews and Nazis there. A Jewish woman was holding a baby in her arms, and the baby started to cry. The SS man took the baby, threw it to the ground, and crushed its head with his boot. I can never forget the sight and the sound of that baby.

That is one of the reasons I came to the United States in 1958. After the war all my friends told me, "You have to go where the memories won't be right in front of you every day." My sister was arrested in a church in Paris, and every time I would see that church, I would remember.

After the war I was disillusioned with Holland; so were a lot of other people. We dreamed of a time when the Nazis would be out of our country and there would be paradise. But when the war was over, many people who were twisted up with the Nazis came back and took some of their old positions back. The people in the underground had these grand ideas of justice taking over the world. So the war was won but the great paradise we dreamed about wasn't realized. Just like Kurt Waldheim becoming president of Austria. He came back on top, right? In every country, they came again. But you have some illusions and they disappear. So we were dis-appointed.

At the end of the war I was an officer in the Dutch army. The government asked me to work on prosecuting those who worked with the Germans, screening them to determine if or how they should be punished. Then they asked me to decorate all the people in the underground and point out the families of the ones who had died, so they could be taken care of by the government. I did this for three years. The bad thing was that many collaborators were punished, but many got their old positions back and escaped any punishment. I realized then that anyone who believed in pure justice is always disappointed because it does not exist.

After these three years I went back into my textile business in Paris, which is what I did before the war. But as I said, every place brought back bad memories for me. In Paris, the church where my sister was arrested on a Saturday morning . . . So I came here in 1958. I'll never forget, but here it's not so active, so direct.

I had always wanted to go into the health-food business. When I finished my studies in 1932, it was the Depression and there were no openings in that business, and I had no money, so I had to go into textiles. But when I came to California, I could do what I wanted, and I chose health food because Seventh-Day Adventists believe that physical health is as important as mental and spiritual health. They promote vegetarianism, not as an article of faith, but for health.

The City of Hope honored me as "Man of the Year." It is always nice to be recognized, but I don't get excited about these things. I did my duty. I just hope to give the message to other people. I am invited often to speak at a synagogue, or to other Jewish groups, about my work during the war.

I work hard for my church. I met my wife at the church shortly after I came to America. Recently I was able to find work and housing for some Ethiopian refugees who became members of the church. I helped some handicapped children in Monterey Park [California] to become educated. You know, American society is probably the most compassionate of all leading

---

countries. I know in our church, four-fifths of all the money we raise is sent outside of America. I'm sorry to say that most Americans didn't do what they should have during the war, but they support Israel now, and that is good.

I am happy about Israel because I saw during the war how few nations did anything for the Jewish people. In 1938, there was a big meeting of all nations in Evian to discuss the problems of the refugees. I attended and was shocked and angry. They had big dinners, poured expensive champagne and wine, but none of the nations offered to accept Jewish people. I have been to Israel twice, and one of the trips was to plant my tree at Yad Vashem.

We all knew in the underground that the tension and physical hardships of the war years would take their toll on us. Many have died before their time. I am lucky to be living this long, but I have had open-heart surgery, and my foot was amputated because of diabetes. During the war when I was tortured, the Gestapo hit me in the head and I had surgery, but I still feel the effects of that. It affected my speech, and that is why I'm difficult to understand. But when I look back over my life, I think that when you do your duty, it's just your duty. On the battlefield or in social life, it's just your duty. After I die, I'll thank God for what I had in this life and I hope God will know I did the best I could to help people.

Dutch-French refugees plow through knee-deep snow-drifts in a rugged Pyrénées pass.

Queen Juliana and Prince Bernhardt of the Netherlands decorating John Weidner.

John Weidner receiving
the Medal of Freedom
award from a U.S.
officer, 1946.

John Weidner (center) and Dr. Gideon Hausner (left) of
Yad Vashem, Jerusalem.

Queen Beatrix of the Netherlands, with
John Weidner, Los Angeles, 1985.

LOUISA STEENSTRA

**Louisa Steenstra with her
daughter, Beatrix.**

*When we ring the doorbell to Louisa Steenstra's apartment in Niagara Falls,
Canada, a cuckoo clock confirms the hour of our appointment. The clock is one
of the few possessions she brought with her from her native Holland. The first
thing she tells us, before the recording equipment is set up, is that her daughter
hadn't wanted her to talk with us. Dredging up the horrible memories of the war
invariably requires several days of recovery. As she tells the particularly cruel
story of how her husband was killed in the last months of the war, her voice and
face seem ageless, as though part of her were still in the past.*

I had been a kindergarten teacher, but when jobs got scarce I took a secre-
tarial course and became a secretary and bookkeeper for a business owned
by Jews. Albert and I were married in 1938. When the Nazi occupation
came, the Germans took over all the Jewish businesses and got rid of the
Jews, but the other workers had to stay on. I told my husband, "I'll kill
myself before I work for Germans." So I lied and told them I was having a
baby so I could quit my job. I had had Jewish friends in school. We didn't
hate Jews; you never thought about those things in Holland.

Albert worked as a supervisor in a wine factory and he got involved in
the Resistance at work. He became a commander of twenty-one men, and
since we had a big house, we rented some rooms to Jews. The first one we
took in was the nephew of my boss. Then Emmanuel Marcus rented a room.
He had been taken to a camp near Groningen but he escaped and came
straight to our house.

One evening I was visiting Emmanuel's sister-in-law, Anna Marie Marcus.
Her husband, Karel, had already been taken to Westerbork. She had five-year-

old twin boys and I often did baby-sitting for her. While I was there, she talked about going into hiding, and all of a sudden there was a pounding on the door and two men, an SS officer and a Dutch collaborator, stormed into the room. It was frightening. I felt so sorry for those Jews. The Nazis would come in the middle of the night and take them out of their houses with nothing. I hated those Germans. When Anna Marie leaned over to kiss me goodbye, she put a key to her house in my hand and asked me to come back later and pack some suitcases of the children's clothes and bring them to her.

They sent Anna Marie and the boys to Westerbork and took me to the police. Luckily a friend of my husband's worked at the police station and got me out. After that, I wanted only to live a quiet life, but a few days later I had to try to go into Westerbork and take the warm clothes for the children. I thought that if I didn't, the winter would take them before the Nazis could. I went back to the police station and got a friend to get me a pass into Westerbork signed by the commanding SS officer in Groningen. I was afraid, but I knew it was something I had to do. As I got near the gate, a woman from that neighborhood asked me what I was doing. When I told her she shook her head and warned me, "No piece of paper will save you. No one goes into Westerbork and walks out again."

I'll never forget what I saw there. Thousands of people crying and grabbing at me. After two hours I found the Marcuses. They took the clothes and told me to leave right away. I was pregnant, and she was afraid for me. I was afraid enough for myself. And I did have a hard time getting out. I was lucky that a man I knew was there, a friend from my office, and he told the Germans, "I know this lady. She doesn't belong in here; you have to let her out." After that I had a new fear of the Nazis. That day I had seen what they could do.

My husband and I then began hiding more Jews. Other young men came; we had a good hiding place in the attic. But because the house was so large, the Dutch government insisted that we take in an elderly Dutch couple whose house had been destroyed by the war. We told this couple that the boys were Dutch Christians who were hiding to avoid being sent to Germany to work. That's what the Germans were doing to all young Dutch boys. But I think they were always suspicious, and they were especially afraid for themselves.

One day the old woman peeked into a pot of soup I was making on the stove, and Emmanuel Marcus said, "It isn't nice manners to open someone else's pot." He was absolutely wrong to say this. She stormed out of the kitchen and right away I knew we were in trouble. This old couple we had taken in, they were so scared but you know what happened? They told that we had Jewish people in hiding to a friend of theirs. But he was not really a friend; he was a traitor. She said to him, "Nothing should happen to this couple"—that was me and my husband—"because they're nice people, but you'll have to take the Jews away." Stupid, because you knew what would happen. She should have known this. So it's Sunday afternoon, you know, and five German soldiers came with a German shepherd. God, oh, God! Barking! They told my husband to sit in a chair and they asked him, "Where are those Jews?" He said, "I don't know what you're talking about." So they sent the dog to him and it bit his ear off. "Oh, my God," I said to Albert, "tell them, because you're lost anyway!" But they didn't ask me nothing.

So my little daughter—she was three years old—she was screaming for Daddy, and he still didn't say anything. And then the German shepherd walked upstairs and was barking. So the Nazis—one sat with me and the other four went upstairs—they found the hiding place. So this man who was sitting with me, I was lucky, boy, and he was stupid. When they were shooting upstairs, he ran up there, and I grabbed my little daughter. I didn't have shoes on, not a coat. I grabbed my daughter and went out of the house. I ran across the street. It was the twenty-first of January 1945, snow and ice and I had not even a coat on! I ran across the street—my mother-in-law was living there. And I said, "Oh, my God! Take care of Trixie, they killed Albert!" And I went right away to the underground, and I stayed there for two days. I didn't even know what happened in my house.

Then I sent for my daughter, and the underground took us somewhere outside Groningen, where we stayed until the end of the war. When the Canadians came I went to the commandant and told my story and he gave me a jeep to go back to my town to see what happened to my husband. I went into my house. It was empty, no furniture or anything. The wall of the hiding place was broken open and the room was full of blood; they had killed my husband and the Jews. Then we went to the house of the traitor—I knew who did it—and he didn't answer the door. The police broke the lock and arrested him. I couldn't live in my house anymore, so they gave me the house of the traitor, but I couldn't live there either. There was a shortage of houses because everything had been bombed. It was a terrible time in Holland. We were so poor that I made a dress from curtains. Food was still short. Most people didn't have anything.

I don't think I would do it a second time, knowing what I know now. I lost too much. But we felt so sorry for those Jewish people with their kids screaming when the Nazis came in the night to pick them up. We had to do what we did. We knew it was dangerous, so many people did it. And we hated those Germans, when we heard how badly they bombed Rotterdam. That's why we helped. And don't forget, I worked so many years for Jewish people, and my husband did, too.

My whole family was involved. My sister hid a Jew and he survived. And then my brother in another city had the brother of the one in my house. We had to keep moving them around every couple of months.

I lost everything in the war, all my furniture, everything. After the war when the Dutch government invited survivors to come look for their jewelry which the Nazis had stolen, I went to try to find my engagement ring which I lost in Westerbork the day I went to take things to the Marcuses. And it was a miracle that I found it! It's this ring I'm wearing today, and it's one of the few things I have from before the war.

Karel and Anna Marie Marcus came back from Bergen Belsen, and the boys survived, too. They went right back to their old house. I got my medal from Yad Vashem in 1985. The Marcuses gave the testimony. You know, it wasn't so important for me, but for my daughter I think it's important. She never had a father, so the medal is like having something of him she can hold onto.

Emmanuel Marcus, one of the Jews who came to stay with Louisa and Albert Steenstra.

Jewish men in Fledders Work Camp, Block 1. Emmanuel Marcus escaped from this camp and fled to the Steenstras' home, where he was killed in January 1945.

ARNOLD DOUWES AND SEINE OTTEN

At eighty-two, Arnold Douwes is a firecracker, still burning with opinions and convictions. We pick him up at his home in Utrecht, on the way to Emmen to do a joint interview with him and his best friend and wartime compatriot, Seine Otten. In the car I fumble for my tape recorder as he begins to talk non-stop in crisp and precise English about his childhood, the war, and the abundant cornfields that flank the highway.

Seine Otten is Arnold's opposite: Seine in muted brown, Arnold in siren red, Seine quiet and gentle, Arnold breathing smoke. Perhaps Seine is more subdued than usual because his wife of over forty years has recently died, and his grief is palpable. Seine and his wife, along with Arnold, were part of a network of 250 people in the town of Nieuwlande who found and provided shelter for hundreds of Jews. Yad Vashem has honored not only the individual rescuers but the town itself.

SEINE: I was born in 1910. I had seven brothers and sisters. Arnold did, too, but we didn't know each other then. My father was a farmer and we belonged to the Dutch Reformed Church. I became a teacher and got married in 1938. My son was born in 1939 and my daughter in 1946. I was teaching in the Christian school and we were living in Nieuwlande [a farming district in the northeast]. My wife and I believed very strongly in the Bible, and we tried to live by it. In 1941, when we began to realize Jews would be persecuted, we told them, "When you are in need, you may come to Nieuwlande."

ARNOLD: In 1941 all the Jews in Holland were ordered to go to Amsterdam. It was like putting them in a ghetto. That's what made it so much more dangerous for a Jew in Amsterdam, because the Nazis could catch them faster if they were all together. They should have stayed in the small towns.

SEINE: They did it to the Jews step by step. First they had to wear the yellow star, then there were signs saying, "Jews forbidden on this street," et cetera.

ARNOLD: In *Mein Kampf*, Hitler had already said it had to be done that way. So we knew years before exactly what he had in mind. That's why I came back to Holland and started doing anything I could to resist the Nazis.

SEINE: Arnold was the first to stay in our house. He was running from the Gestapo. He had to go into hiding because he had been arrested for wearing the yellow star even though he is not a Jew.

ARNOLD: It was a stupid thing to do. It couldn't help anyone. But I had done things like that before. When I was young, in the twenties, I went to the great United States to live. One day during the thirties, I sat down at a lunch counter in Chicago, and there was a black man sitting there, but no one was serving him. I started talking to him and found out what was going on, so when my food came, I gave it to him and I ordered another meal. The owner of the restaurant didn't like that, and he called the police and I was arrested. I was deported as a Communist. My case went all the way to the Supreme Court, and I won. I could have gone back, but by then I was involved in the Resistance.

SEINE: Arnold has been my best friend for almost fifty years. I met him when he came to my house to "dive" [Dutch people who needed to hide or disappear for a while were called *onderduikers*, meaning "one who dives under"]. We started talking about the situation and that led to my neighbor Johannes Post, who had a farm in Nieuwlande. I taught his children. He was the first person I knew who understood what Hitler planned to do to the Jews. He started by looking for people who would give them shelter.

One day Post came to me to ask to use my wife's and my identity cards. I gave them to him and got new ones by saying we had lost them. My wife said, "If Hitler wants to kill all the Jews of Europe, I think we should try to save as many as we can."

A neighbor asked me to take a married Jewish woman into our home, and we said we would. She came in late 1942. The experience with that first woman wasn't good. She was from a rich family and wanted my wife to wait on her all day. While I was out teaching, my wife was left at home to deal with the people we were hiding. This woman was the worst of the fifty who stayed with us. After five months, Arnold placed her in another house, and she survived the war. It was difficult for the housewives because they were home with the Jews all day. The men went off to work, or to do resistance work, or whatever. My wife and I only hid the Jews. Arnold was the one who went out to pick them up.

ARNOLD: I had to lie to everybody. I would go into Amsterdam and tell a Jewish family, "Come with me. I know a wonderful farm where there is plenty of food and you'll be safe." Was there such a place? Of course not. But we'd never have been able to get them out of Amsterdam if we had told them the truth. We'd get them to go with us, and that's where Seine and his wife came in. The Jews would stay with them a few days until we found a place. No matter how many we brought, their door was always open for more. And they had a very small house, only two rooms, and the lavatory was outside in the garden. There was no water, there was a small kitchen, a stairway up to an attic with a false hiding place, and a real hiding place under the house. That was the most important part of the house, this hiding place. It also was a workplace with a mimeograph machine for turning out underground leaflets and where we worked with carrier pigeons that we sent to London. There were usually at least three people hiding, but sometimes they kept twelve or thirteen people at a time, sleeping on the table, under the table, anywhere.

One time I went to a minister who had said he would take Jews, but he got scared when I got there and said no, because he had a family and couldn't take the risk. I said, "Okay, thank you very much," and I walked out of the house. I told the Jews waiting outside, "Everything's fine. Wait here a few minutes and then knock on the door. He'll let you in." I left them standing there in the rain, and I knew that when the minister saw them like that, he'd let them in, and he did. I didn't have any choice; I had nowhere else to take them. That was the best thing about Nieuwlande. Everyone helped. We didn't have any Dutch Nazis here. That's why the whole town was honored at Yad Vashem. Those who didn't actively help kept quiet and let others do the work.

SEINE: Two Jewish boys, Peter [Isador Davids] and Herman [Lou Gans], did resistance work but they couldn't be seen out on the street very much. They stayed in our house for a long time. They worked with pen and ink and paint and paper, drawing and writing all kinds of cards and pamphlets against the Germans to encourage the inhabitants of Nieuwlande. Herman especially was very clever drawing cartoons representing events that ridiculed the Germans. We sold these cards to get money for poor divers and for resistance efforts. A typical one shows a woman carrying packages, holding the hand of a child who's walking behind her. The message is from the New Testament and says in Dutch, "Never forget to be hospitable, for by hospitality some have entertained angels unawares." On the back it reads, "Help the people in hiding and buy this card for more than you can afford."

ARNOLD: Peter and Herman did more than stay inside and draw. Once we were taking a Jewish girl to a hiding place, and we had hired a taxi, which was unusual but necessary that night. A German soldier stopped us and asked for a ride, so we had to let him in. He never guessed what we were really up to.

In 1943 Johannes Post had to leave Nieuwlande because it wasn't safe, so I took over his work. I stole everything from ration cards to bicycles. I sent messages by carrier pigeon to England. I found hiding places for Jews, and I picked them up and took them. I worked twenty hours every day. Our greatest enemy, after the Nazis, was time. We never had enough hours in a day. We could never do enough. I didn't have a family like Seine. He risked more. I think only those with families should have gotten medals from Yad Vashem. Anyway, who needs a medal? I did my job and the Jews did theirs by keeping out of the hands of the Germans. That was their work, and it was very difficult. I could not have done it myself. Just imagine, for two years, to sit in a little hole or some damn place or other. It's enough to make you go mad, but they did what they had to do, and that's quite enough for me. Yes, they saved themselves and their families; they had the courage to sit it out for such a long time. Just imagine what that means.

SEINE: It was terrible sometimes, but we had a lot of fun, too. At night we'd be home after the eight o'clock curfew, and we'd all sit around the table and tell stories. Arnold's were the best. I'll tell you one: I was warned, early in 1944, that my name was on all the Nazi lists and I should get out of Nieuwlande. But I wouldn't leave without my wife and son. So on May 10, 1944, we went to a neighboring farm about six kilometers from home.

ARNOLD: On that night, Seine was gone and Nico [another member of the Resistance] and I were in the basement hiding place trying to put a message on a carrier pigeon's leg informing the Allied forces in England that there were Nazi V-2 rocket parts hidden underground at a nearby airfield. The Gestapo came to the house and searched for three hours, but all they found was the false hiding place in the attic. When they finally left, we let the pigeon go. The next day the Allies bombed the airfield and I got the message back from another pigeon: *"Carpe diem!"* That was a great day. We sent many messages like that. Still we didn't do enough. It's a disgrace that 100,000 Dutch Jews died in Auschwitz. Even in a place like Nieuwlande, it was hard to place Jews.

SEINE: Johannes Post was a real hero. Later on he formed a commando troop to rescue friends who had been captured. In July 1944, he was on such a rescue mission, but there was a traitor in his group and he was arrested. He and two of his comrades were condemned to death, and on July 16 he was executed. You should know that after the war a well-known Dutch writer wrote a book about Post. His wife is still alive and nearly ninety years old. He was a real hero. We were not heroes, not really. We had hope that it would come to an end without disaster.

ARNOLD: It wasn't a question of why we acted. The question is why things weren't done by others. You could do nothing else; it's as simple as that. It was obvious. When you see injustice done you do something against it. When you see people being persecuted, and I didn't care whether they were Jews or Eskimos or Catholics or whatever, they were persecuted people and you had to help them.

SEINE: People ask me if I taught my children to help other people. I don't think that's the point. Look, for the three months since my wife died my daughter has come here three or four times a day. She has cooked meals for me. And besides that, she goes once every fortnight to the old-age home to visit a man who has one leg and who is blind and deaf. I tell her this is nice of her, and she says, "No, it's my duty. It's so we don't feel alone in the world." And that is the whole point. Arnold lives an hour away, and he can't travel by himself, but still he has been to see me three times since my wife died.

ARNOLD: Seine helped me rescue Judith, the woman who became my wife. We went to Israel and lived on a *moshav* [a farm community]. We have three daughters who are still there. I think of the war every day.

SEINE: Perhaps ten or twenty years from now when we are no longer alive there won't be articles in the paper every week about the war, perhaps then the war will be forgotten. But not yet.

Johannes Post, a farmer from Nieuwlande who became the Christian Reformed resistance leader.

Arnold Douwes (right) with Peter and Herman, two Jewish men who were in the Resistance.

Identity cards of Seine Otten and his wife, Dirkje Jantje, during the war.

RESCUERS

PIETER AND JOYCE MIEDEMA

**Reverend Miedema traveling on his bicycle
for rescue activities.**

*Crippled by a stroke in 1979, Presbyterian minister Pieter Miedema, who once
spoke six languages, can with enormous effort speak only a few words. In their
comfortable suburban home in Bowmanville, Ontario, Joyce Miedema recounts
her memories, and, with compassion and respect, tries to tell her husband's
story. He listens carefully, speaking with his eyes, or nodding his head, and only
a few times does he interrupt, frustrated that he can't tell it his way. Although
he saved many people, he refused all medals, believing that receiving an award
for doing what everyone should have done would be inappropriate: it was
enough for him and God to know his deeds. But as he feels the end of his life
approaching, he has decided to tell his story for the sake of his children.*

When the Nazis began deporting Jews in 1941, Pieter was twenty-six
and a minister in the Dutch Reformed Church in Friesland. It was our
Christian belief that Jews were special. Queen Wilhelmina was popular with
the Jews because she had great sympathy and feeling for them. This was in
the Calvinistic tradition. The church held a minister's meeting to talk about
the "relocation" of the Jews. Pieter corrected the senior minister, saying,
"You mean 'deportation,' don't you?" He thought he should practice what
he preached. He was always one step ahead. He was giving Sunday sermons
that said it very clearly. I remember his telling the congregation, "If you opt
against opening your home and heart to an innocent fugitive, you have no
place in the community of the just."

Many congregants didn't like what he was saying and were joining the NSB. In fact, one fellow came to tell Pieter one day that he was joining, and he thought Pieter would be so proud of him. It seems that one of Pieter's sermons several months before had spoken of how Hitler seemed to be helping the farmers, but that was before all the Jewish persecution began. People would say that Jews were sly and clever and always got what they wanted. My husband said they had to be because they were always so downtrodden. You get strength after you go through trials and tribulation like that.

A month after our first daughter was born, in April 1942, an older minister came to Pieter to say that a Jewish boy needed a place to stay. Pieter went all over the countryside, even to my father, and no one would take him, so we took him into our house. He stayed only about three months, and then his older brother came. It was hard for these boys; they were wealthy city people and weren't at all used to our simple life, but that made it harder for us, too.

Then Pieter found places for fourteen children who had to be evacuated from a Jewish children's TB sanatorium. The kids came one by one, and every night for two weeks he picked them up and put them in a different home.

Next came the Lezer family. Their two kids had been badly treated in another hiding place, so Pieter built them an underground bunker in the forest not far from our house. It was furnished and even had a kitchen. He took food and books to them every week, and another fellow visited them every week, too. I'll never forget the dinner they made for us, which we all ate together in the forest.

Then we hid a tailor upstairs. His name was Joseph. Then a medical student came and a Jewish resistance worker, who was later betrayed. When he was shot, we all felt it was too dangerous for us and we moved out of the house. I went to my brother's house with the kids for a while—we had had a second child, a son. I was afraid for Pieter because I didn't know where he was, and I knew he was doing dangerous things all the time. At the end of the war, we all were at Pieter's mother's house. She had taken in two English pilots whose planes had been shot down, and we all celebrated together in the street with our children.

One day about a year after the war, a Jewish father came to find one of his children. He had come right after Liberation but we weren't home, and when he asked someone who wasn't really from our village, they had told him we were gone. But when he returned to the village a year later, we thought we knew who the boy was and where to find him. We had changed his name from Isaac to Bobby. We took the father to the school and he recognized his son, but the boy clung to his stepfather. He didn't recognize his father at all. It seems that all of this man's children had been hidden, and he had gotten all of them back except for this boy.

After the war some of the church members who had helped said that even though it had been a terrible and frightening time, it had been exciting, too. They said, "We felt we were alive, that we had made our presence felt." Pieter received a citation from the Resistance movement in Utrecht, and another one signed by General Eisenhower and Field Marshal Montgomery. We both felt good that he had stood up for what he believed, but the church didn't necessarily agree. Some were angry that he had involved the church in resistance work, so we were transferred to another parish.

In the new church, Pieter's first sermon was met with stern reproach by the wealthy elders of the congregation. They told him they wanted to dictate what he spoke about on Sundays, but he just responded by promising not to meddle in their affairs if they didn't meddle in his. But the next Sunday, the church was empty, and for many Sundays after that. We decided we wanted to make a fresh start in a new country, so in 1952 we moved to Canada.

We weren't honored by Yad Vashem because Pieter said he never wanted recognition. It's what everyone should have done, he thought, so there was nothing special about it. But maybe it would be nice for the children to have. But I don't know if there are any of the Jewish people still alive to give testimony anymore. The Lezers kept in touch with us for a long time, but I'm sure they're gone now. Maybe the children are still there.

Reverend Miedema in Canada, 1960.

SEMMY RIEKERK

**Semmy with Lientje, a nine-month-old
Jewish baby whom Joop brought home
to live with them.**

*When Semmy Riekerk ushers us into her modest, book-lined, sunny apartment
in Amsterdam, she is friendly and direct, but she doesn't know where to begin
her story, or rather on what level of meaning to speak of it. Intelligent, philo-
sophic, and spiritual, midway through the interview she stops worrying about
chronology and detail and begins to relive the war with unusual intensity and
depth, experiencing once again the horror of the arrest of her first husband,
the great Nazi resister Joop Woortman, in 1944. She never saw him again. The
three-hour interview flies by, and in conclusion she tells us, "I told you things
that I have never told anyone before."*

I have thought very much about this war and about things that have happened since the war. I think every human being is like a piano. In every
man and woman lives the whole scale from very bad to very good. It's the
circumstances that bring out the tone. You can't always live by the high
tones. You live very often by the low tones. I don't want you to get the wrong
impression of me. I am as bad as every other person—sometimes.

As a child I knew many Jewish children but not as Jews. I went to a
Lutheran school, and we didn't think of people as Jewish or not. I was born
in 1916 in Amsterdam. My parents used to say to me, "I can't go after you
to watch what you do all day, but someone watches you and don't forget it.
Ask yourself, 'Can I take responsibility for what I'm doing?'" My father was
cosmopolitan; he said he belonged to the world. He felt that religion wasn't
important, but to live religiously was very important. I learned something
else from my father which I didn't understand until many years later. He

died when I was sixteen, but this stayed with me: he would take something he needed from someone else without thinking about it. And if someone else needed something from him, he would give it up even more easily. I understand now that this is better than someone who always obeys the law, never does any wrong, but also never gives.

In 1937 I worked for a Jew from Germany who operated a tobacco shop. His name was Hiller, and since he didn't speak Dutch, I was in charge of dealing with all the customers. Hiller had many other German Jewish refugees living in his apartment.

I met my husband, Joop [Johannes Theodore] Woortman, at about this time. He was eleven years older than I, divorced. We married in 1938, and he was drafted into the army before the occupation. He was a P.O.W. for a while, and then he got a job in the theater. His first attempt to rescue a Jew involved a Jewish musician who also worked in the theater. Joop arranged for false papers for him. Then he asked me to pick them up. That was early in 1942, two years after the Occupation began. The Germans unveiled their face very slowly in Holland.

In 1941 something called the "February Strike" took place. I was working in a factory then, and a Communist came in to say, "We're not going to let them take our Jews," and we in the factory agreed. So did our boss, who was a Russian Jew. That day there was a big demonstration, and the Germans shot people for no reason. We saw a Nazi shoot a boy on his bike who probably had no connection with the strike. I saw his brains hit a tree. That was the first time we realized we really had to do something; words weren't enough anymore.

Joop was a real organizer. He was older than the rest of our group, and he knew a lot about the world. We needed him, because he could guide these young people who really didn't know what to do. In 1942, he started providing false papers for Jews. He got into the underworld and asked pickpockets to steal papers from people. He'd describe the type of person he needed papers for, and they would steal them. In the beginning only the rich Jews could get this kind of help, because Joop had to pay for the papers. I was the one he sent to pay for and pick up the papers. Sometimes it was very frightening because I was carrying a lot of money and dealing with shady characters. After I paid for the papers, someone else took the photos and a Jewish woman who hid in my house for a while painted the German seals on them.

Joop often went to the train station to look for Jews to take into hiding. He didn't tell me everything, because he didn't want to get me mixed up in all of it. But he used me as he used the other people in the group, to do anything that needed doing. Then Joop found out what was happening in the day-care center for young children. He knew politicians who told him that all the Jewish children were being put in the center and transported to camps from there. So he decided to concentrate all his work on saving children. He needed to find people who were willing to hide the children in their homes. Then he had to take them from the center to the new address.

My sister helped, too, but I didn't know it at the time. You never told anyone anything they didn't have to know. My husband used anyone he could trust. One day he brought me a nine-month-old baby. We had no children, but Joop's eleven-year-old daughter was living with us so she and I took care of the baby.

Joop found three religious men who wanted to do something, so they agreed to find hiding places for children. This was really the beginning of the organization. That was the moment we knew we had put a stripe on our lives, that our lives had ended, and any more days we had would be profit. We had to put the baby in another place because our activities would be putting her life in danger. This was very hard for me because I had come to love the baby.

In July 1943 there was a big raid. The Germans closed all the streets, and Joop went from house to house picking up children to take to the day-care center. By then, Walter Suskind, a German Jew, was the director of the center, and he would take any child Joop sent there until my husband could place them. The children we sent there weren't registered, so they weren't in danger of being sent to a camp. My husband would pick them up and tell them to go to the center and say, "Theo DeBrun sent me." That was Joop's code name, and the nurse who answered the door knew to let them in without papers.

I have a foster daughter I adopted during the war. This is how she came to me. She and her sister had been placed in hiding by their father before he was taken. Rachel was twelve and Leah was nine when they were thrown out of their hiding place. They walked around Amsterdam and didn't know where to go, and then they remembered a maid who had worked for their parents. They went to her, and she gave them something to eat but couldn't keep them. She looked out of the window and saw Joop standing on the street. She told them, "You see that man in the raincoat? That is Mr. DeBrun. Go to him and tell him your story and he will help you." He sent them to the center. Then, two days later they were sent to Limburg to be hidden. During the winter, when no one had any food, Rachel came to my house because I was the head of the operation. Instead of finding her a place to live, I kept her myself. I had had a maid for sixteen years and she had just left, so I told everyone Rachel was my new maid.

My mother lived in another neighborhood, on the first floor of an apartment building. A Jewish family with a twelve-year-old son lived on the second floor, and Joop had asked them if he could take the boy. They thought they were safe because they had a *sper* card provided by Germans to important people that could get them released if they were arrested. On the day of the big raid I was at my mother's house, the streets were closed, and the Germans were shouting, "All Jews out."

Suddenly the doorbell rang, and when my mother opened it, she saw the boy standing there. He said, "Aunt Marie, I don't want to die." My mother let him in, but then we had to hide him. We put him in a large cupboard in the kitchen. The Germans were going from house to house, searching for Jews. Soon they rang our bell and asked, "Are you hiding any Jews?" My mother said, "Me? Those dirty Jews! You can take them all as far as I'm concerned." And then she said, "What awful work you have to do. You must be very tired. Do you want a cup of coffee?" My mother was very clever.

So the Gestapo man walked through and looked and opened one closet and one cupboard. Then he said to the Dutch Nazi who was with him, "There's no Jew here. Let's go!" But the Dutch Nazi said, "You didn't look in this cupboard." The Gestapo said, "Can't you see there's no one here? Let's go." How did this happen? Was it God? The boy lived the rest of the war in a hiding place in Limburg. I just saw him last week. He lives in Amsterdam with his wife.

In July 1944 Joop was arrested. We had known it wasn't safe for him anymore, so we had moved to another house. That day I was at my mother's, and when I returned, he was gone. A messenger came from our group to tell me he had been taken. Later I got a note from him, which he had thrown out of the streetcar when they moved him to another jail. Then another note, which he threw out of the window of the train taking him to Germany. But I never heard from him again. A year after the war, the Red Cross told me he had died in Bergen Belsen. I received a letter from a Jewish woman who saw him there, but all I know is that he died. I don't know how he died or why he was arrested. Did someone denounce him? I'll never know. I went to mediums who told me they saw things that made it seem that he had been shot trying to escape, which would have been like him, but I still don't know.

I had to carry on his work until the end of the war. They gave me the book that listed 300 names and said, "These are the people who are hiding children. You have to take them ration cards and money every month." The banks provided money from the Dutch government-in-exile, and our organization provided the ration cards.

My husband must have been an outstanding human being, because he had to decide who should live and who should die. He knew that the people he didn't help would probably be killed. Even when he decided to rescue only children, he was still choosing. I thought, *How could he live afterward?* I think it's a good thing he's dead. How could he live seeing parents come back and asking, "Why didn't you help my child? And you knew me." After the war there were ads from parents in the newspapers asking if anyone knew where their child was. I knew those ads were for him. But I think the circumstances brought this out in him. In a normal society he had never lived up to all that existed in him. I don't know what I would have done if he hadn't been my husband. But

I never had the idea of stopping the rescue work, even after he was arrested. It never occurred to me. Being more careful, yes, but never to stop.

The night I heard we were liberated, I had some children with me, and we all danced in the house. You didn't just resist in that war; you lived, too. Later, my foster daughter cried, because she always had hope that her mother and father would come back. But when we were liberated, she knew they were gone. She had a very difficult time.

I waited a few years to remarry, always thinking that Joop would return. You know, it's impossible to compare people, but I would say that perhaps Joop was a better man but Adolf is a better husband. [Adolf has listened to the entire interview, except when he left to prepare coffee and cakes for us.]

We had many good things during the war. One thing we had that still exists, and that we have nowhere else with other people, is that all of us who worked together feel we belong together. I think now, why do I feel so well after coming home from being with people from the Resistance? Even if they do things I don't like now, still I feel good because I trusted them with my life, and they trusted me. It's a bond—nothing else is as strong as this connection. It's a feeling that's hard to explain. I think it's above all else, even above the bond of the mother to the child. You have been one body. If you heard that one was caught it felt like your arm was cut off. Some names you never forget even if you didn't know them well. You met them maybe only once or twice, but then they were caught. Still that name comes up in your mind even today.

When I visited Yad Vashem in 1977, I asked them to put something up for Walter Suskind, because he lost his life rescuing Jewish children in the crèche. They told me the medals and trees are only for non-Jewish rescuers. They said, "It was the duty of a Jew to help Jews." This made me angry. I asked them, "Was it his duty to sacrifice his wife and daughter to save other people?" Now they have his name there. When I received the medal, it was for all of us—the ones who died and the ones who are still alive, and for Walter Suskind, too.

There's no day that goes by that I don't think about the war. When I go to talk to schoolchildren, they ask me, "Why was this war so much more important than other wars?" I tell them, "It's because it was the intention to wipe out a whole race. That has never happened. It has happened by accident, or in part, but never had it been the intention." When they ask why I rescued Jews, I tell them it's because they were persecuted not because of what they did but because of the way they were born, and that was something they couldn't help. And I relate this to apartheid. I think the children need to realize that all that was bad in the war, that was done by the Germans, could have been done by themselves. This possibility lives inside of them, too.

Joop Woortman, Semmy's first husband.

A Jewish child with her foster mother.

Semmy with her stepdaughter, Hetty (Joop's daughter, left) and her Jewish foster daughter (right) on the dam in Amsterdam, 1944.

Some of the children placed in hiding: the girl in the background is not Jewish but a daughter of the foster parents.

Joop Woortman's book listing the names of Jewish children in hiding. The present mayor of Amsterdam, Eddy van Jhijn, is listed on this page.

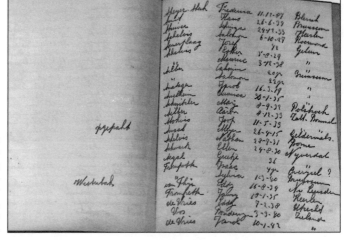

THE NETHERLANDS

AART AND JOHTJE VOS

Johtje and Aart Vos, 1944.

*Aart and Johtje Vos credit their love for each other for giving them the
strength, patience, and courage to harbor Jews in their home in Holland
throughout the war. He is a purely good man whose innate love for all sentient
beings seems to guide his actions. Johtje is no less good, but she is more
intellectual and articulates for both of them their experience of hiding Jews,
with their four small children in the house, during the war. We sit in their
splendid country home in Woodstock, New York, with spring flowers all
around, indoors and out. Their oldest daughter, Hetty, joins us for the first
part of the interview, sharing with us the ambivalent pride and love she feels
for her courageous parents who risked her life as well as theirs. At lunch, after
the formal interview, Aart shyly tells us of the illnesses he has suffered in
recent years. The doctors tell him that it is from the stress of the war.*

JOHTJE: I was born in 1909, in Amersfoort, near Amsterdam. My father was
a career army officer, and my mother was the most wonderful woman I've
ever met in my life. She was highly intelligent and had a terrific sense of
humor. She translated fifty-two books from English, French, and German into
Dutch. She had to do it secretly using my father's name, because women
weren't permitted that kind of recognition then. So my father, who was brilliant in mathematics but couldn't speak a word in any other language, got the
credit for all her work.

My father's father was Abraham Kuyper, a famous prime minister of
Holland. Many streets are named after him. Aart comes from a very famous
father, too. His name was Floris Vos, and he was also in government, but on
the opposite side. My grandfather was very right-wing, and my father-in-law

was very left-wing. Floris Vos was responsible for building a model farm, which is a nature monument in Holland and still attracts many tourists. Aart worked there as a young man; he had a degree in agriculture and was supposed to follow his father, though he was the middle child of seven brothers and two sisters. Aart's mother was lovely and interesting, and was always with her children. Aart grew up in Bussum.

As a young woman, I went to live in Paris to be a free-lance journalist, which was a scandalous thing at the time. My parents were horrified at the idea. I went to Egypt to cover the wedding of King Farouk for the Dutch press. I was already married then, to a painter I met in Paris. He was a German, a good one, not a Jew, but anti-Hitler. We moved back to Holland because I wanted my children to be born and take their first steps on earth in Holland. My father gave us a house in Laren, which is an artists' colony near Amsterdam, very much like Woodstock, where we live now. We had two children, and then we divorced in 1940. Aart and I married in 1942, and continued to live in my home in Laren.

The first thing we did during the war was keep a Jewish couple, friends of ours, overnight. I want to say right away that the words "hero" and "righteous Gentile" are terribly misplaced because, first of all, I don't feel righteous and, secondly, I certainly don't feel Gentile. This is the wrong term for us. And we are certainly not heroes, because we didn't sit at the table when the misery started and say, "Okay, now we are going to risk our lives to save some people."

How it happened is that somebody asked us, "Listen, I have a little suitcase with some valuables and I have to go to the ghetto. Will you keep this suitcase for me?" He was a friend, and to our amazement he was a Jew. We'd never even known that because nobody knew those things in Holland. We never talked about Jews. They were all just Dutch, that's all. So, then you said, "Well, of course I'll keep that suitcase for you." And then a week later, somebody would ask you, "Well, my child is in danger." So we said, "Of course, bring him here." Then two people said, "Well, we don't know where to go." Then by and by we got more involved in the underground. Then we had to make a decision: do we do this, go on with this? That's the moment when we made the decision. And we said yes; we couldn't do differently than say yes. But some people who said no often had very good reasons, and people don't respect that.

AART: Holland was like a family and part of that family was in danger. In this case, the Jewish part. The Germans were threatening our family. We weren't thinking, "What shall we do?" We just did.

JOHTJE: The couple who came to our house that night were both well-known musicians, Nap and Alice de Klijn. We couldn't keep them perma-nently because they were also from Laren and too known there, so the underground found a place for them. They would come back to us from time to time, and their children stayed with us for several months. In fact, their daughter, who was born just after the war, was named for our Barbara. Their Barbara lives in Israel now. And when Nap and Alice played in America, they stayed with us here in Woodstock.

More and more people came to hide in our house. We had mattresses all over the floor, and they had to be camouflaged in case the Germans came. The people didn't have to hide, they could walk around freely, but of course they didn't go outside. The Germans came many times, once during our wedding. They were looking for Jews. We just told them to get out, that this was our wedding. I wouldn't say I'm a brave person. I'm afraid to be alone in the house. But I was never afraid of the Germans. And I was deathly afraid of the bombs.

Only during a raid did the people in our house have to hide, and for that we had a secret tunnel. We lived on a dead-end road, which ended in an area that was acres of bushes, which was marvelous to flee to if you had time. But sometimes there was no time, so we made the tunnel. It went from the art studio, which was a shed on the back of the house, under a false bottom below the coal bin under our garden out into the open woods. It saved lives.

We had a friend who was the chief of police, and he would phone to warn us in code when there was going to be a raid. We didn't lose any of the people who stayed with us, but there was one Jewish couple, the Hilfmans, who refused to come to our house. They said, "We are Jews. This is our fate, and we have to accept it, whatever it is." I asked, "Are you cowards?" They said, "We don't know, but we can't do it." I begged them at least to let me take their three-year-old daughter, Moana, but they insisted on deciding for her. But at the last minute, just hours before the Hilfmans were taken by the Nazis, they let an electrician bring her to us, and she has been our daughter ever since.

Moana was the same age as our youngest daughter, Barbara, and they were like sisters. When the war ended we wanted to adopt Moana, but we weren't allowed to. The Jewish community said, "We have so few Jewish children left that they have to be brought up in Jewish families." She went to live with her mother's sister, who had lived in Indonesia during the war. This turned out to be very difficult, because the mother lost two of her three children on the ship back to Holland, and Moana had the same birthday as one of them, so she had a very difficult childhood. She has said that the only time she was really happy was during the war when she lived with us. She is now married to a Dutchman, not a Jew, and they live in Holland.

I told you that my first husband was German, so that meant that I had German papers. This was good in one respect, because it gave me double food stamps. But sometimes, as I stood in line to get them, someone would spit at me, and I didn't blame them. I would secretly think, "That's good." Somehow, I always had the feeling about the Germans, "You bastards, I can get you. I can be a bastard, too. I'll get you."

My father had died during the first year of the war, and when my mother came to visit me and saw we were hiding Jews, she was upset and said, "You shouldn't do it, even though I agree with what you're doing, because your first responsibility is to your children." I told her, "That's exactly why I'm doing it." I thought we were doing the right thing, giving our children the right model to follow. We had no idea how hard it would be for them.

We played a little game with them. For one hour each day we'd talk about food, and for the rest of the time food was not mentioned. Because when you talk about it continuously, you keep suffering. But during that hour, adults would talk about, "Do you remember that restaurant? Do you remember that dish? What was the best veal that you ever had, the best asparagus, or something, you know." And then we played games with the children. We'd ask, "Who remembers what a banana is?" and then the first to get it, "Is it something to eat?" We said, "Yes, it's something to eat." They wouldn't remember.

For a time, one of my children felt resentment for what we did. She said we risked her life as well, and that all the Jews in the house came first, before her and all the rest of the children. And she has a terrible memory of one night a friend of ours, someone she liked very much, coming to our house. He was a member of the underground and had been caught by the SS. They brought him to our house. My daughter remembers him begging for his life, and we had to deny that we knew him. He survived, and we're still close friends. I couldn't have done any differently because I had lists of all the Jews who were hiding in the neighborhood. I had to deny that I knew anything. That was difficult for a child to understand. But today my daughter is a lovely, radiant woman, successful in her profession, and understands perfectly why we had to do what we did. It all turned out so well.

AART: We had thirty-six people hiding in our house at one time. When you have a home, not a big one, and you have it filled up with Jewish people coming in and out the whole day, every day, not for a week but for four or five years, you can't understand what that takes from a woman. I was out on my bicycle, but she had to keep everyone together.

I was born very near the place where we lived in Holland. I knew every inch of it, every stream and field, so when I had to bring Jews at night, and we sure couldn't use the roads, I could take them through the woods. I picked up a man one night who was very afraid, but I just told him, "Don't worry, just come through the woods with me."

The biggest enemy was people talking. I went to visit at the home of van Gogh's nephew one day, and he gave me an envelope. I asked, "What's in it?" He told me, "It's money for the work you're doing to save Jews." I said, "You have the wrong Vos. I'm not doing that. Look around, you'll find the right person, but it's not me." You just couldn't trust anyone. From the moment the war started, your whole nature changed. I used to trust everyone before the war.

One day after a bombing, I saw a wounded German soldier, so I put him on my bike and took him to his camp. Later everyone asked me, "How could you save a German?" I said, "Listen, you don't know what you'd do unless you were in that situation. My wife and I were brought up to have respect for life."

I wasn't brought up religious. My parents were Dutch Reformed, and I had to go to church as a child, but I spent my ten cents for charity on candy. During the war I thought it wasn't possible that on this little planet people could do things like that to each other. How can God permit it? You have to teach children to respect the planet, but instead we teach them how to make money.

JOHTJE: I was brought up very strictly religious, and I am still religious. When I was a teenager, I was a real religious fanatic. Then I grew up, lived in Paris, and lost it all completely. I thought I didn't even believe in God. During the war I knew I believed in God but I didn't practice my religion at all, and not afterward during the hard years either. But I've gone back to it now. I don't agree with everything the church tells me, but I know now that I don't have to. Religion is much stronger for me now. Most of our children are religious, but not all of them.

During the time of the Vietnam War, our son applied for the status of conscientious objector. He had several interviews, and he was questioned very intensely. The last question on the test was, "Would you kill under any circumstances?" and his answer was, "I hope God never asks me." Well, he didn't get the C.O. status, so he went back to Holland, married a Dutch woman, and they have four children. It was very sad that he could never come here to visit us.

We left Holland in 1951, with our six children, and came to Woodstock. For the first few years we ran a year-round children's camp for the U.N. Then much later it became only a summer camp. We had children here from every country at one time or another.

In the last few years we have been asked to talk about our work during the war more and more. At first we were reluctant, but a rabbi told me, "You must talk about it. You owe it, you have a responsibility. You're the last generation who saw it, and you have no right to be modest about it." But when we had talked about it before, people would sneer, so we didn't want to do it. I guess it sounds nice to be modest but in this case it's cowardice. But we only began talking publicly a few years ago.

If someone heard us talk today with some of those we saved, they would think we were being nostalgic, remembering a beautiful time. But there was something beautiful in it, because we were standing together, for whatever reason, totally together.

Aart Vos died in 1990 while tending flowers in his garden.

Trees Delmonte and her daughter, Saskia, 1945. They and her husband, Koert, lived at the Vos house longer than any of the other Jews—for almost the entire war.

The first Jews to stay in the Vos home were Alice Heksch, Nap de Klijn, and their son. This is a program cover from Alice and Nap's 1950 concert tour.

Moana Hilfman, 1943.

Just after the war—Aart Vos is pointing up at Allied planes. Johtje is between Aart and Koert Delmonte. The Vos children are in the foreground with Moana, the dark-haired girl.

TINA STROBOS

Tina Strobos (right) and her best friend, Tirzah van Amerongen.

Tina Strobos, an attractive, self-possessed woman, speaks slowly and calmly with only a hint of a Dutch accent as she tells us about her childhood in a close-knit, distinguished family in Amsterdam. This strong background seems to be the major influence that led her to rescue Jews. Her family was exceptional not only in accomplishment but in its open atheism. Strobos herself, a psychiatrist, is an independent thinker who continues to try to improve the world in her hometown. We sit in her book-lined office shaded by ancient trees in Larchmont, New York, trying to capture her deep and original thoughts on the Holocaust and its meaning for our times.

My family were Social Democrats and atheists. They were people who acted on their ideals of education and helping people. They had brought in Belgian refugees during World War I. I was born in Amsterdam in 1920. When Hitler came to power, it was natural that they took in refugees right away. After the invasion a well-known Jewish columnist and writer, Henry Pollack, called my grandmother and asked to stay with her. They were at our house from day one. There's a statue of him in Amsterdam and also a home for the elderly named for him.

I was very close to my grandparents and, though my grandfather died when I was five, he was a legend in our family. In Holland at the end of the nineteenth century, there was great fear of the power of the clergy. My grandfather and some of his friends started a free-thinking movement to rid Holland of this tyranny of the clergy. They started a newspaper which still exists. In fact, I'm named after Tina, the wife of Max Havelaar, a well-known writer and one of the first anticolonial atheists in Holland.

Even in the 1930s, we had miners' children staying in our house, so there was a tradition. My mother was the secretary of the women's peace movement, and she helped German and Austrian refugees. Father was a smart, self-taught businessman, but they divorced and he left when I was ten years old, so he wasn't a part of our house during the war.

At the time of the invasion in May 1940, I was in medical school. My best friend was Tirzah van Amerongen. She was Jewish. Her family were all Zionists, and I was very involved with them. She was hidden in our house and cared for by my grandmother. After the war she and her husband moved to Israel, and I visited them there.

My family had many Jewish friends, which wasn't unusual in the socialist group of artists and intellectuals in Amsterdam. Bram [Abraham] Pais was another good friend. When he earned his Ph.D., my mother and I gave a party for him. He was the last Jew before the war to receive a doctorate from the university in Amsterdam. We were very close, and many Jewish and non-Jewish friends came to the party.

When the Germans occupied Holland, they set up a civil government headed by Artur von Seyss-Inquart, the Austrian Nazi responsible for Austria's quick integration into the Reich. He tried to calm everyone by giving a speech saying that anything we had done in the past was okay; "sponge it over" was the famous expression. He said, "As long as you don't hinder our efforts to win the war, it's okay." So people began to come out of hiding, but then the Germans began slowly to tighten things. They made all the Jews congregate in Amsterdam, and in 1942 they had to begin wearing the yellow star. I always wondered why the Jews complied. Because the ones who didn't went free. Those who did had to register formally as Jews. Why did they register and put the "J" on their I.D. cards? It was so stupid in hindsight.

First there was tremendous fear, and Jews began to commit suicide. People tried to go to England in rowboats, or to France or Switzerland. I helped some of them escape. One was Leah Gitter. She was one of the most courageous people. She was seven months pregnant when I took her and her husband, Sieg, with her sister and brother-in-law across the Belgian border and turned them over to the underground railroad that took them to Spain. They walked for two months, only at night, and she had her baby just after she crossed the border. Now they live in Israel.

People began to disappear, and you didn't see them come back again. We just thought they'd been put to work in factories. We didn't know of systematic gassing until after the war. Then the curfews and shootings started, if you were out after 8 P.M. Then the raids started. The Jews were put into the ghetto, and then the ghettos were emptied into two camps, one for hostages, political prisoners, Jews, and important people whom they would shoot if there was an act of sabotage, and one a way station to Poland. That one was Westerbork. There were no killings there. The Jews could get packages at first, and they had a school and entertainment and weren't really treated too badly.

I was in medical school, because I had read Freud at sixteen and had already decided to become a psychiatrist. But in 1942 all university students were required to sign a loyalty oath to the Nazis, and that drove the medical school underground. I purposely joined a sorority, even though I'm not that type, and it became a network for finding places and hiding Jews, for getting false papers and food cards, and doing whatever was needed. I was in a study group that read *Mein Kampf* and Marx, and we became active, but it scared me because they carried guns. My boy friend was killed that way. They were all killed. I separated myself from them because I'm nonviolent. I participated only with the women's group, which was geared to hiding people and nonviolent acts. But occasion-ally I hid weapons and trans-ported radio senders.

We lived in a big house, which had been a city school. We lived on the second floor, with the bedrooms on the third floor. A carpenter from the underground came to make a hiding place. He did it so well that when I took my youngest daughter back to Amsterdam last year, I had to ask the woman who lives there now to find it for me. After the hiding place was built, my mother said to me, "We're hiding people; do you know you can be killed?" I said, "Yes," and we never talked about it again. I was more the leader; my mother was in her fifties and was a little afraid although still quite brave.

Over the years we hid about one hundred people, but never more than about five at one time. Some we knew, some we didn't; some for a couple of nights, some for a couple of months. But I always looked for safer houses because our house was raided eight times. They searched for hours, ripped up rugs, knocked on walls, took off pictures. The secret hiding place would hold only two people, so it was a good thing we had a counterspy at Gestapo headquarters who would call us when they were about to come for a raid. It was better in Holland—not like Poland where your neighbors would turn you in. We had a network—the Dutch were 90 percent good. Anne Frank was hidden in a warehouse, which in my mind wasn't safe.

I was always afraid when I was interrogated or arrested, because they would come in and take both wrists and throw you against the wall. But you learned certain tactics so you didn't look afraid. First, I'd ask for an interpreter in order to have time to organize my defense, even though I spoke fluent German. And then once I crossed my legs and my skirt flew up accidentally, and the Nazi said, "I'm not impressed with your legs." That helped to relax me, because I realized that he was just a man and he was interested in my legs. So that gave me a sense of power. I got cocky. I could say, "I didn't know he was a Jew" in a stronger, more convincing way.

We actually rented rooms to people for money so that we could say to the Gestapo that we didn't know this or that person was a Jew. Our housekeeper, Lize, stole from us all the time, but we could do nothing about it because she knew so much. You could get $100 for turning in a Jew, and Lize would threaten to turn us in. Once the Gestapo arrested her for black marketeering, and we were sure she would betray us, but she didn't. There were always difficult things happening in the house. My grandmother kept the food supply in a certain place, and once she found there were rations missing. It turned out that the culprit was a man who was my grandmother's favorite, so she wouldn't confront him. We just moved the food to another place so no one would know where to find it.

My mother, Marie Buchter Schotte, was very close to the de Leeuw family, and went there often for Friday night dinners. One night when she was there, the ghetto was closed, so she hurried home on her bike, not knowing what might happen to her friends. As she rode through the ghetto, people were begging her to take their babies. The ghetto was emptied out that night, but she went back the next day to see if anyone was left. She went into the house and it looked deserted, but she called out to ask if anyone was there, and the de Leeuws' seventeen-year-old daughter and her husband were hiding in a closet. She brought them out, and I found a place for them to hide in a tomato hothouse, where they survived the war. After the war they were very close to our family, and my mother became like their mother, and like a grandmother to their son. They had a china shop and gave me a beautiful set of dishes for my wedding. But when their son grew up, he turned into a rotten, spoiled kid, and began accusing my mother and grandmother of stealing his grandparents' money. He asked my mother, "Where is their money? They were wealthy before the war. You must have taken their money." But of course, there hadn't been that much money, and whatever there was, we used to take care of them. We never had any money left over after the war. But the son got the parents believing his story, and they and my mother stopped speaking. This was a very sad thing, because they had been so close, and even though they finally apologized, my mother never would be close with them again.

Once one of my friends was arrested, and when I found out what jail she was in, I sent her a package which included my red pajamas. She told me later that this made her feel so much better because then she knew someone knew where she was and cared about her.

We were all very clever and never were arrested, but my uncle spent a year in a concentration camp, my other best friend's father spent a year in jail, and two first cousins spent several months in jail, all for helping Jews. During the "hunger winter" especially, there wasn't a week that went by when someone wasn't picked up and sent away.

I felt guilty for many years that I didn't do enough. I knew people who needed shelter and I couldn't find it for them. And some things you did came

---

out wrong. This very dear friend we helped got caught anyway and perished. I wouldn't call what I did a sacrifice because we believed so strongly that we were doing the right thing. I felt like a heroine and virtuous, and the boys my age swaggered around with their guns. But today I simply feel that if there are altruists and egoists, I'd like to be counted as one of the good guys.

We were hungry and afraid for so long that when Liberation came, there was such celebration, dancing, and music in the streets that we didn't even notice that we were still hungry. And people were hungry in Holland for a long time.

After the war you just wanted to forget about everything. I married a doctor, and when we left for the West Indies in 1947, we still didn't have meat, eggs, or milk. I practiced psychiatry there for two years and our first son was born in the West Indies. Then we went to England to study neurology for six months, and then my husband began a residency in Holland. But we didn't like being back there so my husband got a fellowship to Columbia, and we came to America. I trained at Valhalla and Cornell, and now I'm a family therapist. We had three children, made careers, became citizens, and didn't talk about the war. It weakens you in a way to remember all that. I had nightmares about being arrested, so who wanted to remember it? My mother would come to visit and at one point we made a list of everyone we saved, but I promptly lost it. Now I'm asked to talk to Jewish groups about that time and what I did to help. It took a long time for anyone here to ask to talk about the war, but when I return to Holland, I get together with friends and we talk about it. As I said, I felt guilty for many years that I didn't do enough, but gradually I started having some good feelings, too, thinking about how many we did save in our little house.

I can't be called a Christian rescuer because I am not a Christian and never was. The rescuers were often Christian in the country, but not in Amsterdam. It wasn't unusual for Dutch to not be Christian. I don't believe in a personal God, but I believe in the sacredness of life. I have a more conservative attitude about food and nature than many other people: I'm sad if a plant dies, and I won't throw away food. When I wanted to be a doctor, I was very attached to younger children.

My children are twenty-seven, thirty-five, and thirty-eight years old, and on the one hand they are very proud of what I did during the war, but on the other hand, they don't ask me questions about it like you do. My son is a doctor and helps people. My daughter helps illiterate people learn to read; she has always done that as a volunteer. And all my children and I have tutored in Harlem, and we painted houses there. There was a time in the sixties when we helped fix up poor neighborhoods. It was a project called "I Give a Damn." We cleaned out streets in the South Bronx, had block parties. When my husband died, I remarried an American Jew who worked for the United Nations, helping Third World countries raise their standards of living.

I believe you can make the next generation better by teaching, but also by treating your children very well. Don't hit them, don't be cruel to your children—that still happens, you know. People who have been treated with cruelty will be cruel.

I go out and talk to schoolchildren today and I tell them that people like to join groups which think like they do, and dress the same, just to feel like you belong. And then they become cruel to those who don't belong, who limp, or are different, and we have to be careful not to hurt others who don't belong to our little group.

I'm glad people are now becoming interested in the rescuers because we have paid enough attention to the bad guys. Hitler, Himmler, Goering. And we don't think as much about the good people who helped. I think that's true in our personal lives, too. We remember much more who did us harm than who did us good.

Tina Strobos (left), Bram Pais, and Tina's mother, Marie Schotte.

The room everyone lived in, 1944–45.

The house that Tina lived in—it had been a city school.

Marie Schotte Abrahams, Tina's grandmother.

RESCUERS

BELGIUM

When Jews were an integral part of national life, as in Italy and Denmark, the native population protected them as fellow citizens. But when they were isolated from the broader society, as in Poland and Hungary, the population did not identify with them and allowed their removal. Ninety percent of the Jews in Belgium were refugees and, therefore, especially vulnerable. Jews from Eastern Europe had flocked to Belgium's large cities, especially Antwerp, following World War I, because they found acceptance and some opportunity there. Nevertheless, their great numbers triggered prejudice against them, with Debus de Warnaffe, minister of justice, saying in 1936, "There are already 90,000 Jews in Belgium and I can't allow others in because they will invade and overwhelm us." Gerts and Yvonne Jospa, immigrants from Romania in the 1920s, helped to smuggle fellow Jews in and find them work.

Belgian Jews were conspicuous in their speech and dress, less socially integrated, and had less money than Dutch Jews; yet more than half of them survived the Occupation, whereas in Holland almost 90 percent perished. The Belgians weren't more compassionate than the Dutch, and surely Belgian Jews didn't possess a greater will to live. Many reasons have been offered to explain this difference, including the fact that Belgium had been overrun by the Germans in World War I, provoking the hostility and resistance of its people to German domination, while the Netherlands had remained neutral. In any case, the Belgians responded to the Nazi invasion in a significantly different way: they saw the threat as collective, and they transformed their compassion into organized cooperation. Belgian Jews were slow to answer the Nazi calls for deportation, and the local military authorities were insufficiently eager to enforce them. According to one source, the German Foreign Ministry in Belgium complained of difficulties in organizing deportations because the Belgians failed to display "sufficient understanding" of the Germans' objectives. When Jews stopped reporting voluntarily altogether, deportations had to be carried out through police raids. When Jews were ordered to don the yellow star in 1942, the burgomasters of Brussels unanimously refused to distribute them, and burgomasters of other municipalities supported this action. Consequently, the Belgian Judenrat was given the task of branding its own people. Finally, appeals to Hitler on behalf of the Jews were made by Queen Mother Elizabeth through the military governor, General Alexander von Falkenhausen. These included protesting the separation of Jewish families, and requesting that elderly and native-born Belgian Jews not be liable to deportation. Additionally, the cardinal archbishop of Malines, Joseph-Ernst van Roey, denounced the "inhuman," "brutal," and "cruel" treatment of the Jews. While their attempts at intervention did not succeed on a grand scale, Queen Elizabeth and Cardinal van Roey did manage to show support for the Jews of Belgium, to save the lives of a least five leading members of the Jewish community, and to delay the deportation process, albeit briefly.

The underground, the Front Indépendance (FI), was organized to thwart the Nazis, and in the process it also helped the Jews. It published flyers that read, "To inform against a Jew is to murder him or her!" and it threatened collaborators with their lives. Despite this effort, however, most of the underground's work did not specifically protect the Jewish population; its members concentrated on sabotaging the Nazis and collaborators. Jewish Communists and Socialists working in the underground therefore asked for a separate unit that would act to save Jews. After three months the FI consented and the Comité de Défense des Juifs (CDJ), founded by Gerts Jospa, began its work. Although Jews worked in resistance movements throughout Europe, Belgian Jews did more to help their own people than Jews in any other country.

The committee, headed by Jospa and Maurice Heiber, included non-Jews as well. It helped adults by providing them with false papers identifying them as Aryans and gave them money to go into hiding. But the committee's main thrust and greatest accomplishment was to save three-fourths of the 4,000 Jewish children in Belgium.

Yvonne Jospa, a key figure in the Jewish Resistance, recalled, "In 1941 we were required to wear the Jewish star, and it was then my husband began trying to form a special Jewish committee inside the Resistance. We were both always politically active, Communist party members, and involved with Jewish problems because of all the injustice in the world.

"We all got false papers, and moved to a new municipality and never registered as Jews. It was easier to hide a child who was separated from its parents, so one section concentrated on finding homes and placing Jewish children with Christians. For the adults we had a special committee which tried to find them a place to stay and give them false papers, and money for rent. And a third committee was financial.

"I was the head of the children's committee within the CDJ. Of Belgium"s 4,000 Jewish children, the CDJ placed and saved more than 3,000. Every day about sixteen people worked day and night to organize the work.

"I worked with Esta Heiber and Ida Sterno. We kept three books: the first listed the real names and addresses of the children, the second listed the false names and where they were hidden, and the third book was the connection between the first two books, all in code. One night each month we came together with all the books, and the financial committee brought the money, and someone else brought the ration cards and letters to be distributed to the child. Only three of us had access to the three books, and only we knew the code."

Because the CDJ had the cooperation of some local authorities, isolated clergy, and the Resistance, its people were able to hide children in convents, religious schools, and private homes. Belgian government departments and banks provided material assistance and ration stamps. Despite the tremendous Jewish effort in Belgium, without the support of the rest of the country they would not have been able to save themselves.

Yvonne Jospa said, "Many Belgians participated; even if they didn't hide a Jew, they might get us false I.D. cards and food rations. There were also many non-Jews working with the CDJ. I want to speak now for the Belgian population. I'm against the people who say that most people did it only for money or personal gain. I'll tell you one of many stories which illustrates what I mean. Once the Germans were sending 450 non-Jewish children from the cities to the countryside to prove that they were concerned with people's welfare, and the CDJ clandestinely included about 175 Jewish children in the transport. The peasants were paid to do this, but were not told that the children were Jewish. However, when they were told that the children *were* Jewish, none refused to continue to take care of those children. In order to put the Jewish children on the train, I got up very early that day and took the first tram and told the driver, 'I must get to the station early, right away.' He never even looked at me, but he passed up many other tram stops where people were waiting and took me with no hesitation. He understood the urgency, and he helped me save all those children."

After the war most of the children could not return to their families, because many parents had not survived. The committee then worked to place the children in new homes. Mme. Jospa recalled, "We had trouble after the war, not only with the people who had kept Jewish children who wanted them to stay with them after the parents returned, but also with the Jewish community about the children whose parents did not return. The Jewish Committee wanted them to go to Israel. I fought for them to stay in Belgium. I said, 'They are Belgian. Let them stay here until they are adults and then they can decide for themselves where to go.' I was only partly successful. I understand that they were afraid the children would not remain Jewish and they needed Jewish children to help build Israel. But it was a difficult choice."

Of the 57,000 Jews who lived in Belgium at the time of the German occupation, 29,000 survived. Like all Belgian resistants, the CDJ members paid a higher price than those they defended. Of its eight founding members, six were deported, and of those, only two survived.

All but one of the eleven Belgians interviewed had worked in the CDJ. Yvonne Jospa and Esta Heiber ran the office devoted to saving children;

Andrée Herscovici and Fela Herman persuaded parents to relinquish their children. Under the direction of Abbé André of St. Jean Baptiste Church in Namur, Gustave Collet transported children to hiding places that the CDJ had found. Alice Schiffer and Marcelle and Therèse Lacroix hid a child in their homes; Marie Taquet and Marie-Henriette Feremans-Ceulemans hid many Jewish children in the schools where they worked and lived. Paul Pensis, only a boy, did daring rescue missions for the committee. Germaine Belinne and her daughter, Liliane Gaffney, performed the kind of rescue of friends and acquaintances more typical of the independent acts of rescue that took place in all other countries.

David Inowlocki, a Jewish child hidden in Château du Faing by Marie Taquet, recalled, "We had fun! We played in the forest and spent our days like boy scouts. I didn't want to leave when my father picked me up. I didn't recognize him." Most children, however, did not acquire pleasant memories. Many were wrenched from their families, given new names, told to forget their past and never to say they had been Jewish.

In 1991, at the Conference on the Hidden Child held in New York City, Belgium—because of the high number of children hidden there—claimed the greatest attendance. Andrée Herscovici, a participant in the conference, said that talking about that painful time is essential for the healing of the children she saved.

Yvonne and Gerts Jospa with their son, Paul, 1946.

Gustave Collet.

GERMAINE BELINNE AND LILIANE GAFFNEY

**Germaine and Liliane,
summer 1943.**

*Germaine Belinne and Liliane Gaffney, mother and daughter rescuers from
La Louvière in Belgium, live in adjacent houses in Northvale, New Jersey. We
meet them at Liliane's home. They both smoke continuously and although
they frequently contradict each other, mutual respect is evident. Because Germaine still feels somewhat lost in America, she volunteers in a home for the
aged even though she is in her late seventies. Helping others is what gives her
life meaning. Liliane also expresses a sense of alienation but, perhaps
because she is younger, was able to make a full life for herself in America.
She is married, has two grown sons and two grown daughters, and is a professor of linguistics at Fairleigh Dickinson University. Although they are neither bitter nor unhappy, they miss the time when people cared more about
one another and less about themselves.*

*Germaine and Liliane are the only Belgian rescuers we interviewed who
were not involved with the CDJ, but acted independently to save over thirty
Jews who were their friends.*

GERMAINE: My mother was a wonderful person, always giving. During the
first war I saw her giving away her own dinner. She said, "They need it
more than I do." I went to work when I was fifteen years old, proofreading
at the local newspaper. I was married when I was seventeen. We were living
in La Louvière, and I worked in my husband's tailor shop. Liliane was my
first child. When the Germans invaded, my husband, Charles, served as a
commander in the Resistance.

121

LILIANE: My grandmother had adopted two Jewish brothers from Poland, Simon and Charles Moncarz. Not really adopted, but she looked after them because they lived nearby. Other cousins of theirs came later to get married, and mother sort of grew up with all of them. She was about twelve at the time.

Beginning in 1938 or 1939, there was much emotional sentiment being fermented against the Jews. In those days I didn't know what a Jew was. In 1940 my father was captured and was sent to Munich for two years as a P.O.W. In 1941 Jews began to be arrested or to disappear. When mother heard that Charles and his wife, Blanche, would be arrested, she told him, "Just disappear with your family."

GERMAINE: Charles and Simon sold furniture across the street from our shop. Our children played together. One day someone told me, "You know, they're going to arrest Charles." That was the start of it. The first thing I did was give the papers of my sister, brother-in-law, and niece who were in Africa to Charles, Blanche, and their daughter, Elsa. Then Tova, Charles and Simon's niece, came from Poland and moved into our house. Tova stayed with us for more than two years because there was no possibility to place her anywhere else since she spoke no French or Flemish at all. She pretended to be a deaf mute whenever visitors came.

Charles and Simon had many other relatives, so we needed a lot of papers. We got the help of someone from City Hall who would get papers for us that belonged to someone else. So they were legal papers, just like my sister's. We ended up helping about thirty people disappear, and they all had legal papers and ration cards. There was Betty, Charles's sister, and her husband, Joseph, their son, Albert, and then they had two more children during the war. There was Myriam and Maurice Berkenbaum, cousins of cousins, whose son, Willie, was born during the war. There was Max and Reinette Konigsman with their daughter, Danielle, or Danny, as we all called her, and Reinette's mother, too. And Charles and Simon had a third brother, Sammy, who stayed with us for a while until he married and moved in with his wife.

We took them to places where they weren't known, and we told people they were Flemish, to explain their accents. Even though everything looked legal, it was still very dangerous.

LILIANE: I was fourteen at the time, and it didn't seem as if it was all that tragic. I shared my room with Tova. We had a lot of fun with those families we were hiding. There was nowhere to go out, no dancing, no restaurants, but we'd gather and have a heck of a good time. That's when I started smoking. We wrote flowery letters to each other. So time passed very nicely most of the time. Evenings with Reinette, Max, Maurice . . .

GERMAINE: But the next day we would be scared to death again. It was a good thing we had a little fun every once in a while. Otherwise we would have died.

LILIANE: Willie was born in 1943. Mother picked him up because his mother looked too Jewish. He had a *bris* [circumcision] in 1946, and he came over to our house and pulled his pants down and said, "Liliane, look! Isn't it pretty now?"

GERMAINE: Once one of the Jews we were hiding got a paper with the name I had given him, telling him he had to go to Germany to work. I thought, *Oh, no. Now I'm caught.* All of a sudden I remembered that I knew the man who was in charge of work permits. I went to him and said, "Please help me. Could you get his name off the list?" And he did it. That was a close call.

Today people ask me why I could do this and others couldn't, and I just don't know. They were friends, of course, so it felt very natural. I guess other people were more afraid than I was.

LILIANE: She has always been a rebel. She's afraid but she doesn't show it. The one thing I could never stand as a child is injustice. It always brings out the worst in me. I suppose it's an inherited trait.

GERMAINE: I don't go to church but every night I pray for the world to be better.

LILIANE: Did you pray in 1942, Mother?

GERMAINE: I always pray, Liliane, yes, every night.

LILIANE: Why did you never train me to do that?

GERMAINE: Because you were a big girl with a typical French cultural attitude: even at two years old they tell you to be reasonable.

After the war I got so depressed because I had nothing to take care of anymore. I could cry more about that time than during the war, and also because I felt maybe I didn't do enough. It seems to me maybe I could have done more. I had this feeling, also when we first came to this country, that there was nothing to do here. You didn't have to risk your life every day. Everything was safe and you always had enough to eat. Before, you had a reason for living without bothering to find one every day. This left me with problems for a long time.

You know, something just came back to my mind. This Jewish boy who was in the army said to me just after the war, "You know, you were stupid. You could have been a millionaire." I told him I would never have done it for money. I could never.

LILIANE: Maybe he was testing you, Mother.

Our entire family came to the United States together in 1948. It was a sort of promise I had made to a friend of my father who had become a surrogate father to me. He was killed in Germany, but he had said to me, "If I don't come back, you must go to America for me." He never came back and I came to America for him.

I married a man here who seemed reckless to me, like a cowboy. My brother, Francis Belinne, became the Number One test pilot in America. He followed Chuck Yeager. It's funny to remember him playing with neighborhood children of Belgian Nazis in order to avoid suspicion that we were hiding Jews.

We thought perhaps the children of the rescuers should get together because to see someone thrown on the floor repeatedly when you're just fourteen does change your perspective on life. Or to have helped your father, as I did, carry machine guns and ammunition, and feeling so afraid and excited at the same time. You can become a cynic and think that people are bad. Or at least it makes you leery. I have many Jewish friends because I grew up with Jews at a crucial age. Most are Europeans. It frightens us to hear people say it can't happen in America. So I think children must be raised with careful trust in their hearts. Not blind trust to think that it can't happen here, because it could, but careful trust.

GERMAINE: When we came to the United States we said, "Well, at last it's okay to like Jews."

LILIANE: I was thinking, Why did people do things like that and risk their lives? It's very difficult for a generation raised looking out for Number One to understand it. This is something totally unknown here. But there, if you didn't live for others as well as yourself it wasn't worth living. To be human we need each other.

Tova with Francis Belinne, summer 1943.

From left to right: Reinette, Danny, Max Konigsman, and Reinette's mother, May 1944.

From upper left: Myriam Berkenbaum, Germaine Belinne, and Germaine's husband. From lower left: Francis Belinne, Willie Berkenbaum, and Liliane's cousin, Claudine, July 1944.

Danny Konigsman, 1944.

ESTA HEIBER

Esta and Maurice Heiber, 1955.

Madame Heiber's elegant Brussels apartment, filled with tasteful modern art, seems far away from the dark years of working in the clandestine Committee for the Defense of the Jews that her husband cofounded. She talks of the war carefully, not to awaken feelings, but despite these efforts and the difficulty inherent in communicating through a translator, it is obvious that the war has marked her. Still a stylish woman, she is reluctant to tell us her age; she continually tries to hide her arthritic hands. She doesn't want to reveal much about her personal life, but abundant snapshots in the room reflect her deep connection to family. She hurries toward the end of the interview because one of her granddaughters is coming for lunch.

At the university in Warsaw in the 1920s, I remember pogroms in which non-Jewish students beat the Jews. Finally, in 1925, I was glad to leave for Liège, Belgium, where I met my husband, Maurice. He was from a wealthy family in Galicia in Poland, but he had been brought up in England.

I was born in Warsaw in 1905, the youngest of six sisters and one brother. My father trained to be a rabbi but when he married my mother he gave all that up and went into business. At that time the Jews dressed in long black coats and hats, but he changed all that when they married. My mother was very strong; she was the one who held the whole house together. My family wasn't traditional in terms of religion, but Jewish holidays were important because they became family occasions. Both my parents and my eldest sister died in the ghetto, and so did other family members, but others managed to escape to Israel.

Maurice and I married and had a few good years before the war. Many of our friends went to Switzerland and we could have gone, too, but we decided to join the Resistance instead. It seemed like the normal thing to do. The time was already very dramatic and something had to be done.

What happened was that, little by little, you couldn't do this, you couldn't have a radio, you couldn't go out in the street after dark. Eventually you couldn't even be a person, you had to walk with a star. And after a while the star had no purpose because whenever they saw someone with a star they would arrest him and send him to the barracks. That's the way it was. You can't believe it, but we weren't people anymore, we just had to hide. All that remained on the surface was the association with the council that the Germans set up. I always hid my star so that it couldn't be seen, but you had to have it on.

My husband headed the department to save Jewish children for the Committee for the Defense of the Jews [CDJ]. We weren't political, as was Gerts Jospa, who founded the CDJ. He was a Communist, but we were interested only in resistance and saving Jews. So Maurice organized the operation for saving the children and I was in charge of the office, of putting all the information about children into five books, in code, so the Germans wouldn't know anything if they found the books. This was information like the child's name, birth date, parents' names, and where the parents were, and with which family the child was hidden. I also oversaw the distribution of money and food stamps which we gave to the families who were hiding the children.

We had hidden our own son, born in 1934, with a Catholic family in Liège. We weren't permitted to know, of course, where he was. That was information that no parent could have. We wrote to him through the committee, just as other parents did. He lived with that family as if he were their son, and in those few years he became a Catholic.

I usually worked alone in the office, but one day another office worker came in and, fortunately, I told her everything about the records, because three weeks later I was arrested.

It happened this way: On May 20, 1943, Gestapo agents, led by a traitor known as Jacques, walked into a convent in Anderlecht where we had hidden twenty Jewish children. The Nazis recognized the kids, and ordered the nuns to keep them until the next day, under penalty of death, when they said they would return to fetch them in a truck. The nuns called Maurice, and he informed the Partisans. It was important to allow the transfer of the children to a Jewish boarding school without putting the sisters in danger. That night the Partisans, with the complicity of the nuns, simulated a kidnapping, tying up the nuns and cutting phone lines. The children were taken to a safe place.

Hours after the Gestapo discovered they were too late to get the children, Maurice and I were arrested. The Gestapo said, "Only a Jew could have gone into a convent with a gun."

The next day we were taken to a prison camp in Belgium called Malines. Maurice had been able to set up his program so well that it could be carried out in his absence. In prison he managed to establish a clandestine contact with the outside, someone who could relay important information. He didn't reveal anything when he was tortured, so the work of the CDJ continued.

The prison was made up of military barracks with huge rooms in which a hundred people lived on bunk beds. Every time there were 2,000 people in the camp there would be a transport to Auschwitz.

Three months after we arrived a group of Gypsies was brought into the prison. They were put in a room and the windows were barred. There were so many of them, and the commander forbade anyone to bring milk to them, but my husband did it anyway. For this we were punished and put in the part of the camp from which transports were chosen. We stayed in that area until one day, only three days before we were to be transported to Auschwitz, we were mysteriously called into the courtyard and given different numbers, which kept us out of the transport. I think the Resistance was responsible for this, which, of course, saved our lives.

On January 11, 1944, we were released because the Gestapo had accepted money for the freedom of some Jews. They were setting up old people's homes, and they needed Jews to staff them. Maurice directed one of them until we were liberated in September 1944.

A thirteen-year-old girl slept next to us in prison. Her parents had died in the camps, and we became very close to her. Unfortunately, she was eventually transported to Auschwitz where she spent a year. When she returned to Brussels after the war, we adopted her. She's the same age as our son. When I went to get him after the war, I couldn't believe how much I had missed him. I hadn't seen him for three years. I have four granddaughters. I haven't told them specifically about what I did during the war, only about the resistance work in general.

When we were in prison, Maurice would visit children there who had tuberculosis. As a result, he contracted the disease and spent three years in a sanatorium after the war. But while he was there he wrote the history of the organization of the Jewish rescue in Belgium as accomplished by the CDJ.

I went back to Poland in 1957 and saw one cousin who survived. He had married a Catholic and never told his daughter he was Jewish until she was twenty years old. He felt it was too dangerous because of all the anti-Semitism there.

Until the war I wasn't interested in politics at all. During the war everybody was concerned. Someone had to do it because a lot of the Jews were hiding, so someone had to try to save the children. It was just life. It was natural. It wasn't because I wanted to do it; it just happened. I had to do it. I never could have imagined it or foreseen it.

For an entire generation you couldn't talk about the war because you couldn't live if you talked about it. If you remained in those memories you couldn't live. My granddaughters knew nothing about it until they were adults.

The war changed me completely. I can't even remember who I was before.

After the war, A. Manaster (second from left), and on his left, Andrée Herscovici and Ida Sterno, surrounded by Jewish children they saved.

ANDRÉE GEULEN HERSCOVICI

**Charles and Jacques Skalka
with Andrée Geulen Herscovici.**

*Andrée Herscovici did not have to travel far in the world to find adventure,
security, and meaning. She still lives in Brussels, the city in which she was
born to a liberal, bourgeois Catholic family with a social conscience. In her
beautiful apartment, filled with antiques and photographs of grandchildren,
Andrée, speaking French, describes how she joined the Committee for the
Defense of the Jews, and volunteered to help save Jewish children by taking
them from their families, a violence she didn't fully understand until she had
children of her own. After the war Andrée married a Jew and became a social
worker. "Today I'm more Jewish than he is," she says.*

The children I rescued, for forty years they would not talk about the war.
Only now, when they have become adults, do they have an urge to talk
about it. After forty years in which we would meet and talk about movies and
food, anything but the war. Now these kids talk, talk, talk all the time. They
come out and express emotions which they felt when they were five or six
years old. These emotions are so strong that I cry whenever I'm with them
now. It's terrible to hear how a five-year-old child felt when I told her, "Your
name is not Sarah, your name is Suzanne. You're not Jewish and you never
were Jewish, and you never were called Sarah." And the child does not understand. She does not know why she cannot use her real name. It's only now,
forty years later, that these emotions are surfacing. It's really terrible to hear;
they describe such anguish.

I was born in Brussels in 1921, the middle child of three sisters. My mother and I were opposites; it was like a chicken who had given birth to a duck. She was a simple woman who was dominated by her husband. My father was cultivated and intellectual, and as preoccupied with justice as I was. He never worked because he was born with a physical handicap, but his parents had left enough money and land to support us.

At the age of twelve I told my father I didn't have faith and didn't believe in God, and my father didn't insist. I realized that it was such a cruel world that God could not possibly exist. I was a difficult child because I didn't conform. At fifteen I had already defended the Republicans against Franco. My father was amazed, but it was my idea of injustice which made me react this way then and which guided me for the rest of my life. You must understand that the entire generation of people born around 1920 was influenced by two events: (1) the beginning of the persecution of Jews in Germany—our professors spoke about it in school; and (2) the Spanish Civil War. My response to this was to take care of Spanish refugee children and to collect food and goods to send to Spain.

In 1941, I was teaching school and noticed that children were disappearing from my class. I asked questions and learned they were Jewish children being taken by the Nazis. I asked around some more and found Mmes. Yvonne Jospa and Ida Sterno, who were working with the Committee for the Defense of the Jews [CDJ]. They were in charge of placing Jewish children. They asked me if I would be willing to risk my life, to change my identity, to take children away from their parents and take them to Flanders or to the Ardennes. They asked if I would be willing to change my name, to take a false identity, to risk deportation to Germany. So right away I knew where I stood. I agreed to do it. I never exactly felt afraid. I think when you feel you're doing something absolutely necessary, fear is in the background. You don't really think about it.

The Gestapo had a list of all the Jews who still lived at their official addresses, and the CDJ had this same list. It became a race between the Gestapo and me, who would get there first, who would get the children out first.

This was the procedure: a family would make a request to the CDJ that their child or children be taken to a safe house. It was almost impossible for a family to survive together, but separated, they all had some chance. The CDJ concentrated on finding homes for the children so the parents would be free to try to survive on their own. On my first visit, I would identify myself with the letter requesting help which they had written to the committee, and I would explain everything to the parents. I would get information about all the names and the family history so that, after the war, if the child or the parents didn't survive, there would be enough information to identify the family. Twenty-four hours later I would return and take the child. I wrote down in this book the name and age of the child, and if they looked Jewish. That would determine where I could place the child. When the child was placed, a line was drawn through the name. There are approximately 1,000 names in this book.

A different group in the CDJ would go visit the child every month, try to talk to the child alone to be sure he or she was being well treated, and give money and ration cards to the rescuing family for food for the child. I was involved only in picking up and placing children, and I did this for two and a half years.

It was very difficult for a parent to give up a child. Once I went to a home where a mother lived with her three children, twelve, ten, and six years old. The father had already been taken, and the mother couldn't part with the little one. I placed the two older children, and eight days later the mother and the six-year-old were taken to the camps.

When I was twenty years old I was unsure of myself, and what I did during the war gave me confidence. Everything I am today I owe to that period of my life, those three years. I spent the war in fear, hunger, and constant dread, so I can't say that it was a good time, but I grew up very fast. I knew very few Jews before the war, but during the war I learned a lot by being around Jews. I continued in social services after the war until I retired at sixty.

Immediately after the war, I was involved with the Joint Distribution Committee in working to reunite parents with children. The parents would come into the office and ask, "Where are my children?" and I would bring them to the parents. I would go get the child out of school, or wherever they were, and bring them to Brussels where the parents would pick them up. Unfortunately there were few reunions, because most parents didn't survive. We placed the orphaned children in Israel.

I married in 1948. My husband is a Jew who escaped to Switzerland in 1943. His eldest brother was deported to Auschwitz but luckily he returned. His parents, grandparents, and another brother all died in Auschwitz. When I had my two daughters I imagined what it would have been like to have someone come and take my own children away. This work would have been much harder if I had already been a mother.

I began talking with my grandchildren early about being tolerant and caring about others. All five of them go to the school across the street, and they come here every day for lunch. It's hard to explain to them that war was being waged against children, that trucks would come in the night into neighborhoods and children would be thrown in like animals, that we had to take them away from their homes to save them.

Therèse Rosenblatt, one of the children rescued by the CDJ.

Michel, Maximillien, and Elizabeth Ackerman with their mother.

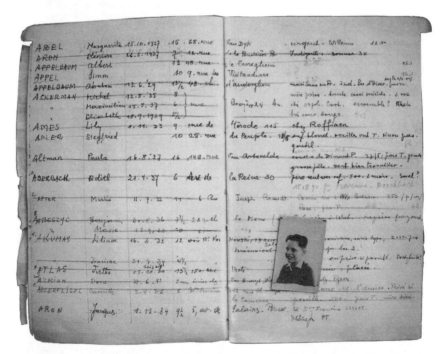

Notebook in which Andrée recorded information about the children she placed, with a photo of Martin Apter. Apter is listed on line 11 of the left facing page.

MARIE TAQUET
WITH DAVID INOWLOCKI

Marie Taquet, 1940.

We meet Madame Taquet at an especially welcoming and attractive nursing home outside Brussels, with David Inowlocki, who is alive because of this frail old woman. Although Marie Taquet never had children of her own, at least eighty Jewish boys regard her as the woman to whom they owe their lives. Raised to live a retiring life as the wife of a military officer, Mme. Taquet found herself headmistress at the Castle of Jamoigne, a school for boys whose fathers were in the military. Half the children were Jews in hiding. David Inowlocki has arranged for her to live in this well-maintained facility and has also offered the testimony necessary for her to receive the medal from Yad Vashem at a 1988 reunion, held at the castle, of the boys she saved. He brings her sweets, and when her dinner arrives, he helps feed her; he also helps when her memory fails. Although his English is rudimentary, he translates her French well enough for us to understand why David Inowlocki feels such love and gratitude toward this modest, gentle woman.

MADAME TAQUET: I was born in 1898, in Luxembourg. We were practicing Catholics, but not very strict. My father was a very sociable man and a wonderful musician; we were very proud of him. My mother was very discreet and didn't like social events. She was actually against my having any friends, but it was the time of the First World War when I was sixteen years old. That war changed everything in my life because it interrupted my studies.

When I was twenty, I married a career officer in the Belgian army. We moved to Germany for a few years while we occupied their country after the war, and then we returned to Belgium. In early 1942, after Belgium had been occupied, my husband was assigned to direct the Reine Elizabeth Castle in Jamoigne, to take care of children of the military. The castle was staffed by nuns, but we moved in to run it. My husband did the administrative work and I did everything else.

I was brought up in such an old-fashioned way that I never thought I could work. I just didn't think I had the character. The first boys came to the castle in 1942, and soon there were eighty boys. Then in March 1943 I was told that another eighty would arrive, and only after they came was I told, "They're Jews, but no one has to know it. Will you keep them?" I said I would.

It put the other chil-dren in danger because you could tell they were Jewish, but the children didn't know it. We changed all the names of the Jewish children from David and Yankel to Pierre and Jean. David's name was Daniel.

DAVID: I was four and my brother was six when we left home. I remember my mother telling me, "David, you have beautiful brown eyes. Never let a German see them." So whenever I saw a Nazi soldier, I kept my head down. But we had very little awareness of the war while we were at the castle. We were hidden in full freedom. It was harder for the parents than the children because we remember it as a good time. We had classes in the morning and in the afternoon we played in the forest. When we returned from the forest, Mme. Taquet was always standing on the steps of the castle. We thought she was showing her authority, but she was counting us to be sure no one was missing.

MME. TAQUET: It was such a big responsibility that I couldn't even think about it. If I had, I wouldn't have been able to do it.

DAVID: We always did things children like to do. We were raised like scouts and we marched on the road. People in the village thought we were like Hitler Youth. My most vivid memory is of Mme. Taquet kissing each of us goodnight every night. We never went to sleep until she had kissed us. The good boys and the bad ones.

MME. TAQUET: The Nazis paid us many visits but I always spoke to them in German and in a very strong, cold way, just as they spoke to me, so they thought, *She's one of us.* One night the Nazis came looking for an English pilot who had apparently parachuted into the neighborhood. We all had to get out of bed and be counted. One of our teachers had escaped from being sent to work in Germany and was afraid he'd be caught, so he hid on the roof. When the Nazis counted and one person was missing, they sent the dogs out to find him, and they did. As he was saying goodbye to me I told him never to try to escape from the Germans because it might put the children in danger. He survived and later told me he had had many opportunities to escape but he remembered my words and never did it.

DAVID: When Liberation came in September 1944, I had been away from home for almost three years. Since I was so young I didn't even remem-

---

ber my family. When my father came to pick me up he walked up to me and I didn't recognize him. I looked up at him and said, "Hello, Monsieur." I remember being very sad when I had to leave the castle.

MME. TAQUET: The castle stayed open until June 1946, because many parents of the Jewish children did not return. After that the Jewish organizations took care of these children, and I continued doing the same kind of work for vacation camps and other children's groups until I retired in 1952.

The war years were very good years for me. It was the war, but for us it was the best, most interesting, and challenging time of my life. I was surprised to be able to do what I did. I was thrown into it, and I took the devil by the horns and I did it.

DAVID: I didn't see her from September 1944 until February 1987. I think our parents were trying to get our lives back to normal as completely as possible. They probably wanted us to forget what to them had been a horrible time, and besides, they wanted us to forget our Christian names and be Jewish again.

MME. TAQUET: I received some letters from parents thanking me for what I had done, but that was all. I lived one mile from the castle for eleven years after the war and no one came to look for me. But I've always been realistic. I understood that the boys had their own lives and their own parents, so I knew why they didn't get in touch with me before. I thought I would never see any of them again.

DAVID: In May 1988, we organized a reunion of the boys and the teachers, and we arranged for Mme. Taquet to be honored by Yad Vashem. Many people came from all over the world to be at the castle to remember and pay homage to Mme. Taquet. Now I come to visit her and bring her cakes. She took care of me and now I must take care of her. For most of us it's the past, but as long as she lives, we have to be thankful.

Marie Taquet died in September 1989.

Château du Faing, the Castle of Jamoigne, 1940.

RESCUERS

M. Taquet, major of the Belgian army, at his desk in the castle.

A group of Jewish and non-Jewish children who were called "the little ducks" because they were under six years old. David Inowlocki is in the top row, second from right.

Dormitory at the Castle of Jamoigne.

Marie Taquet and David Inowlocki, 1988.

FRANCE

*If we take the capsulation of minorities within the nation-state as a given con-
dition, the implication of the Holocaust is that the life and liberties of minorities
depend primarily upon whether the dominant group includes them within its
universe of obligation; these are the bonds that hold or the bonds that break.*
　　　　　　　　　　　　　　—Helen Fein, *Accounting for Genocide*

In 1987 Klaus Barbie, the infamous "butcher of Lyon," was put on trial in
Paris for deporting forty-four children in 1944 from the mountain village
of Izieu. The trial created a furor in France, because many feared that court-
room testimony would reveal new information about French collaboration
with the Nazis. Just as the present generation in Germany wrestles with the
Holocaust, trying to understand why its people followed Hitler, so France
also struggles with its past, specifically with the Vichy government's collaboration with the Third Reich.

Although the Jewish population in France was only 1 percent, roughly
350,000, since 1875 Jews had enjoyed equality and prosperity in French
society under the democratic government of the Third Republic. To be sure,
anti-Semitism existed, sometimes with great intensity, as in the case of the
Dreyfus affair, but French Jews still felt part of the country.

In the 1930s, right-wing opposition to the liberal government increased
with high and growing unemployment and a large influx of refugees, including Jews. Many in France, fearing communism and a war with Nazi Germany, looked to the right for a solution to the nation's problems. Some
20,000 refugees were put in internment camps in 1939 and 1940.

The quick defeat of the French by the Nazis in May 1940 led to an
equally easy victory of the right-wing parties over the Third Republic. In an
effort to be on the winning side, the Vichy government, newly formed to
negotiate an armistice and headed by eighty-four-year-old Marshal Philippe
Pétain, made a deal with the Germans. The French turned over Alsace-Lor-
raine to the Germans and invited them to occupy the northwestern part of
their country. In return, the Nazis allowed France to control the "free zone"
and gave them administrative and legal powers in the occupied zone, as long
as they didn't conflict with Nazi rule.

Vichy supporters defended their decision by asserting that they prevented
all of France from being occupied by the Nazis. When asked about the popu-
larity of the Vichy government, Gilbert Lesage, a rescuer who worked with the
Quakers in Lyon, said, "Ninety percent of the French supported Pétain until the
Allies began to win the war in 1944. Then 90 percent supported de Gaulle."

Because the French are so patriotic, the Nazis knew they would resist the deportation of French citizens, even if they were Jews. So at first the Nazis left the deportations to the French government. Vichy cooperated with the Germans by deliberately abandoning Jewish refugees who had flocked to the free zone from Germany and the Netherlands, only to be interned in detention camps such as Gurs and Rivesaltes. They surrendered these Jewish refugees to the Germans while protecting native-born French Jews, who made up about half of the Jewish population of France in 1940. It was from these camps that John Weidner, the Dutch rescuer, saved more than 800, and Fritz Heine, from Germany, rescued many German Jews and political prisoners.

No other occupied country cooperated more with Germany's efforts against the Jews than France. The French wrote their own anti-Semitic legislation, provided French police for deportation, and voluntarily deported Jews from the south of France, the area not occupied by the Germans. Why did they offer such cooperation? Helen Fein writes: "The Jews were instrumental to Vichy as a medium of barter with the Germans—like wampum, gold, or potatoes—in order to obtain a place in the New Order."

Given the cooperation of the Vichy government, it seems remarkable that only 29 percent of France's Jews were killed. This low statistic is not the result of heroic efforts to save Jews. Rather, what saved so many Jews in France was the dispersion of Jews all over the country; France's proximity to safe havens such as Switzerland, Spain, and Portugal; the lack of sufficient Nazi personnel; and a shortage of trains. Individual citizens also helped: Jean Boete, Ivan Beltrami, and Robert Gachet joined the Resistance in France primarily to save Jews. Simone Monnier and Mireille Gardère took Jewish children into their schools; Claudine Gilain kept five-year-old Roger Kauffman, a friend of her son's, for three years. Adele Defarges took a Polish-Jewish woman into her home posing as a maid.

When the Vichy government refused to allow Jews to hold civil service jobs and began its discriminatory legislation against French and foreign Jews in 1940–41, no group spoke out. Only when Himmler ordered Jews to wear the yellow star did Vichy protest, because the order did not distinguish between native and foreign-born Jews.

When the government of an occupied country did not resist Nazi persecution—for example, as Denmark did—the clergy's role in saving lives became vital. Unfortunately, in France the Catholic Church and Vichy were on the same side; the government enjoyed the blessing of the Church and the Church appreciated Vichy's efforts to protect France from communism and the Jews. In a letter to Pétain, Léon Bérard, ambassador to the Vatican, wrote: "It would be unreasonable, in a Christian state, to permit them [the Jews] to exercise the functions of government and thus to submit the

Catholics to their authority. Consequently it is legitimate to bar them from public functions. . . . ”

Locally, there were notable exceptions. Père Marie Benoît, a priest of the Capuchin order, was known as “father of the Jews” in Marseilles, where he provided false papers and helped 4,000 Jews to get to safe countries. Marie-Rose Gineste traveled more than sixty miles surrounding Montauban, a town in southwestern France, to distribute a letter written by Monsignor Théas to Catholic bishops protesting Nazi persecution of Jews. When a bishop spoke out, the priests felt protected in their own rescue efforts.

Huguenots, French Protestants, were more sensitive to the plight of the Jews, perhaps because of their own long history of persecution in a Catholic country. They organized CIMADE *(Comité d'Inter-Mouvements auprès des Evacués)* to resettle refugees. They smuggled Jews to Switzerland, or hid them in the Haute-Loire region in villages such as Le Chambon-sur-Lignon, where no Jew was ever turned away. The 5,000 inhabitants of this village, under the leadership of Pastor Trocmé, saved 5,000 Jews, many of whom Pastor Marc Donadille, Ermine Orsi, and Emilie Guth escorted there.

Not until the Nazis began deporting both foreign- and native-born Jews from the free zone in mid-1942 did the French Catholic Church finally respond with a protest. The French cardinals and the Pope also objected to Vichy premier Pierre Laval's proposed law to make it easier to deport Jews by rescinding their newly acquired French citizenship. The Church's veto of the law saved lives, but by the time “the bonds that hold” came to include France's Jews, 93,000 of them had died.

In 1943, the pastor of Le Chambon, André Trocmé (last row) poses with the children from one of the village's new homes for children.

Photo from *Weapons of the Spirit* (courtesy of the director, Pierre Sauvage, and Friends of Le Chambon)

RESCUERS

Père Marie Benoît.

MARC DONADILLE

**Pastor Donadille with
his wife and children.**

*Protestant minister Marc Donadille lives in a house in a suburb of Marseilles in
the Cévennes district of France. His home is very large for just one person, but
he has lived in it for over fifty years, raising his family there while serving as
pastor. At the beginning of the interview he announces apologetically that he
will have to cut the interview short in order to officiate at a funeral. Donadille
gently fingers the book he has written,* Comment participe au occulte, *as he
speaks French slowly and clearly for the benefit of our young American translator. He describes his wartime work in providing false identities for Jews, getting
them to Le Chambon, and hiding about eighty in the Cévennes. His eyes twinkle
when he recounts people in the village whispering to him about some pastor who
was hiding and saving Jews: "I would tell them to be careful talking about it
because he could get in trouble."*

My Protestant ancestors were very strong in the belief that it was inad-
missible to persecute people because of their race or religion. They
taught me that Jews are the people of the Bible. We have the same Bible and
are also responsible for our own lives, unlike the Catholics who have the priest
as an intermediary. I was born in 1911, in St. Croix du Belle Française, the
middle child of three brothers. St. Croix was mostly a Protestant community,
and my father was the minister. He was so well liked, so important in the community that I wanted to follow in his footsteps. During the First World War,
my father was away and my grandfather came often to spend time with me.

In Nîmes, where I went to high school, there was an important Jewish
community and I had many Jewish friends. The small Protestant and Jewish

communities identified with each other because we both had always been persecuted by the Catholics. In high school I began to have trouble, as a Protestant, with the Catholics.

Later when I studied in Geneva, I learned a lot about the rising anti-Semitism in Germany. I married in 1935, and my wife, who was Swiss, was equally anti-Nazi. We were both aware from the beginning of the German persecution of the Jews, which was beginning to happen in France, too. In 1939, we moved to the Cévennes, in the south of France.

All the pastors there were aware of the persecution of the Jews in Germany. Everyone agreed on the issue of saving the Jews. I worked with CIMADE, a Protestant resistance organization, which was helping Jews. Madeleine Barrault was the director of CIMADE, and she was helping Jewish refugees, primarily the ones from Germany who were fleeing into the Alsace region. She would go down to those refugee camps and set up schools and find the people places to live outside the camps. She was trying to help them learn how to live without fear. I would go to those camps and take Jews out. Staying in the camps was dangerous because the Vichy government regularly pulled Jews out and handed them over to the Nazis.

I also picked them up from Aix or Marseilles and took them to the Cévennes and hid them in churches and on farms, and I took them to the Protestant village of Le Chambon in the mountains that never refused refuge to a Jew. All along the way, we had set up welcoming houses where people could stop for a night to eat and sleep.

My family went to Geneva to be safe, so I was alone, but my parish knew what I was doing. People could tell I was saving Jews; when I arrived with twelve people, strangers carrying boxes, it was obvious. We provided the peasants who were hiding Jews with extra food, which we got from the surrounding farms.

In 1943 my wife left the children there with her family and returned from Geneva. One day she was at home when two Vichy policemen came to search the house. They didn't go into this special room where I made false I.D. papers, but she did have an exchange with them which shows how everyone in the area agreed that the Jews should be saved. The window was open when they came in and you could hear that a neighbor was listening to BBC News. One of the policemen said to my wife, "You should tell them to lower the volume. It's illegal to listen to BBC; you're supposed to listen only to the news from Paris or Germany." My wife replied, "Everyone listens to it! If one plays Vichy or Paris radio, they shut the windows and doors. But when one listens to English radio, one leaves everything open."

In my three townships there were no collaborators. But the authorities eventually found out, and it became more dangerous. The chief of police had been watching me, but he never arrested me. Some Jews weren't careful and did things that caused them to get caught, but everyone in the region was willing to take Jews.

We knew it was dangerous but we had accepted the risk once and for all, and that was that. Fear never haunted me. One day on a train someone said, "There's a pastor in the Cévennes who's hiding Jews!" I said, "You shouldn't say that. The pastor could get in trouble for that," not telling him that he was talking about me. He replied, "Really? You can get into trouble for that?" Some of the people were very naive.

Often I would bring people to my house and then take them to other houses to hide. I think I hid about eighty people, and I took about a hundred people to Le Chambon.

My younger brother also did dangerous things during the war. He was the director of the railroad and in charge of the train that went to Le Chambon. Railroads played a very big part in bringing Jews to Chambon, and my brother was partly responsible for that village being able to save 5,000 Jews.

What I did was something useful, that's all. The memory of these events doesn't cause me anguish. There were happy times and sad times. We think now of happy things. When we managed to save someone, we were happy; when we failed, we were sad. I never had nightmares, exactly, after the war; but for a while I would wake up very easily at the slightest noise and be ready to jump out the window. Otherwise, I've been fine. My wife and I raised seven children. The two oldest participated a little during the war. They certainly learned to keep a secret then. Since the war I have continued to do what I can for people, through the church.

I received the Yad Vashem medal in 1981. When I went to Israel to accept it and to plant my tree, I met many people I had saved. One family I saw, I had saved the entire family.

I'm sad to say that anti-Semitism still exists in France. Le Pen still has many supporters in Marseilles. I heard a woman shout just the other day, "Let's get rid of the Jews once and for all!" There's less anti-Semitism now than during the war, but unfortunately, some still exists. The world doesn't learn completely from history.

The children of Pastor Donadille with a little refugee, Eva Ahlfeld, near the church at St. Privat-de-Vallongue, 1943.

RESCUERS

COLOR PORTRAITS

When I began this series of portraits I wasn't sure whether to use black and white or color so I shot both at the first thirty-five sessions. My initial preference had been the black and white, but when I studied the images, only the color seemed to represent what I had seen and felt during the sitting. Only after all the pictures had been made and I was working on selecting and printing did I discover the rationale for the color.

These people had told us stories of unbelievable heroism but they were all unassuming and modest. Therefore I did not need to add drama to their images, which is sometimes the effect of black-and-white portraits. On the contrary, I wanted the photographs to represent the rescuers with as much reality as possible, and black and white, with its qualities of abstraction, moved the images one step further away. Furthermore, although these are stories about the past, I wanted the photographs to be contemporary, to bring viewers into the present, so that they could relate to the rescuers as people living today whose acts of goodness and courage are timeless.

—from the Photographer's Note on page 268 by Gay Block

PAGE 1
Row 1: Helena Orchon, Pol./USA; Arie Verduijn, Neth./Can.; Stefan Korbonski, Pol./USA
Row 2: Paul Pensis with his mother, Belg.; Yvonne Jospa, Belg.; Marie-Henriette Feremans Ceulemans, Belg.
Row 3: Andries van der Meer, Neth.; Johannes and Boukje Stenekes, Neth./Can.; Nienke Veenstra, Neth./Can.
Row 4: Jan de Haan, Neth.; Anna Dobrucki with Lusia Schimmel, Pol./Isr.; Pelagia Springer, Pol./Isr.

PAGE 2
Row 1: Claudine Gilain, Fr.; Heinz & Irmgard Jonass, Ger./USA; Gertrude von Egloffstein, Ger.
Row 2: Jean Boete, Fr.; Denise Siekierski, Fr.; Wladyslaw Wyrwa, Pol./USA
Row 3: Fela Herman, Belg.; Dr. Paul Kerner, Czech./Ger.; Janina Pavlitska, Pol./Isr.
Row 4: Jansje and Jan Sevinga-Brower, Neth.; Mireille Gardere with her husband, Pierre, Fr.; Marcelle and Therese Lacroix, Belg.

PAGE 3
Row 1: Wijbren and Mieke Streekstra, the Neth./Can.; Zofia Wieczorek Avni with her granddaughter, Pol./Isr.; Took Heroma, Neth.
Row 2: Skoukje and Rinze Bouwma, Neth./Can.; Irena Yakira with her husband, Eliahu, Pol./Isr.; Robert Gachet, Fr.
Row 3: Yaraslaw Klymowsky, Ukr./USA; Margot Lawson, Neth./USA; Gilbert Lesage, Fr.
Row 4: Helena Toth-Elias with her husband, Benjamin, Hun./Isr.; Veronica Parocai with Itzhak Grossman, Hun./Isr.; Jacob Oversloot and his wife, Neth./USA

PAGE 4
Row 1: Willie and Jan Brinkers, Neth.; Mary Szul Diaczok, Pol./Can.; Adele Defarges, Fr.
Row 2: Simone Monnier, Fr.; Ala Sztajnert, Pol./Isr.; Henryka Kowalski, Pol./Isr.
Row 3: Piotr Budnik, Pol./Isr.; Gerrit van Lochen & wife, Anna, Neth./Can.; Wilhem Hak, Neth.
Row 4: Irena Landau with daughter, Chava Zadok, and Chava's sons, Pol./Isr.; Kalman and Karolin Dreisziger with her grandson, Hung./Can.; Ruth and Johan de Jong, Neth.

PAGE 5
Row 1: Maria Dobrowicz, Pol./Isr.; Christine Hilaum-Beuckens, Neth.
Row 2: Christine Zilverberg, Neth.; Wilhelm and Maria Tarnawski, Pol./Isr.
Row 3: Alice Schiffer, Belg./USA; Shimon and Irena Noskowicz, Pol./Isr.
Row 4: Klaas van Houten, Neth.; Willem LaBruyère and Elizabeth Wilhelmina, Neth.

Johannes DeVries, the Netherlands *(p. 48)*

John Weidner, the Netherlands *(p. 80)*

Louisa Steenstra, the Netherlands *(p. 86)*

Semmy Riekerk, the Netherlands *(p. 98)*

Arie van Mansum, the Netherlands *(p. 53)*

Bert Berchove, the Netherlands *(p. 69)*

Marion P. van Binsbergen Pritchard,
the Netherlands *(p. 59)*

Marguerite Mulder, the Netherlands
(p. 75)

Arnold Douwes, the Netherlands *(p. 90)*

Seine Otten, the Netherlands *(p. 90)*

Andrée Geulen Herscovici, Belgium *(p. 130)*

Marie Taquet, Belgium *(p. 134)*

Aart and Johtie Vos, the Netherlands *(p. 104)*

Tina Strobos, the Netherlands *(p. 110)*

Pieter and Joyce Miedema, the Netherlands *(p. 95)*

Germaine Belinne and Liliane Gaffney, Belgium *(p. 121)*

Marc Donadille, France *(p. 142)*

Ermine Orsi, France *(p. 145)*

Emilie Guth, France *(p. 145)*

Ivan Beltrami, France *(p. 151)*

Marie-Rose Gineste, France *(p. 154)*

Gertrude Luckner,
Germany *(p. 173)*

Helena Jacobs,
Germany *(p. 176)*

Maria Countess von Maltzen, Germany *(p. 179)*

Gertruda Babilenska, Poland *(p. 192)*

Jan Karski, Poland *(p. 195)*

Fritz Heine, Germany *(p. 169)*

Zofia Baniecka, Poland *(p. 189)*

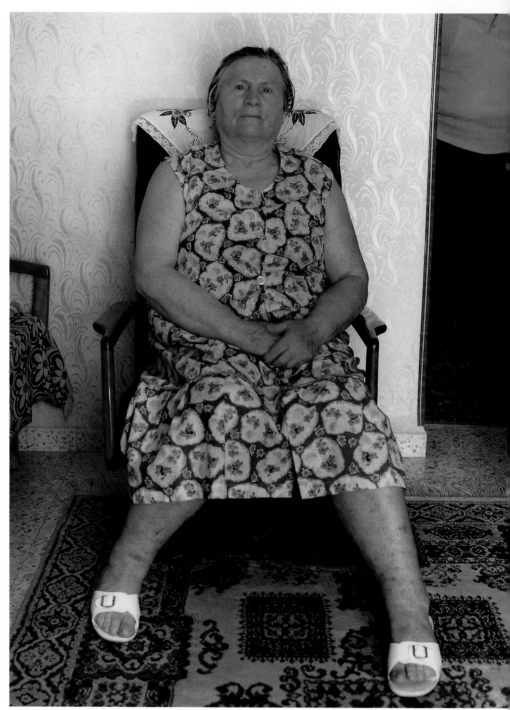

Agnieszka Budna-Widerschal, Poland *(p. 202)*

Alex and Mela Roslan, Poland *(p. 214)*

Irene Gut Opdyke, Poland *(p. 222)*

Antonín Kalina, Chechoslavakia
(p. 234)

Stefania Podgorska Burzminski
with her husband Joe, Poland *(p. 206)*

Stefan Raczynski, Poland *(p. 227)*

Gustav Mikulai, Hungary *(p. 250)*

Mihael Michaelov, Bulgaria *(p. 260)*

Libus Fries, Chechoslavakia *(p. 238)*

Malka Csizmadia, Hungary *(p. 245)*

Ivan Vranetic, Yugoslavia *(p. 254)*

Jean Kowalyk Berger, Ukraine *(p. 264)*

Orest Zahaikewycz and Helena Melnyczuk, Ukraine *(p. 268)*

Amfian Gerasimov, Latvia *(p. 273)*

EMILIE GUTH AND ERMINE ORSI

Emilie Guth, 1938.   Ermine Orsi, 1940.

Old people often talk of the past, but Ermine Orsi and Emilie Guth offer each other something more than memories of youth: they remain witnesses to each other's selflessness and courage, and they remain best friends. They met when they both worked together in Marseilles in the French underground network, "Combat."

The first interview took place in Madame Orsi's ornate dining room in Marseilles, where the two friends remember their own and each other's stories with laughter and tears, and always with honesty. But we sensed that Madame Guth had more to tell, so we accepted her invitation for a second visit the next morning.

Mme. Guth's nearby apartment is much simpler, filled with her crochet work. She displays the hope chests she has made for each of her grandchildren filled with this handiwork, and she gives us each a doily. After the interview, she serves handmade pastries, and we meet her charming grandchildren who visit every day. She asks us to meet her son a few doors away, and he bears a strong resemblance to the father he never knew.

MADAME GUTH: I was born in 1911, in a small village, Buste, the oldest of four children. The village was mostly Protestant merchants. We were Protestant, and my mother and grandfather were very religious. I had many Jewish friends before the war, but this was not well received by other villagers. I had a Jewish boy friend, and a man in our village threatened to beat him if he entered our town again.

My father had died in the First World War, and it was very difficult to grow up without a man in the house. My mother was very generous. Everyone in town knew to come to her house. We weren't rich, but she always gave wheat and flour to people who needed something to eat. If there was someone who was alone and not being cared for, she would go. In the spring she grew vegetables, and in the winter she crocheted. She taught me how to do everything. When children see people in the house helping others, it makes them want to help. The things you learn in your own house are the things you grow up to do.

When I was sixteen years old, I became a nurse and had to go to work.

MADAME ORSI: My mother was one of only four Protestants in the village of Carrara, Italy, where I was born in 1909. Italy is such a Catholic country that to be Protestant there was like being a bastard. My mother and grandmother helped people and cared for the sick, but still my mother was discriminated against because of her religion. I'm sure that's when I learned to fight for any kind of justice. I've always known how to defend myself.

My mother died when I was seven, and my grandmother raised me. My grandmother would walk four kilometers just to bring me sewing needles. When I was sixteen years old I married a man twenty-four, and we had to leave Italy because he was anti-Fascist. At seventeen I moved to Marseilles. My first daughter was born in 1927, and my second one in 1930. My husband was never able to get identity papers from another country, so he was always on the move.

In 1936, during the Spanish War, I went to Spain to help children and sick people. My older daughter was living with her father's family in Italy, and I sent my younger daughter, Odette, to school in Paris so I could do this work. In 1942, Paris was occupied by the Nazis. I became very upset because I couldn't find a way to get her out.

Then I met a man, a Polish Jew, Benjamin Feingold, hiding in a trench near a Paris train station. He was a journalist who had come to France for safety. He told me not to worry, that he would get my daughter. Ten days later she was back home with me. I then hid Feingold in my house for a long time. One day, he went out to get oranges for my daughter, who was sick, and he never returned. I'm sure he was caught and deported.

I think I got started in the resistance movement and helping Jews because of Feingold. I had helped people in Spain, so it was natural to want to help French people.

MME. GUTH: I was working as a nurse in a children's home where Jewish refugees were brought from Germany, Poland, all over. I began trying to help the Jews through this institution. When the Germans closed this home I continued the work undercover, and I became part of the network called "Combat."

MME. ORSI: In Marseilles, there were many refugees because it was in the free zone. I had heard about what the people in Le Chambon were doing. That was a Protestant village in the mountains not far from Marseilles, where all the people were hiding Jews. The pastor there, André Trocmé, was a pacifist and a deeply moral person who inspired that village of 5,000 Protestants to save 5,000 Jews. What I did was find the Jews and take them to Le Chambon. I rode the train every day back and forth. Mme. Guth stayed in Marseilles, distributing false I.D. cards and money to Jews, and hiding them until I could take them to Le Chambon, and I did all the transporting.

MME. GUTH: We both began doing resistance work in 1942, but we didn't meet until 1943. She was working in a fruit-pie market where many Jewish refugees, artists and journalists, were working. I was living with my sister and brother-in-law. They worked so that I could spend my time in the Resistance. Since I was a nurse, it was natural for me to find hiding places for Jews in psychiatric hospitals or in maternity wards. I also got food cards for them, and money which mostly came from the United States, but when they needed to be moved from one place to another, Mme. Orsi did that. You know, we both just began doing this work, and once you started to do one thing you couldn't stop because people came to you and begged for help. Even if you had just a little bit of feeling and were very afraid, you had to keep doing it.

Then I met a Jewish man, André Weingarten, and we fell in love. He was also working in the Resistance. He moved into our house, and we wanted to marry, but it was too dangerous. I was arrested by the Gestapo in November 1943, and they held me for a month. I think they let me go because I was bold and I spoke to them in German. But I knew they suspected I was a resistance worker.

MME. ORSI: One day a man whom I had placed in Le Chambon told me he had a nephew who was hiding in a woman's house. He asked if I would go to the house to see if his nephew was okay. When I walked in, there was no one in sight. Then all of a sudden I saw this big piano move, and it scared me. Then, from behind the wall where the piano was, five Jews came out from their hiding place, on their hands and knees. They were so scared and thin, they looked as if they had been in a concentration camp. They told me that one woman had been taken that morning by the Gestapo, and they begged me to help them get to Le Chambon. I took them home because Dr. Ginsberg, a Jewish man I hid in my house for two years, could help them get strong enough to make the trip. Then I took them on the train, though by then it was very dangerous to travel. Anyone who says they weren't afraid is either lying or crazy. We got to Le Chambon and they stayed in a hotel. Even if there was no room for a Jew to stay in Le Chambon, there was room.

At one time I kept a three-month-old baby in my house for a few weeks, because his mother was in the hospital in Paris. I became so attached to that baby that when she returned to pick him up, I knew I could never see him again, that it would be too painful for me. I had about five or six people living in my house all the time. One woman was so scared that she trembled all the time, and when there was a knock on the door she would really shake. She made me crazy.

Once I was arrested in the Avignon train station, and I was held for eight days. My daughter suffered as much as I did during that time because she guessed what had happened. I was put on display for all the citizens to see. But then I was released, and my daughter was so happy when she saw me come back home.

It's painful to think of the war years. Sometimes I went a long time without eating so I could give food to other people in my house. The hardest time for me was when the Gestapo took Pastor Trocmé from Le Chambon. His wife, Magda, was also very brave and believed in the work as much as he did. I'm just glad they survived.

MME. GUTH: The war had a terrible end for me. I still, after all these years, cannot accept what happened. We had a double agent in the Resistance who was telling the Nazis all our plans and operations. This woman took Jews as if to liberate them, but instead she would turn them over to the Germans. Once she even turned an entire convoy of children over to the Nazis. None of them was ever heard from again. This double agent was a terrible woman, and it's unbelievable that she wasn't punished after the war. Just at the time of Liberation in August 1944 she had me, André, and my brother-in-law arrested because she didn't want us to have her punished for what she had done. She had the cooperation of the French police, who worked with the Germans during the war, and sometimes they were even worse than the Germans. I was released from prison after a few days, and two days later I learned that the police had beaten André to death. My brother-in-law was beaten also, but he was more physically fit. And André probably had it worse because he was Jewish.

I had become pregnant with André's child just before Liberation. My son looks a lot like his father. My grandson looks even more like him. I will never digest it. André had a sister in America and he could have moved there with her, but he wanted to stay here to work in the Resistance.

MME. ORSI: What I did during the war came naturally; because I had lost my mother I identified with the children who had sustained loss. I can't stand to see someone sad. And sometimes I think we were unconscious, not aware of the danger we were taking on.

MME. GUTH: Don't diminish yourself. We didn't see danger because sometimes we were unconscious.

MME. ORSI: I don't know if the Jews would do for us what we did for them. There are some good ones but I have the impression that they will help one another, but not non-Jews.

MME. GUTH: Mme. Orsi worked for so long during the war and had no social security for that, so she's bitter. She sold all her mother's jewelry to help people and never asked for anything. After the war almost all the children she saved disappeared. Of all those in the photos, she saw very few ever again.

MME. ORSI: There were times I didn't have enough to eat.

MME. GUTH: After the war, many people had troubles and it was hard to show appreciation. But I am still in contact with a Jewish woman I saved. She's eighty-four years old now. I found her a hiding place and went there two or three times a week to take her food and anything she needed. I think the most important thing is to be good.

MME. ORSI: Before the war I thought everyone was nice; after the war I saw that this wasn't true, and that hurt me a lot. Some people are very selfish. I don't know if I would do it again.

MME. GUTH: I would do it again, even with what I lost, and I'm sure Mme. Orsi would, too. She is sick now because of what she did. During the war she walked from village to village, and now her legs are bad. And I am also sick from some of the things I went through. We're both a little disappointed. Mme. Orsi spends too much time alone. She doesn't like old people; she thinks she's young!

In 1985, we went to Israel with a senior citizens' group, and that was when we received our medals and planted our trees at Yad Vashem. Two Jewish women on our bus heard there were two "Righteous Gentiles" on the bus and they asked what that was! And after I returned home, there was an article about us in the Marseilles newspaper, with a picture and everything. A woman I knew came to my apartment and asked, "Are you the one who did all that for the Jews?" When I said, "Yes, that was me," she said, "You shouldn't have done it; it wasn't worth it." I slammed the door in her face.

MME. ORSI: Well, it's hard to know what is happening in this world. The Jews were in concentration camps, so why are they occupying territory in the West Bank and Gaza? But Mme. Guth and I get together often to talk about the war, and about the people who do remember us.

Benjamin Feingold.

André Weingarten.

Mmes. Guth and Orsi, 1988.

(courtesy of Friends of Le Chambon)

Ermine Orsi holding the Jewish baby and
future filmmaker Pierre Sauvage in Le
Chambon-sur-Lignon, 1944.

RESCUERS

IVAN BELTRAMI

Ivan Beltrami, 1944.

*Dapper and ebullient, Dr. Ivan Beltrami welcomes us into his large, graceful
home in Marseilles, the house in which he was born and the one in which he
and his family had hidden Jews. His young wife offers us refreshments, soda and
cookies, while Dr. Beltrami drinks fruit juice, explaining that he doesn't eat
sweets; he is in superb physical condition. Perpetually in motion and speaking
rapid French, he pulls out scrapbooks chronicling his wartime experiences and
shows us exactly where in the house Jews had been hidden. An unquestioning
supporter of Israel, he was disappointed in 1967 when they rejected his offer to
serve as a paratrooper in the army.*

Our family is Catholic but I always had Jewish friends in school. From
the time I was very young, I tried to defend them because of my feeling
of justice. I was born in 1920, in Marseilles. My father was a physician, and
he was the chairman of the French faculty of medicine. I have one older
brother; he and I are both physicians. My parents also had Jewish friends.
My mother was very strong; she was more courageous than I because she
healed people during the war. They took care of some Jews on the second
floor of their apartment building when there were German army personnel
on the first floor. My father was a big French patriot. When my brother came
back from almost two years in Buchenwald and people congratulated him
for his bravery, my father said, "Don't congratulate him; it was his duty!" I
think I'm most like my father because for us he was the boss. In fact, I
always called him "boss" instead of "father."

I learned in 1933 what the Germans were planning to do, and then when
Kristallnacht happened in 1938, it just confirmed our fears. I had friends in

Spain who talked about what the Germans did there, like the Guernica bombing. In 1939, I volunteered for the French air force, but they never flew. I continued my studies after the occupation as I watched Jewish refugees arrive here from Germany.

In 1941, when Pétain created his armed forces—it wasn't really an official army—I began defending the Jews because Pétain's forces were obviously anti-Semitic. A Jewish boy was supposed to go to prison, but instead I managed to get him into the infirmary where he'd be safe for a while. I hid some Jewish friends in my apartment, which proved to be very dangerous. In January 1943, the Germans began rounding up Jews, and my entire apartment building was surrounded. I hid the Jews in the courtyard, under an overhang, until the Germans left.

I joined the Resistance in September 1942. I wasn't political—I was both anti-Communist and anti-Nazi. I became the major of the underground forces in charge of transmitting messages between Resistance centers. At the time, I was an intern in a hospital where many Resistance members and Jews were sent to be treated. Instead of just trying to heal them, we tried to keep them there longer to prevent them from being deported.

My brother was the chief of another Resistance network, but neither of us knew the other was working in the Resistance. And our parents didn't know about either of us. It wasn't safe to tell anyone who didn't absolutely have to know. Most of my work was warning Jews when the raids and roundups would occur. But many Jews refused to leave even after they were warned. They just had no idea what they faced if they were picked up. From 1939 to 1942 we were able to save some refugee Jews in a camp thirty kilometers from Marseilles, but when the Germans occupied the free zone, they emptied the camp and all of them were deported.

After my brother was arrested on May 23, 1943, I stopped all my activity for a while. Then I became com-mander of those underground forces made up mostly of Spanish people. We were in charge of killing French militia [Nazi collaborators] and Gestapo. This was a special satisfaction! I killed people myself, and I don't regret it. Especially after what happened to my brother. When he was arrested he was tortured brutally for eighteen days, but he never talked. In April 1945, in Buchenwald, my brother was on one of those wagons of dead people about to go to the ovens, when a friend of his noticed he was still alive and took him to the infirmary. For some reason the Gestapo let him live. Even when he was in Buchenwald he helped his Jewish friends.

One of the Jewish men I helped, Maurice Bernard, recently died, but we had remained best friends all through the years. He wanted me to receive the award from Yad Vashem, so he told the story of what I did for him, which served as the testimony. Many French people who helped Jews

---

have never been recognized by Yad Vashem, so I work on trying to find the people who did rescue others, and I help those who were rescued to write the necessary testimony.

You know, I'm surprised you're so interested in this. To me it seems so ordinary, so natural. When I was at Yad Vashem, going up to plant my tree on the Avenue of the Righteous, I said to Paldiel, director of the righteous at Yad Vashem, that I didn't think I really deserved this. He told me that all the righteous say the same thing. "But," he asked, "why didn't everyone do this ordinary thing?"

I understood his point. In the beginning, it seemed that 80 percent of the French were collaborators, and when they saw that Germany would lose, 80 percent said they had always been in the Resistance. I'm against the French government because of their political stance against Israel. There's nothing to be proud of when you consider what France did after the war. If I hadn't been the chairman of the surgery faculty, I would have stayed in Pittsburgh when I went there a few years ago.

I support Israel completely; I've been there seven times in the last three years. During the Yom Kippur War, I immediately went to Israel and replaced doctors and surgeons who had to fight. I worked at the Hadassah Hospital. Now the hospital has my name and will call me if there's another emergency. For two thousand years people said, "Next year in Jerusalem!" Now that they have a country, it must be defended. In 1973, I created the Association France/Israel to support Israel and speak against the PLO. I organize conferences between Israel and France. The Israeli embassy is often criticized by French TV, and we work against that.

My brother and I never talked about the war. Never. He moved to Canada because he was disappointed with France. The French people aren't interested in hearing about the war, either. But my grandson is now interested in the stories. My son is the director of a perfume factory, my daughter is a dentist. They wouldn't have done what I did. They don't have the same opinions and feelings, but they're proud of me and of what I did. My son went to Yad Vashem after I had planted my tree, and now I have a photo of him by my tree.

Front row (center): Ivan Beltrami
with Maurice Bernard on his left.

MARIE-ROSE GINESTE

Marie-Rose Gineste, 1946.

*Honored throughout the world for her courage during the Holocaust and the
subject of a French television documentary, Madame Gineste has been interviewed many times and is wary of journalists: "They put words in my mouth."
Despite her physical slightness and her retiring nature—she has lived in the
same house for over sixty years—she is an adventurer whose world extends
well beyond Montauban, a small town an hour's drive west from Toulouse.
Her home reflects her universal interests, with photographs of her mother and
friends of all ages from all over the world. A simple cross of twigs is flanked by
two Israeli menorahs, and books about religion and the Holocaust dominate
the room. Flowers from her garden brighten the sitting room, which also serves
as her office. Her wartime bicycle, which she still rides around town, is in the
main hallway.*

M y father was very interested in politics and wanted a son to take to
council meetings with him, but he had two daughters. So I became the
one to accompany him to these meetings. Perhaps that's why I've been
involved in municipal government for fifty years. I was born in 1911, in a
small village on the canals near Montauban. I went to school until I got my
certificate when I was twelve. My parents were Catholics but not as religious
as I am now. They were just peasants who worked in the fields, and I worked
with them until I was twenty, when there was a terrible flood that killed
many people. So we left the canals and moved to Montauban.

I learned how to sew and got a job as a seamstress. There was a Polish
Jew working there. I didn't really get to know him well, and I left that shop
in 1937, but forty years later when I was on a bus in Israel and I mentioned

Montauban, someone asked me about this Polish Jew. He had been his best friend, and he told me that the Jew from Montauban had been deported and died in the camps. But isn't that something—forty years later!

In 1942 we knew that the Jews were being arrested and taken to Germany, but we didn't know what they were doing with them there. On August 27 I volunteered to take a letter from Monsignor Théas to all the priests within 100 kilometers of Montauban. This letter stated clearly that the actions against the Jews are abhorrent to us and that we do not support this violent anti-Semitism. All the priests were to read the letter aloud in Sunday services. We were afraid it would be stopped by the Germans or the French police if it were mailed, so for four days I rode my bicycle, delivering the letter by hand to all priests in the diocese. All except one, that is, because I knew he was pro-Nazi; he had denounced an Allied airman who had parachuted near him.

After that, Monsignor Théas asked me to be in charge of the hiding of every Jew in Montauban. I became head of the Maquis and I could tell no one what I was doing, not even my best friends. I was in the secret order, in the Resistance, and I was saving Jews. I couldn't refuse. I did many, many things. One thing led to another. I never refused anything that was asked of me. I didn't know they were exterminating people, not until after the war. But I did see children torn from their parents.

I asked convents if I could put Jews in there. They wanted to take only children, but I convinced them to hide families. The Resistance stole food from farms and brought it to me in suitcases, and I took it to the convents that were hiding Jews. A Jewish man named Levi came to me to ask if I could find friends who could also help and who could give money. I was able to find some money at the university to send to them. I acquired false documents from a comrade in the Resistance in Toulouse and passed them out to Jews. After October 1943, I had to begin making the documents myself, and some of the Jews helped me: Nicole Bloch, Armand Alkimof, Réné Klein, and Berthe Delmas. There was a vicar at the cathedral who gave me real baptism certificates. And on two occasions I even brought plastic explosives, on my bicycle, to Monsieur Ginesty, a painter in Moissac, who made them into bombs to blow up railroads and trains.

My mother had been living with me since my father had died in 1937. She wasn't quite aware of what I was doing until the police came to the house and questioned her about me. They searched all the cupboards, but they didn't find anything. After that I was worried about my mother and stayed home in dangerous times, but I didn't stop my work. I had an English intelligence agent living in my house, and it was through these activities that mother finally realized what was going on. I began bringing in all sorts of people—Belgian, British, and American airmen were always coming through on their way to safety in Spain. My mother was at home so she prepared all the meals.

My house was only fifty meters from Gestapo headquarters. Every night when I heard cars leaving I was in agony, because I knew they were either going to round up Jews or I thought, *Maybe they're coming for me*. I lived in constant fear. And today, whenever I talk about it, I relive it. I can never watch a film about the war, but I did see *Au Revoir les Enfants*, which reminded me so much of that time. It was so true.

The man who was in charge of the parachuting of airmen was killed by the Montauban militia because he stayed in a dangerous place so he wouldn't compromise me in any way. I went often to his grave. It was very hard. I often visited his wife and children.

Emilie Braun was a lawyer to whom I gave false papers and a baptism certificate. She was harbored thirty kilometers from here until her house was bombed. First she hid in the bushes and then she came to stay with me in Montauban. She lives in Israel now, and I saw her when I went there to receive my medal last year.

I don't know why I was never arrested. They searched my house only once, and one time I was followed all over town for eight days. I stopped going to work because I didn't want my mother to be taken on account of me, but nothing ever happened. You know, de Gaulle gave us hope that we would be able to overcome, but even so, there were many days I wondered how we could get through the day.

Immediately after Liberation, people who had been strong supporters of the Germans wanted to be members of the Resistance. We thought people would be different after the war, that they would have learned something, but we were very disappointed.

In Toulouse, I was made a member of the jury for war criminals and I judged those who denounced Jews. Some were condemned to death but none were actually executed. Being a woman, they expected me to be more lenient, but I wasn't. They deserved punishment. There was one criminal who was being paid by Jews to take them to the Spanish border, and paid by Germans to hand them over to them. Despicable! And he had his sentence revoked!

I think that the reason people collaborated was that they lacked courage; it was easier to go with the stronger side, and the Germans looked strong. But for some it was also anti-Semitism. A priest recently came out with a book about what the Christians did in this area, but I don't like it; it tries to say that everyone helped, and that was not the way it was. If I could do it again, I'd do everything I did before.

For one month after Liberation I occupied the mayor's office. Later, I served on the Montauban municipal council for seventeen years, and then I was an administrator of social security. I'm a feminist and I think women should have the same rights to jobs as men, but frankly, I prefer men to women in politics. I've spent all my life in meetings with men. I'm pretty well known in Montauban because I perform marriage ceremonies with the mayor.

I received many awards for my work: the National Order of Merit, the Legion of Honor, the Croix de Guerre, and my favorite, the Military Medal of the Resistance. Only forty women in France have received the military medal. But the most important of all is the medal from Yad Vashem because it is specifically for saving Jews. Nicole Bloch and Réné Klein are the ones who offered the attestation to Yad Vashem.

The war years were important and good for me. The camaraderie in the Resistance was very dear to me. I have some strong relationships from that time. There's a Jewish family here in Montauban whom I see frequently, and I love them dearly. I helped them late in the war when they jumped from a deportation train. Just recently a ninety-year-old neighbor lady who now lives in Israel called me regarding the false papers I made for her. I hadn't seen her in a long time and she wanted to ask me so many questions because I saved her. And there are some people I saved who now live in Paris who have asked me to come visit them and stay at their home. But I'm seventy-seven years old and I don't travel much.

If the war were to happen now, I wonder if we'd find people who would save the Jews. There's more anti-Semitism now and, also, the young people have too much freedom and don't take responsibility. But I still think people would help. It's just a matter of egotism. You must think of others and not so much of yourself. Here in Montauban I ask people every day not to park their cars in front of my house because I can't get my bicycle out the door, but they do it anyway. And some people get mad at me for going too slowly on my bike. One day a woman with children in her car yelled at me for riding my bike too slowly, and I said, "Look what you're teaching your children! When I was young I was taught to respect the elderly!"

People still ask me why I helped. I guess it's a question of temperament. I think I've always had courage. The hardest thing for me was that I was putting my mother in danger. It was all about human justice and helping the Jews and hating the Germans. Before the war I wasn't so patriotic but during and after the war I was. I always said that if anything happens to me, put a tricolor flag in my coffin.

GERMANY

Know, Christian, that next to the devil thou hast no enemy more cruel, more venomous and violent than a true Jew. Their synagogues should be set on fire, and whatever does not burn up should be covered or spread over with dirt so that no one may ever be able to see a cinder or stone of it.

—Martin Luther, *On the Jews and Their Lies*, Wittenberg, 1543

Hence today I believe I am acting in accordance with the will of the Almighty Creator: by defending myself against the Jew, I am fighting for the work of the Lord.

—Adolf Hitler, *Mein Kampf*, 1923

The word "holocaust" means a burnt sacrifice. It may be no coincidence that the Third Reich and Martin Luther were born in Germany, yet shocking as Luther's writings may seem to the post-Holocaust world, they reflect the common prejudice toward the Jews in Europe during the Middle Ages. Most European countries either expelled Jews or at least denied them citizenship, and Germany was no different from any other.

Indeed, one reason why so few German Jews responded to the anti-Semitism following World War I was that as long as Jews had lived in Europe they had known hatred and persecution. Frightening though this environment might have been, it still allowed a Jewish culture to survive and, at times, even flourish. The emancipation of the Jews that characterized much of Western Europe after the French Revolution brought Jews into national communities through the arts, sciences, and government. German Jews, among the most assimilated on the continent, were proud of their national citizenship; many even regarded it as more important to their identity than their Judaism.

In World War I, 100,000 Jews fought proudly as Germans for the Fatherland, and afterward, Jewish government officials were instrumental in rebuilding a modern democratic Germany. The nation had been badly defeated, and the postwar mood throughout the country was grim. The Versailles Treaty further punished a Germany thoroughly humiliated by defeat in the war by keeping it economically and militarily weak. Because of the high cost of reparations and rebuilding, the country suffered overwhelming inflation and unemployment. Growing industrialization and urbanization also contributed to social displacement. In addition, Germany feared Russian as well as internal communism. Such times are ripe for a scapegoat.

In 1919, a new political party, formed with a nationalistic and racist platform, asserted that Jews were to blame for these problems and were responsible for Germany's military defeat. Adolf Hitler drafted the anti-Semitic part of the campaign. "The Jews are undoubtedly a race, but not human. They cannot be human in the sense of being an image of God, the Eternal. The Jews are an image of the devil. Jewry means the racial tuberculosis of the nation," Hitler wrote in *Mein Kampf*. The National Socialist German Workers' Party, shortened to Nazi by the first two syllables of the first word, was small, and few paid attention to it, not even the Jews. They were used to anti-Semitism, and they believed that even though they represented less than 1 percent of the population, they contributed too much to the culture for anyone to take Hitler seriously.

But by 1930, Jews being beaten by party thugs in the streets and cafes was not unusual. Synagogue services were interrupted by the Storm Troops Hitler created "for the coming struggle for liberty." Fifty synagogues were desecrated during the High Holy Days, but few knew about it, because the newspapers were more interested in headlining the growing unemployment.

In 1933, Hitler was elected chancellor of Germany, and even those who were uncomfortable with his anti-Semitic rantings appreciated Hitler's ability to bolster pride in a shamed nation. That it was at the Jews' expense was unfortunate but worth the price to many who were not themselves anti-Semites.

From the beginning of his rule, Hitler's intentions were clear: to drive the Jews from Germany. He did it with two of the instruments of civilization, law and the media. Step by step, he took away Jewish rights of ownership, employment, and education. The Nuremberg laws of 1935 demanded expulsion of anyone who was not Aryan, declaring Jews noncitizens. Scurrilous propaganda films such as *The Eternal Jew* and anti-Semitic pamphlets convinced even many nonracist Germans that Jews were different, not really part of German society. Fritz Heine and other members of the opposing political party, the Social Democrats, fled Germany and helped Jews and other party members to escape. None of this persecution was new to Jews; many hoped it would pass, yet a few agreed with Leo Baeck, writer, teacher, and leading rabbi of the Reform movement, who declared in 1933, "The one- thousand-year history of the German Jews has come to an end."

The international press had begun to report beatings in the streets, and Hitler, sensitive to public opinion, moved the arena of cruelty away from the cities to a concentration camp, Dachau, where Jews and political dissidents were imprisoned and tortured. When Hitler announced a boycott of Jewish shops, American Jews

Rabbi Leo Baeck.

held a protest rally at Madison Square Garden. The Nazis retreated and limited the boycott to just one day, a Saturday. Lady Rumbold, wife of the British ambassador to Berlin, was an eyewitness: "On every Jewish shop was plastered a large notice warning people not to buy in Jewish shops. And often you saw caricatures of Jewish noses. To see people pilloried in this fashion, a very large number of them quite harmless, hard-working people, was altogether revolting, and left a very nasty taste in the mouth. I shall never forget it."*

German Jews could not believe what was happening in their cultured society. Though most chose to ride out the storm, some 150,000 of Germany's 500,000 Jews left the country.

With the Storm Troops, the Gestapo, and concentration camps, Hitler had built the apparatus for dictatorship. In October 1938, he bullied England, France, and Italy into allowing the Czechoslovak Sudetenland to become part of Germany. This capitulation was what he needed to achieve his ends. The world now knew what he was doing, and it was silent. He immediately expelled 18,000 German-speaking Jews from the Sudetenland. One of them, Zindel Grynszpan, sent a postcard to his seventeen-year-old son, Hirsch, in Paris about the inhuman treatment the family had suffered. On November 6, 1938, the youth walked into the German Embassy and assassinated Ernst von Rath, a secretary.

Within a day virtually every Jewish neighborhood in Germany was vandalized, and more than 30,000 Jews were beaten and arrested. Many committed suicide. During the night of November 9, the Storm Troops smashed and burned 191 synagogues. Kristallnacht, "the night for the broken windows," as the Nazis derisively called the nationwide participation in violence, caused another 200,000 Jews to flee the country. Few could take anything of value with them. They continued to emigrate until war broke out in 1939. Many who couldn't leave the country went to Berlin, the most politically liberal city in Germany. Its large population made it easier to hide and a few actually survived the war in Berlin with the help of people such as Countess von Maltzan, Gitta Bauer, Helene Jacobs, and Irmgard Jonass. Of the 5,000 Jews who were in hiding, however, 4,000 died.

No one knows whether Hitler had always planned to exterminate the Jews or merely to drive them out of Germany, but in the beginning he moved slowly, and initially his efforts to make Germany *judenrein*, "Jew free," were without mass bloodshed: propaganda and laws to segregate and vilify Jews in Germany were working well enough to drive them out. In fact, despite the seeming impossibility of it, Hitler disclaimed prior knowledge of Kristallnacht, explaining it as a series of spontaneous uprisings all over the country.

When Hitler invaded Poland in 1939, that country's 3 million Jews

---

*Martin Gilbert. *The Holocaust: A History of the Jews in Europe During the Second World War.*

became his problem. It was "solved" in various ways, none of them satisfactory to the Nazi leadership. Then in January 1942 at Wannsee, a group of top Nazis devised the "Final Solution," the plan to systematically murder every Jew in the world, to consign them to *Nacht und Nebel*, night and fog.

The only exceptions would be Jews over sixty-five, those with high military honors, invalids, and Jewish officials and celebrities whose absence would attract international attention. Those exceptions would be sent to Theresienstadt, the model concentration camp without death machinery. In fact, most of those who went to Theresienstadt were soon sent on to Auschwitz and death.

The systematic and efficient extermination was made easier by the 1941 law that required all Jews to wear the yellow Star of David. The prohibition against immigration made them helpless to escape. When the deportations to the camps began in 1942, the 150,000 Jews who remained in Germany had become stateless under the Nuremberg Laws. No other government would help them. The Nazis commanded the Jewish-run Reich Association for Jews in Germany to participate in the legal deportation of 150,000 Jews to the death camps in the east. By June 1943, the Nazis proclaimed Germany itself *judenrein*. In fact, 25,000 German Jews survived the war, and most of them owe their lives to at least one other person, more than likely a non-Jew who was not affiliated with any resistance organization.

By the time the Final Solution was devised, German resistance was almost nonexistent, and the resistance that remained had no interest in saving Jews, only in getting rid of Hitler and taking power. With the exception of people such as Gertrud Luckner, who worked with the Catholic Caritas, the Church did little to stop the Nazis. Most Germans didn't care enough to protest the gradual elimination of the Jews. They remembered how Hitler had restored their pride and morale. The Nazis attempted to keep the camps a secret; the stories about death camps and torture were thought to be enemy propaganda. Those few Germans who wanted to help the Jews escape had nowhere to take them: every surrounding country was occupied, and neutral Switzerland had stopped admitting Jews in 1942.

That there were very few German rescuers does not mean that the Germans were more anti-Semitic than people in other countries. The Resistance in German-occupied countries certainly helped the Jews, but not necessarily because they favored them in any way. Often they simply hated the German invaders and viewed saving a Jew as revenge against Germany.

Ancient prejudice, poverty, national humiliation, and technology all conspired to permit the murder of 25 million civilians during World War II. The Holocaust holds special terror because the perpetrator was so scientifically advanced and cultured a nation. If it could happen in Germany, it could happen anywhere.

GITTA BAUER

Gitta Bauer, 1942.

We call Gitta Bauer the moment we land in Frankfurt to get directions to her home. She is warm and patient, and in her precise English gives the complicated instructions necessary to find her house. It is in the hamlet of Wetter, a charming place of old renovated cottages. This is our first interview in Germany and we wonder how much emotional baggage we will bring to it. Perhaps because she was a journalist, she understands our purpose, takes in our questions, and answers them more deeply than is comfortable. She is direct and frank, cries with the pain of her country's crime, and repeatedly talks of the shame of Germany and her own shame for not doing more. After the interview, she calls several rescuers and sets up appointments for us. We are so moved by this woman's generosity and her brave confrontation with the past that we drive on to Bonn without the handbag containing our passports, tickets, and money. The next day we find someone to make the four-hour round trip to retrieve them.

We never spoke to Gitta Bauer after that day in July 1988, but we communicated several times by letter. When the notice of her death arrived from her son, André, in 1990, we felt as if we had lost a lifelong friend.

W ell, I must tell you, when the Israeli Embassy called me, I called my friend, the one I saved, she told them the story, she still lives in Berlin, you know. I asked her, "Can one do that? We never did this for anything, I mean, not for an award or anything." And she said, "You know, there are so few people in the world who know that not *all* Germans were bad." And this was what made me accept the Yad Vashem medal.

I was born in Berlin in 1919, and I think I was very lucky to be born into my family. For instance, my father took us to museums before modern art was banned. I remember we saw paintings by Liebermann, and in Berlin, he was known as the greatest painter. And then, after 1933, so many of these things which I saw were forbidden, but they were already in my mind.

We were four girls, and our father and mother opposed the Nazis. My father voted for the Social Democrats, the liberal party, and my mother voted for the Catholic [Center] Party. My father was a pharmacist, a simple man. When I asked him, "What are Jews?" he said, "Jews are people like you and me only with a different religion. And that's it." That was the rule in our family. We knew so many Jews and they were no threat to us. I have many memories of my father. When I was about ten years old I saw an SA [Storm Trooper], and I asked my father, "Who are those people?" And he said, "They want war again." He was very upset about the things Hitler was doing.

My father was Protestant and my mother was Catholic, and we were raised Catholic. I left Catholicism because I couldn't live with someone else telling me I couldn't do things. Today I'm agnostic. But that was much later. I was in a Catholic youth movement which was made illegal in 1935, but before that we tried at least to be resistant to the Nazis. But we were required to be in the Hitler Youth. In 1942 I was arrested by the Gestapo with my whole group of six girls and one boy. They thought we were Communists. When they found out we were harmless, just singing folk songs, preaching and praying, they let us go. When the Gestapo came into the house they were looking at our books and one of them said, "I see that you have many books but you do not have *Mein Kampf*!" My mother was very brave. She said to him, "You look to me as if you have read only *Mein Kampf* and nothing else!" She was East Prussian, you know. I think I have some of that in me also.

We had a seminar the other day at the university, people of my age. They said, "We didn't know a thing." I said, "How could you not have known? Your park must have had benches which said 'Not for Jews' and you must have had restaurants where it said 'No Jews allowed'! You didn't have to read *Mein Kampf* to know Hitler had it in for the Jews. You saw photos of Jews marched through the street carrying a sign saying, 'I am a Jewish pig.' And all of us saw Kristallnacht in 1938. Even if you didn't see it yourself, you had to be aware. Everyone must have realized." Especially here in Essen, where there was a synagogue and a Jewish cemetery.

The Jews here were usually the people who sold cows and horses, and this didn't make them popular, because everyone thinks he has been cheated. I remember this from Harlem. I lived in New York during the time of the race riots in 1967, and I realized that when the blacks said, "You know, the Jew at the corner store charges more than. . . ," they always felt cheated, so the anti-Semitism of the blacks stemmed sometimes from economic reasons as it did in Germany. In Harlem, I tried to explain that the small Jewish store at the corner charged more because he had to deal with a lot of theft in this neighborhood.

What happened was that I had an aunt who had all these Jewish friends and we met them all. My aunt had a special Jewish friend and she took that friend's entire family to Amsterdam and saved them all. My aunt's friend had a twin sister who came to me in 1944 and said that her daughter was in danger. What else could I say but "I'll take her into my home"? This was no big moral or religious decision. She was a friend and she needed help. We knew it was dangerous, and we were careful, but we didn't consider not taking her. Her name was Ilse Baumgart; I was twenty-four and she was twenty-one.

Ilse was half Jewish: her mother was Jewish and her father was not. In 1933, he was told to divorce her or he would lose his job. He didn't, so he lost his job. Marriages where the woman was the Jew were in less danger than vice versa. You can't follow this thinking, but I found similar things in U.S. racists toward blacks. A black man and a white woman is very bad but a white man and a black woman isn't as bad. So it's the same kind of thinking in a way. Anyway, Ilse's parents managed to survive.

Ilse had been able to get false papers for herself and was working as a secretary for the Luftwaffe on the night shift when her superior awakened her one night to tell her that an attempt had been made on the Fuehrer's life. She replied, "Is the pig dead?" So this woman turned her in to an officer who said, "I'll have to turn you in to my superior, but first I'll give you fifteen minutes by yourself to think it over." And of course she fled. This SS man went looking for her at her parents' house, so her mother came here to ask for help.

We never told our parents even though I'm sure they would have wanted us to do it. This was the time of the big bombings in Berlin, and only my older sister and I were in the city. Our mother and younger sisters were in the countryside, and my father was always on the road. We didn't want to burden them with knowing about Ilse, so whenever my father came home, friends would take Ilse without asking questions.

Ilse lived with me for nine months, until the end of the war. In January 1945, a young friend stopped at my house to say goodbye. He was going into the army, he said, "to celebrate the victory." I said, "Franz, if you celebrate a victory, this girl," meaning Ilse, "will die." And would you believe that he is the one who read about Yad Vashem in 1984 and wrote to them about me. Then they got the testimony from Ilse and I was asked to accept the medal.

I didn't want to accept it because I still feel ashamed to be German, one of the generation that killed 6 million. You know, what really put me to shame is what is written on the Yad Vashem medal. It says, "Who saves one life, it is as if they saved the whole world." When I said to Yitzhak Ben Ari from the Israeli Embassy, "My God, I have only saved one life," he asked me if Ilse has children.

I said she does. "And grandchildren?" But that doesn't help. I am still deeply ashamed for my people, my country, still ashamed, deeply ashamed. And it doesn't help me that I was able to save one life. It doesn't help me. *We did it!*

It's an entirely different story, what we did and what the Americans did not do. I think they could have helped and saved . . . if they had done something, you know. They were able to. They didn't even bomb Auschwitz.

I met my husband after the war, in 1945. He was Jewish and had just returned from spending the war in Switzerland. I became a journalist—I always wanted to be one but wouldn't compromise myself before. I was sent to the Nuremberg Trials and learned things that many of my generation did not know. It was terrible to know you were from this country. What finally came out was that for twelve years we had been ruled by these gangsters and not done anything against it. That is not easy to swallow. My father used to say, "Enjoy the war; the peace will be terrible." In fact, I can remember my father talking about World War I quite often, but the next generation didn't talk about this war at all, especially those who fought in Russia.

In 1950 our son, André, was born. We were living in East Berlin, and my husband and I were arrested. I was imprisoned for four years and he was sent to Siberia and was gone five years. We were the opposition, though of course we weren't spies or hadn't done any of the things they accused us of. The trouble was that André was just two months old when I was arrested and they wouldn't tell me what happened to him. They said, "Tell us that your husband is an American spy and then we'll let you know where your son is." In the fourth year of my imprisonment I was allowed to write my first letter, and my father wrote back to me and there were greetings from my son. I was released soon after this and a year later my husband returned. But he was very sick and didn't live long.

Strangely enough, his father didn't want André to know that he was of Jewish origin. I said, "But what will we do if he becomes an anti-Semite? We have to tell him." But he was ten years old when I finally wrung it from my husband. He said, "I don't want him to feel Jewish, to feel persecuted." I said, "He won't be feeling that way." So one day I took André and his cousin to *Exodus*, the movie in which Jews were heroes. After the film they asked, "Where were those people on the ship coming from?" I said, "From German concentration camps and in one of those, Auschwitz, your grandmother, grandfather, one uncle, and two aunts died." "Ah," he said, "that means I'm Jewish, or half Jewish?" "Yes," I said. And do you know what he said? "That's funny!" And then he wanted to know everything about Judaism and Israel, and I said I had a big library. That was, of course, exactly what I wanted.

In 1964 I went to New York, at the height of the race riots, to cover the stories for a German magazine. No one could tell me why it was happening, what was in their minds. So I went to Adam Clayton Powell and I asked him if I could live in Harlem. He said, "I live in Harlem, why would you?" I said, "Congressman, you pass for white but everyone knows you're black!" He advised me to go to a home for single black women. It was in the midst of Harlem and belonged to his church. The women had mostly come from the South and at first they weren't too happy with me, but we became friends. I got into the political scene and was with many different kinds of people. They saw me home at night and nothing happened to me. After living with blacks for months and months I felt strange among whites. People looked different to me. I learned that I have no inhibition at all as far as race is concerned. Anyway, I wrote many stories and got a Theodore Wolff Prize for one of them—that's the equivalent of your Pulitzer Prize.

I have always been most concerned about racism of any kind. I spoke both to blacks and to Arabs about anti-Semitism while I was in New York. One day at the U.N., I was with the Libyan ambassador and his delegation when they started one of their anti-Israel tirades. He was a rabid anti-Semite. I told them, "I am German and of the generation which killed 6 million Jews. You cannot talk that way in front of me!" And they understood. I think there wasn't as much anti-Semitism among blacks then as there is now, with Jesse Jackson and "Hymietown" and the like. I bought this sculpture by Valerie Maynard in memory of my Harlem days. It's called *Rufus*, and symbolizes the battle for civil rights. I have one of four casts of it. The other three are owned by Harry Belafonte, Lena Horne, and *Ebony* magazine in Chicago.

I owe my first visit to Israel to a senator in Berlin who made it a custom that all retribution cases that involved rescuers should pass through his office. One day in 1960 this Senator Lipschicz called to tell me I could go to Israel with funds provided by the Jewish Community of Berlin. It was a very early time for a German to go to Israel. You know, Israel has changed everything. Now Jews have a country.

Something upsetting happened on that trip. In Haifa we were staying at a Catholic home where many German survivors lived. I was traveling with a group of Protestants and they would pray, and of course I didn't pray, but they asked me if I would sing folk songs with them. Since I love to sing, I said I would. Then these people living in this home asked us to sing German folk songs for them. Can you believe it? We began singing and the survivors of what we had done were listening and crying. I was standing there feeling so rotten.

My poor aunt, who did so much, much more than I did, in Amsterdam, was honored and everything. There are four trees planted for her in the Queen Juliana woods in Jerusalem. She died in a Jewish home in Frankfurt. She said, "I have lived with Jews, I want to die with Jews," and she did. Anyway, when she returned to Germany after the war she lived on the street where the Franks had lived before going to Holland. One evening she was walking home and an American man asked her, "Do you know where the Anne Frank house was?" She said, "Yes, you're standing right in front of it." And he spit on her! She nearly broke down, and I don't think she ever recovered from that. You cannot explain to a total stranger what you have been and what you have done. You just cannot do that.

It's this kind of thing which makes me sometimes wish I had stayed in America. My generation is absolutely lost. We have all first to die and then, maybe. . . . My son told me that his fellow students in medical school—he's a surgeon now—envied him that he had parents who were not Nazis. They *envied* him. That means that many of their parents *were* Nazis. The generation of my son, they are afraid there will be another Fascist regime. And he asked me, "How do you know when the Fascists are coming?" I said, "When Storm Troopers march through the streets and when Jews are persecuted because they are Jews." He said, "By that time it may be too late."

When that ghastly Hollywood TV series "The Holocaust" came to Germany, I didn't think it would have had such a reaction. We had had documentaries like "The Yellow Star," but this was the first one that touched the nerve of the younger generation. It started all the questioning again. People asking their parents, "Where were you? What did you do?" All of a sudden they woke up. Isn't that strange?

I'm studying history at the local university and shortly after I was honored by Yad Vashem I came to the seminar—it's a large class, about one hundred people—and the professor said, "I must tell you that among our senior people here there is one who is special." And he told about me and they all knocked on their desks in approval. So many of the young students came up to me after the class. I think some of them are suspicious of the old people, but then they thought that I, at least, was all right.

Ilse Baumgart with her
mother and her grand-
children, 1985.

Ilse Baumgart with
Gitta's son, André, 1953.

FRITZ HEINE

Fritz Heine, 1944.

Fritz Heine lives on a country estate in Bad Münstereifel, Scheuren, not far from Bonn, surrounded by stately trees and extensive lawn. The home he shares with his wife, built and furnished in the finest style of the 1950s, is gracious and lends itself to large gatherings. Although he is eighty-four, he seems at least a decade younger, and actively participates in the gardening. Considered a political enemy because he was a leading member of the Social Democratic party, Heine rescued many Jews and political prisoners as he fled Germany for England where he continued to fight the Nazis. Despite his importance in rebuilding Germany after the war and his high position in government, he is a modest man who generously shares his experiences in soft-spoken English.

I was born in 1904 in Hannover, a city of about 90,000 at that time. My mother died while Father was away during the First War, and I was alone with her when she died. The last years were very difficult because we were very poor, and this made a deep impression on me. My father, who was an organ builder, remarried a widow. I tell you these things because it gives you an idea of the human surroundings in which I grew up. I had no money to go to high school, so I went to a trade school. My family was Protestant but I left the church at thirteen because I didn't feel like a churchgoer. I'm sure I had Jewish friends in Hannover, but no one made a distinction between people of other religions. It was of no importance.

My father had always been a Social Democrat, all the family was, so I became active in the party. In 1925, the party in Berlin needed candidates and I was asked to be the adjunct secretary. I was only twenty-five. Until 1933, I organized the propaganda department for the party. We were very concerned about the rise of the Nazi party and we tried to organize some resistance. The problem was this rise of nationalistic feelings in the right-wing party because we had 6 million people without work, and they were easy prey for the Nazis. Hitler and Goebbels were brilliant speakers from their point of view. Personally, I never listened to Hitler because he was boring to me.

People didn't realize at first that the Nazis were dangerous, but in 1928, '29, and '30 when street fights began to break out between Nazis and Social Democrats, it became clear what was happening. There were months when 150 people would die in these street fights.

We built an underground radio station, which didn't function because the Nazis overran everything. In 1933 our party was banned and the leaders had to go abroad, underground, or be arrested. I was a good skier, and I knew the way to Czechoslovakia. So in March I took several dozen of my friends, both political and Jewish, over the border. It was clear that the problems were worse for the Jews, but it was bad for all party members. I stayed in Czechoslovakia until 1936, but I returned to Germany about ten times with false passports to meet with political friends, make resistance plans, and bring more people out. When the Germans forced the Czechs to make us stop our activities from there, we asked the premier of France, Léon Blum, a Jew, if we could relocate our political work there. He gave permission, and we went to France early in 1938.

Most of my friends and I lost our German passports and citizenship. We got refugee passports from Czechoslovakia so that we could move our operations to France. After the German occupation of France, people were on the roads every day trying to get to the free zone in the south of France. Thousands of these people lined the road, often walking with two suitcases and more things on their backs. I was among them. As we walked, German planes flew over and machine-gunned the masses of people. Everyone would throw down their luggage and run. So for hundreds of kilometers there was luggage strewn all over the roads. It was a terrible sight.

Along with most German refugees, I had to go into an internment camp in May 1940. I was with my political friends, and it appeared that we would be extradited to Germany and the Nazis. So we asked friends in New York to help us. The Jewish Labor Committee was the first to understand. Then William Green, president of the American Federation of Labor, went to Eleanor Roosevelt to ask her to persuade her husband to get visas for us. It was our only chance to get out of France. Finally, in the autumn of 1940, we got 600 visas from America.

Because I was the youngest member of headquarters leadership and I spoke English and French, I was asked to try to help our political friends get out of France. We then received 300,000 francs from the American Jewish

Labor Committee and, with Varian Fry, we launched a gigantic refugee organization. I tried to get French exit visas for those for whom the Americans had sent American visas, but it was difficult because France was in alliance with the Nazis. So many people had to be escorted over the Pyrénées into Spain. I found someone to make false passports, and about twenty-four people got out that way. And we had the help of the Quakers and the Unitarian Church.

While I was doing this work in Marseilles, several Jews who were not Social Democrats came to me for help. I tried, but I couldn't help everyone. The main task of the rescue was left to the Emergency Rescue Committee.

One of the best known Jews we rescued was Georg Bernhard, who had been the editor-in-chief of a great liberal paper in Berlin until 1933, when he came to Marseilles. When we told him that going through Spain was dangerous because they might arrest him and his wife, he said, "What do you think the chance is? If it's ninety-nine to one against me, then it's still a good chance. We'll go." They reached Portugal and then the United States.

I was deeply involved in efforts to rescue a friend of mine, Dr. Rudolf Hilferding, a prominent Jew and the minister of finance in Germany, who was arrested in Arles by Pétain's French police. His wife was in Paris and got a smuggler to bring her to Arles, but she arrived two days after he was either murdered or committed suicide. We managed to get her to the United States. This is one of the many chapters which is still in my mind and dreadful to remember.

I could stay in France only until February 1941, when it became too dangerous, so I escaped to Lisbon. I remained there several months and arrived in London in June. In Great Britain I helped organize the German liberal refugees. I worked with a radio station reading German newspapers every day and made suggestions about radio news. In 1943 I went to Algiers when the German army was defeated. There were 20,000 to 30,000 German prisoners of war, and I was asked to separate the Nazis from the anti-Nazis. It took three or four months.

I returned to Germany in February 1946 and I became a member of the executive committee of the Social Democratic Party. There were six of us, five men and a woman, and she was Jewish, a friend who had been with us in Great Britain. I served on the committee until 1958. Then I served as chairman of the party newspaper until I was seventy.

In 1987 I was awarded the medal from Yad Vashem, and several Jews I helped, most of whom live in the United States, gave the testimony. The Germans did a very black deed during those years. I wrote a dozen or more memos about what to do with the Nazis and how to deal with them after they were defeated. It was a terrible period in German history.

Fritz Heine (middle, against wall) with members of the Fry committee and other rescue groups, Marseilles, 1940.

Alexander Stein, Rudolf Leeb, Fritz Heine, and Dr. Erich Rinner in New York, 1947. Heine helped Rinner, Leeb, and Leeb's family escape from France during the war.

GERTRUD LUCKNER

At first glance, Gertrud Luckner might be mistaken for a gnome rather than the respected philosopher she is. Hunchbacked and very deaf, everything about her seems ancient except her remarkable mind. Her two-room apartment in a Catholic old-age home in Freiburg, a hamlet in the Black Forest, barely provides enough space for her to live and work. We cannot enter into the "living room": books, journals, and manuscripts cover all surfaces, filling the room from floor to ceiling. A photo of her standing between Leo Baeck and Albert Schweitzer is propped against a book-lined wall. Near the entrance to the room she sits in one chair; we stand at the threshold. She points to two small hassocks for us to sit on. As we squeeze into the space one of us inadvertently brushes her arm. She screams, "Don't touch me! I was in a concentration camp!"

Setting up a tripod for video recording is not possible, and she doesn't permit photographs. The video camera is hand-held as she begins to talk in perfect English. She is very deaf; I shout, "We interviewed a rescuer in Israel at the Gertrud Luckner Home for the Aged." No response, and most questions go unheard. When asked if she thinks about the war often, she erupts, "How can you ask that? When you have been in a concentration camp and have seen people gassed every morning, how could I not think about it?" She trembles with rage. "Stop the interview! I don't want to talk anymore."

Apologies and persuasion make it possible to continue. After only an hour she grows tired and asks us to leave, but by now she seems to have become fond of us and follows us to the parking lot where Gay manages to take a few snapshots.

I was born in 1900, and my parents died young, after World War I. We were Catholics, but I had no brother or sister, so my family was a small part of my life. I was always against war so I got involved with a very international group. I received my degree from Frankfurt am Main in 1920, in the political science department. You could concentrate on economic or social-political science, and I took the social. Then I received my Ph.D. in Freiburg.

In 1926, I went to Poland when they were having such a bad time after the First War. I met people, made contacts. The Poles have suffered such a lot. You know, there were many Poles in concentration camps.

In the 1920s, I saw the Nazi era coming and was surprised that others couldn't recognize it; I was an old pacifist. I was interested in slums, and I worked in England, in 1930, for a year before moving to Freiburg in 1931. In Freiburg I was shocked to see students enthusiastic about Hitler. I had seen it coming for so long that by 1933 I was prepared. I began a little discussion circle, and fetched pupils from the upper classes, to prepare them and to give them literature about the Nazis and the anti-Nazi movements.

In 1933, knowing Dr. Leo Baeck, who was a prominent rabbi in Berlin, I got from him the addresses of all the Jewish institutions in Germany—the names and addresses in every town. And so I visited them, to tell them what was happening. In this way I was very much connected with the Jewish community. Then when the Nazis became more powerful, I went again from place to place to see what we could do, how we could help, personally help, from one person to another.

I always told the Jews to leave, but it was very difficult. In the United States you needed an affidavit from someone who would also give a lot of money to sponsor you. And you could go to England but you weren't allowed to work, and that was the difficult thing. People couldn't get into other countries. I had some Swiss friends in Basel, so when the Nazis came I went there and wrote to friends in the United States and England. These were people who knew me through my international work. And that was how I helped some people get out of Germany.

So I had the Jewish contacts through Dr. Baeck, and I had the contacts in Basel from whose homes I could mail the international letters asking for help. This was the only way to help, person to person. I also worked for the Church War Relief Office in the German Caritas Association in Freiburg.

I had known Dr. Baeck very early in Berlin. You know, he wouldn't emigrate because he wouldn't leave his Jews. Many people offered him exit visas, but he wouldn't go as long as there were Jews in Berlin. I was still going around trying to help, all day and night on the trains; but the day he was arrested, January 24, 1943, I was also in Berlin. I was arrested two months later. The police fetched me from the train and took me to Ravensbruck. It was clear that I had been going everywhere to meet the Jews.

I spent two years in that concentration camp, seeing Jews gassed every day and not being able to do anything about it. I can't talk about it at all. When I was released from the camp in May 1945, I was in the Russian zone so there were no letters, nothing. I saw some English soldiers and I gave them a letter to my English friends saying, "I have survived the camp! I'm out!" Dr. Baeck received one of these letters. He had also survived the camps and was in London with his daughter. The first letter I received from abroad after the war was from him. It was something!

Right away I began to try to repair the relations between Christians and Jews. I started the *Freiburg Newsletter*, a publication of dialogues between Christians and Jews. At first it was only a few pages, but it has grown over the years. It is published annually, and just now there has been published a book containing the documents from 1945 to 1985, all the dialogues. This has been a very great step for relations between people. I am just now editing the next journal. We have a circulation of 13,000, but it is published only in German. The editorial board is made up of Catholics. For years there has been hatred between Christians and Jews, and I hope that will pass.

I think Israel is very important. I was the first German to be invited to go to Israel when Dr. Baeck invited me in 1951. Now I've been there thirty times, the last time in 1986. I love Israel. I stayed with the Sisters. I met Martin Buber there many times; he lived in the German Colony, and I visited him in his home often. In honor of my sixtieth birthday, the Jewish National Fund planted a Gertrud Luckner Grove, and then a few years later I was honored at Yad Vashem.

I have great hope, also for the Russian people. They have suffered a lot. I'm glad about the things that Gorbachev is doing. In all I'm quite hopeful.

HELENE JACOBS

"1933–1945. My grief remains predominant. That we did not stop it. That we destroyed ourselves. A community which destroys a part of itself on purpose, out of hatred, gives itself up. It degenerates. This happened in our country. . . . It struck all of us. Even if many among us did not notice it at all and did not want to notice. . . . it directly concerned us, even if it was not directed against us."

These remarks are from an acceptance speech delivered by Helene Jacobs when presented with the Buber-Rosenzweig Medal by the German Coordinating Council for the Societies for Christian-Jewish Cooperation on March 6, 1983, in Stuttgart. Helene Jacobs lives in a modest, officelike Berlin apartment: one room serving as a place to sleep and the other a space to eat and work. Despite her renown as a Nazi foe, she is shy and does not want to be videotaped or photographed. Speaking both in English and German, she prefers to talk about broad philosophical themes rather than tell us about her specific wartime experiences. After much cajoling and asking us to comb her hair, she finally agrees to the picture. Then she speaks passionately about the importance of teaching children about the Holocaust: they must know where intolerance will lead so that it will not happen again. After her initial reticence she does not want us to leave, so we take her to her favorite neighborhood trattoria for dinner.

As early as 1923, when Hitler was just coming to power, I understood that I had to fight him. I was born in Berlin in 1906. From childhood I believed that each of us who is given the gift of life is responsible for our own life and for what and whom we decide to surround ourselves. This is why I fought Nazism.

Beginning in 1932, in Berlin-Dahlem, I was a member of a group who gathered for Bible study. Because of our sense of responsibility, which came from our religious beliefs, we undertook to assist those who were being persecuted by the Nazis, especially Jews. We began to look for people who would be willing to give refuge to Jews.

During this time, I was studying to become a lawyer and was working for a patent lawyer who was Jewish. I had to leave school because the war interfered with education in Germany. My rescue work began with this patent lawyer and his family. They were people who were in danger and I wanted to help them. It was as simple as that.

I was associated with the Confessing Church and we went to Jewish groups to tell them we were sympathetic and wanted to help. We needed false identification papers for Jews, and at first they were procured on the black market. Then a young painter named Gunther Rugoff joined the group. He could make the counterfeit cards on his own. I then passed on these counterfeit I.D.'s to agents or to the Jews themselves. The food-ration cards we needed were collected from the Lutheran congregation, but there weren't enough for everyone. We had to do business with dealers in stolen cards, and for this we needed money, which we continually sought from people.

The Gestapo finally tracked down our counterfeiting operation. I tried to find a hiding place where Gunther could go on making the cards. But when this was unsuccessful, I took him under my own roof in the spring of 1943. The trouble was that my apartment was no longer safe from police raids.

Our underground movement collapsed when one of the people hidden was arrested and confessed where he had obtained the false documents. I and other members of the group were arrested on August 17, 1943. When I didn't return home that night, Gunther fled my apartment just before the Gestapo arrived to search it. He succeeded in reaching Switzerland.

A special trial was conducted against our entire group and the penalties were severe for all of us. I was condemned to two and a half years in jail. My Aunt Lischen also worked to rescue Jews, but I knew nothing about her work; it was too dangerous. We later discussed how both of us had encountered many Jews who were willing to turn themselves in to avoid risking the lives of rescuers.

I believe that Christian theology is responsible for anti-Semitism, though I can't persuade many of my friends of this. I wanted to save Jews because I hated Hitler's ideology. The Germans lost their dignity by following Hitler. So many people thought it was an honor to be an Aryan. Germany was in a state of war with the whole world. I remember seeing soldiers everywhere, and feeling offended that they were a part of my world. I feel there is no difference between the self and the world, and the Nazis made it impossible for me to keep my world intact.

I was released from prison on April 17, 1945, twenty months after I had been arrested. Berlin was in chaos and the Russians were coming. I found my house; everything was burning.

After the war there was no money for me to return to school, and I had to search for meaningful work. I felt that there ought to be money and laws to help the Jews who survived, and I was very committed to bringing together Christians and Jews. But even more important, I felt that Christians must reflect on themselves to try to understand why this could happen, and to change the theological interpretations which allowed it. Today many people still have problems freeing themselves from deeply rooted prejudices. I'm encouraged, however, to see important theologians of the two churches seeking new responses, in the true sense of the Gospel, to the questions which in the past caused so much trouble in the relations between Jews and Christians.

I am often asked how I had the strength to stand so firmly, in the face of such risk, on the side of the persecuted Jews. My answer is that I followed my drive for self-preservation. If Hitler had already destroyed my country, I wanted at least to keep my personal world intact. I always knew how dangerous it was, but I did it for humanity, and because I was a patriot. I was ashamed of what the German people were doing. During that time the forces of injustice pervaded everything. These were the forces which came from the outside. Could we then regain the destroyed community from the inside? Until today, only in fragments.

It is difficult to learn from one's own history, especially in this case, because the disaster was incomprehensible. Who could have the courage to admit that he had participated in any way? But it has been possible to express our grief about the crimes committed in our name. We could express it by doing something. I turned to the so-called reparation. I worked in the office of reparations from its founding until my retirement in December 1970.

There I experienced strange things. The one who causes something is completely responsible for the consequences of the things caused. This is a fundamental principle of law. This general obligation was limited, however, by the reparation law. On the federal and later the state level, responsibility was taken only for special aspects. Therefore it was necessary to make full use of the possibilities provided by the law. Because I always sought to find such interpretations of the complicated regulations which were the most favorable for the people concerned, I was said to be partial.

In spite of huge material expenses and many laws, it has been difficult to restore the destroyed consciousness of right and wrong. In my work with the reparations board I became deeply involved in many individual cases. On the day of my retirement, December 30, 1970, the director pulled out a proceedings form from his drawer and said, "We have a claim against you." They were going to present me with a summons. I replied that he should send it to me right away so I could defend myself. I heard no more of the matter.

I was awarded the medal as a "Righteous Among the Nations" by Yad Vashem in 1985.

MARIA COUNTESS VON MALTZAN

Countess von Maltzan as
a veterinarian, 1947.

*The taxi asks us to check our address in West Berlin—this is not a good
neighborhood. But we soon learn that Countess von Maltzan, born to
enormous wealth in Silesia, in Germany, lives in this primarily Turkish "slum,"
as she calls it, with pride and conviction. Although the apartments around her
have been burglarized, hers is left unharmed because her neighbors know her
as a friend of the weak and powerless.*

*We walk through her veterinarian's office to reach the large, light-filled
living room where the antique furniture and large portrait of her father, the
Count, reveal Maltzan's distinguished origins. Her English is clear and her
stories substantive and personal. Nearly eighty, her mind travels from one
global problem to another. Anger and toughness are balanced by a
compassion and sympathy for others. Her sweet-faced mutt gnaws happily on
a rubber Margaret Thatcher chew-toy.*

I was born in 1909 on our family's 18,000-acre estate in Silesia in south-
eastern Germany. I was the youngest of eight children. I adored my father
and he adored me. He was a very social person, a count, and governed all of
Silesia. The land had belonged to our family until the Russians took it after
the war. My father was respected for all the good things he did. He built
orphanages and an old-age home for the peasants living in our province. I
remember, when I was seven, telling my father that the cottage of my nurse
had burned down. He asked me how much money I had. I told him 217
marks. He said, "I suggest you go get it. Berta has taken care of you for a long
time; now you must take care of her." I gave her 200 marks.

My mother was a different story. Just after my older brother's birth she was burned very badly, and four years later I came along. My delivery took twenty-seven hours, and since all the other children had been born in three or four hours, she was always very angry with me. She was the most unjust person I have ever known. She adored her eldest daughter because she was so attractive, and she favored my brothers over her four daughters, and she was always angry with me for the long labor.

My mother hated Jews and told me never to marry one. It was easy for me to resist Nazi authority because I had always resisted my mother's authority.

I was always very active with my eyes. I would come home and tell my mother what I had seen and she'd say, "Stop your lying!" So one day I stopped, and she couldn't get me into a conversation after that. It nearly drove her mad, but why should I talk? I had my school friends to talk with.

When I was thirteen my father called me to his deathbed to say, "You know your mother doesn't like you. Try to be polite and do what you should do." I think it was because she was such an unjust person and treated me so unjustly that I have such a strong feeling of justice.

As a schoolgirl I read *Mein Kampf*, and from the beginning I despised Hitler. I was heartsick at what he was doing to my country. My brother became a Nazi and was killed, which, of course, was the best thing that could have happened to him. I have a very silly sister who said to me, "Your brother fell for you." I wrote her back that I didn't know what got into her head—he fell for Adolf Hitler, not for me.

When I was fourteen years old I moved to Berlin and soon began studying to be a veterinarian. I traveled a lot and had a fine life even though times were hard in Germany. Beginning in 1936, I helped any Nazi opponent hide to avoid being thrown in prison. I escorted many Jews out of Berlin. This was complicated and dangerous work. I took groups into outlying woods where they hid in furniture boxes, and then we put them on a train to Sweden—we had already bribed the conductor. The SS hunted us with guns and dogs, but we all escaped.

By 1942 my flat was always crammed with people. That was when Hans Hirschel came, and of course he stayed until the end of the war when we married. Most people don't understand that there were a lot of Jews in Berlin who were just sort of wandering about. In the daytime they went to the zoo, or anywhere, and at night they went to the woods, or slept in shops, or at my place. But on May 27, 1943, Goebbels said, "Germany is *judenrein*." They put out a notice that Jews who told where other Jews were hidden wouldn't be killed. Suddenly you could rely on no one. When people live in terror and fright, they simply can't use their brains anymore. The Jews were in a condition that caused them to stop thinking.

I've been in some very tough situations in my life and mostly I've pulled myself through because I can think. Once the SS came to my flat and Hans was hiding in the couch. I had fixed the couch so that it was impossible to open, and covered his hiding place with a thin material. I drilled holes in it for air, and every day I put a glass of water in there with a little codeine to suppress a cough. I was a veterinarian and had access to medicine. The soldier asked, "How do we know nobody is hiding in there?" I said, "If you're sure someone is in there, shoot. But before you do that, I want a written signed paper from you that you will pay for new material and the work to have the couch recovered after you put holes in it." Of course, he didn't do a thing. He left!

In the winter I left the flat very early in the morning for work, and the Jews in my house couldn't light a stove or turn on a light. They couldn't even go to the w.c.—disgusting, when you think about it. And I even had to put one out; I was sad about it but I had to do it. He would leave the flat when I went out, and would run all over and then come back. Everyone could see my door and it was much too dangerous for the others.

I had a very good hairdresser, and I made him teach me how to do men's hair and beards. I could never let them go to the barber because it's the place where you sit for a long time and people talk—many people were caught at the barber's.

I didn't help only Jews. I helped everyone who was being oppressed because of their politics or ideas. So many terrible things happened. I became pregnant with Hans's baby. But the night the baby was born he was placed in an incubator and the hospital was bombed. The electricity running the incubator stopped and the baby died.

I was a queen on the black market all during the war, but I had to be good at it because I had so many extra people to feed. I always said, no matter what came along, "I prefer to be in a tough situation than to go to bed with a bad conscience."

But after the war things were so difficult for me. My whole thing with drugs was because of the war. I'm not the type to become addicted to drugs, but I did. And at that time we were treated awfully. They threw everyone in together in an insane asylum and we had to scrub floors. It was horrible. I went on a talk show recently to discuss drugs. It's treated much better these days.

Leonard Gross wrote that book about me, *The Last Jews in Berlin*, and then they made a film from it; Jacqueline Bisset played my role. They betrayed me out of my life story. They came from Hollywood with a contract like I've never seen before. I should have never signed it without a lawyer. I'm writing my own book now, and the title will be Heinrich Heine's words, "Beat the Drum and Be Without Fright."*

Now the East Germans want to do a film about me. The first part would

---

*The book was published in 1989 by Ulstein (Berlin).

be about my childhood, the second about Jews and the Third Reich, and the last part about the work I'm doing now. I'm quite engaged in social things now because this part of Berlin is a perfect slum. They don't like me to say it. I really stand up for this part of Berlin, Kreuzberg. They've shoved everybody into this area—Turks, colored people, Poles, everyone is stuck into this corner! We have houses with eight flats on one floor with one w.c. on the staircase. The police, you can't imagine how brutal they are down here, beating. If I see it—because you can see I have big corner windows with a clear view—I go down and get hold of the police and say, "Why are you beating these people?" And the silly police say to me, "Perhaps you like colored here!" "Well," I say, "I prefer them to helmets!"

You see, I was trained for these things. I'm the youngest child from a big family so I had to be quick to get my ideas in every once in a while.

As I said, because my mother was unjust I have a very strong feeling of justice. That's the real matter of the whole thing. That's why I'm furious with Israel. They wanted me to plant a eucalyptus tree and get a medal pricked to my breast! Such things I really don't care for. And they told me they wanted to make a very big kick-up in Bonn for me, but the letter inviting me for this arrived the day after the attack on Sidon. I wrote back saying that all my life I've been for the peaceful coexistence of all people, of all colors and religions, and I don't see that Israel has anything to do with my ideals. So I don't think I want to have a medal from you. And I didn't go.

I used to wear all old clothes. My friends said they were all clothes from dead people. Now I stopped that and my tailor loves me! I have all nice clothes now. Would you please send me an extra photo for my tailor? He is so proud of this suit.

The 18,000-acre estate of Countess von Maltzan's family in Silesia.

RESCUERS

Hans Hirschel, 1939.

At the premiere of the film *The Last Jews in Berlin*: Countess von Maltzan with Jacqueline Bisset, who played her role in the film. Jürgen Prochnow played her husband, Hans Hirschel.

POLAND

You Poles are a strange people. Nowhere in the world is there another nation which has so many heroes and so many denouncers.

—An SS officer

Before World War II, 3.5 million Jews lived in Poland. By war's end only 50,000 to 100,000 were left: Partisans, death-camp survivors, and those who hid or were hidden. Although the Nazis bear full responsibility for the decision to exterminate the Jews, the Poles helped. After all, anti-Semitism had been a part of Polish national and religious life since 1100, when the first Jews arrived.

Even many of the Poles who risked their own lives to rescue Jews continued to view them at least as aberrant and often as unnatural and loathsome. When asked if a person they had hidden looked Jewish, a rescuer might laugh and say, "She looked like ten Jews!" Or "He walked just like a Jew." A Polish child even in a tolerant family might be told, "If you're bad, I'll turn you over to the Jews!" Because the word "Jew" is so derogatory in Polish, sympathetic, educated Poles prefer "Israelite" or "Hebrew."

During the impoverished twenties and thirties, anti-Semitism was part of almost every Polish political party's platform. Jewish businesses were often boycotted, pogroms were frequent, universities had segregated sections for Jews, and, in 1937, the Polish government supported an early Nazi plan to send all Jews to Madagascar.

The Germans picked Poland as the most convenient killing ground for Jews because of its large Jewish population (transport was simpler) and its virulent anti-Semitism (who would object?). At first, the Nazis were concerned about what Western Europe thought of their actions against the Jews, so they were careful to hide their atrocities in France, Holland, and Belgium. But they felt no shame in allowing the Poles to witness and even assist in the Final Solution, because they considered all Slavs to be inferior. By 1939, when the Germans invaded Poland, they already had six years of experience in anti-Jewish policies. Their efficiency coupled with traditional hatred for Jews in Poland made the country the most monstrous place for the Jews of Europe. The Nazis guessed correctly: the Poles offered little resistance to the slaughter of the Jews. In fact, Poles often led Nazis to Jewish apartments, eager to loot and take over the property. Polish children hunted Jews for sport.

In 1940, the Germans began moving Jews from all over Poland into Warsaw, creating the infamous ghetto. More than 500,000 were herded into an impossibly small area and isolated from the Poles. Alex Roslan, who did business with Jews, at first could not understand what had happened to his customers; curiosity led him to risk entering the ghetto. He still grows emotional when he speaks of the starving children he saw there. Despite the inhuman conditions, many Jews didn't leave the ghetto while they still could, because they were more afraid of the Poles than of the Germans. The Nazis even told Jews they would protect them from Polish anti-Semitism. Deportations to the extermination camps began in 1942.

By the time the Jews in the Warsaw Ghetto did decide to fight back, in April 1943, most of them had been killed. Alexander Donat, publisher of Warsaw's largest newspaper before the war, described the response of bystanders to the burning of the Warsaw Ghetto:

> Then came Easter Sunday. . . . Mass over, the holiday crowds poured out into the sundrenched streets. Hearts filled with Christian love, people went to look at the new unprecedented attraction that lay halfway across the city to the north, on the other side of the Ghetto wall, where Christ's Jewish brethren suffered a new and terrible Calvary not by crucifixion but by fire. What a unique spectacle! Bemused, the crowds stared at the hanging curtains of flame, listened to the roar of the conflagration, and whispered to one another, "But the Jews—they're being roasted alive!" There was awe and relief that not they but the others had attracted the fury and vengeance of the conqueror. There was also satisfaction.
>
> Batteries of artillery had set up in Nowiniarska Street and were shelling objectives in the Ghetto from there. The explosions of grenades and dynamite could be heard as well, as Jews scrambled from their hiding places. Pain-crazed figures leaped from balconies and windows to smash on the streets below. From time to time a living torch would crouch on a window sill for one unbearably long moment before flashing like a comet through the air. When such figures caught on some obstruction and hung there suspended in agony, the spectators were quick to attract the attention of German riflemen. "Hey, look over there! No, over there!" Love of neatness and efficiency were appeased by a well-placed shot; the flaming comet was made to complete its trajectory; and the crowds cheered.*

Another description of the ghetto burning is contained in the illustrated words of Aaron Landau, who wrote a newspaper he called the *New Warsaw*

Quoted in Fein, *Waiting for Genocide*, p. 259.

Daily while he was hiding in an eighteen-inch space between two walls in the home of a Polish Catholic woman.

Stefan Korbonski, one of the leaders of the Polish underground, said of the brave spirit of the Jews: "On July 22, 1942, was the first day of the daily transports, and that's when the Jews opened their eyes and said, 'No, we shall not survive!' On that day they began to think about fighting, not with any hope to win, only to dearly sell their lives. On April 19, 1943, I sent an underground telegram to England, telling the Allies, 'Speak to the Ghetto today!' They broadcast a message, 'We know you are heroes!' "

Despite the Jews being 10 percent of the population and the hundreds of years they had lived in Poland, they were not part of the life of the country; no one considered the Jews Poles. Besides looking, dressing, and behaving differently, Jews went to segregated schools, and only 12 percent spoke Polish as their first language. Most Poles were peasants and farmers, but most Jews were in manufacturing and commerce. Polish Jews didn't know where to look for help. Even blond, blue-eyed Jews felt uneasy "passing" among people who excluded and oppressed them. Some went to fight with the Partisans but soon discovered that they were often put in the front lines to be shot first or turned over to the Germans. Many put their faith in Polish underground leaders such as Stefan Korbonski and Jan Karski to inform the free world what Germany was doing to them. They hoped that would stop the genocide. But the Allied leaders did nothing.

The Jews who survived owed their lives to Poles who put aside deep prejudice and risked their own lives to save them. In Poland, those who wanted to help Jews worked alone and in great secrecy, because no one could be trusted.

One of the first steps in the rescue process was to get the Jews out of the ghetto. Alex Roslan slipped into the ghetto to take eight-year-old Jacob Gutgelt. Even though the ghetto was sealed, it was possible to enter and leave, but getting Jews out was just the beginning of the problem. Besides needing shelter and food, they needed Christian papers and some Catholicism. When a Nazi stopped a person suspected of being a Jew, he might ask questions about the Church. A few beauty parlors not only bleached dark hair but also served as classrooms in religion. Some doctors reshaped noses and disguised circumcisions.

Children were easiest to hide, but Jewish families often perished rather than be separated from their children. The Church took Jewish children into convents and boarding schools and baptized them so they could receive communion. Sometimes a priest asked permission of the parents; it was almost always granted. Some survivors describe their Catholic childhoods with ambivalence. Many felt security in the Church and remained Catholics, while others struggled after the war to become Jewish again. Whether the

Church helped keep these children alive for the sake of humanity or to gain converts didn't matter much to those who survived.

Nazi theory held that killing a Pole would "purify" the world's races, so they had no problem stringing up Polish rescuers in the town square with a warning: "This family hid Jews!" Although more than 2,000 Poles have been honored at Yad Vashem, recent evidence suggests that thousands more helped Jews, and no one will ever know how many righteous Poles were murdered along with those they tried to save.

To save a Jew in Poland required an independence of mind and an iron spirit. Intellectuals, leftists, and free thinkers such as Zofia Baniecka and Helena Orchon were more likely to help than any other segment of the population. Peasants responded out of simple compassion, although some also appreciated the immediate jump in status they gained when they helped middle-class Jews. Often a maid such as Stefania Burzminski turned out to be the savior of the family or the new mother of the children. One survivor described a peasant's house as being filled not only with Jews but with stray animals: "She couldn't turn away anything helpless and needy."

Even a few prominent rightists with a tradition of anti-Semitism rescued Jews because, whatever contempt they felt, they could not condone genocide. Poles who had done business with Jews before the war sent gift packages into the ghetto. Despite Polish feelings against the Jews, Nazi cruelty and violence formed bonds of sympathy between them. When hoodlums beat up Jews before the war there was no public protest, but after 1941 there were accounts of Poles trying to stop such beatings.

Polish anti-Semitism did not disappear with the war's end. Thousands of Jews and their rescuers were attacked and killed by Poles after Liberation. Agnieszka Budna-Widerschal's daughter was killed by Polish children. Many rescuers were forced to leave the country; nearly forty of them live in Israel, some with or near the people they saved. Those who stayed in Poland remain silent about their work during the war. Although only 6,000 Jews live in Poland today, anti-Jewish feeling persists. Again, Stefan Korbonski emphasizes the opposite perspective: "Poland was the cultural, scientific, and religious Jewish center—Warsaw, Vilna, Lublin. It was something unbelievable. It's hard to believe such a loss, that two generations of Poles have never seen Jews in Poland."

Polish rescuers are sensitive to the rage many Jews feel toward their country. Some told their stories simply because they want the world to know there were good Poles.

Taken from Aaron Landau's newspaper: *New Warsaw Daily* of 08-18-43

I, who write these words
I state, as an eye-witness
that all the theatres, movie theatres,
show-places, and all sorts of casinos
and other places of amusement
were open and operating according
to their daily routines, at the
time when up above, in the
   Warsaw skies,
were rising coils of smoke
   from the
burning Ghetto, and inside
   burning alive
tens of thousands of souls.

April 1943
04-19-43
Warsaw Ghetto in Flames

Taken from Landau's book. This drawing pictures the Jews as flowers or plants, with Yiddish letters on each one, growing in a field about to be cut by a sickle. On the top it reads, "Hitler's Autumn Harvest," and on the bottom, "The sad harvest of the beautiful autumn flowers. . . . The Holy Capital City and her provinces were desecrated and divided. All new beauties flooded [perished] and lost. They even deprived us of this Holy Tradition. . . ."

RESCUERS

ZOFIA BANIECKA

Zofia Baniecka.

This interview with Zofia Baniecka takes place on a perfect October day on Staten Island at the home of Ruth Curtin, one of the people Zofia saved. She does not speak a word of English, so Ruth translates from Polish, with her own memories as a filter. Despite the barrier of language, we feel immediate connection with Zofia because of her warmth. Her physical presence conveys the spirit of an intellectually rigorous mind clear in its path to action. She smokes throughout the interview, but this is not a nervous gesture, more a mark of her passionate, independent character. Zofia and Ruth were schoolmates in Warsaw, and although Zofia still lives in that city, the women have maintained a close friendship. This is not Zofia's first visit to Ruth's home.

I was born in Warsaw in 1917, the only child of a father who was a sculptor and a mother who was a teacher. I came along after they had been married fifteen years, so I was a bit spoiled. I had a beautiful childhood. I went to the finest Catholic school even though we weren't religious. There were many Jewish students in my school, but only during the war did I find out which students were Jewish. They were children from assimilated homes and many of them had converted. My parents had high ideals and our house was always full of their friends talking about politics or music and art.

My father was my greatest love. When I went to the university and openly anti-Semitic behavior became even worse than before, we spoke about it often and, of course, he was against it. He had a very close friend who was a sculptor and a Jew. My father often went into the ghetto to take food and books to friends. But during the Russian strike on Warsaw in 1941, my father was killed. We were in our home when he was hit, and Mother was hit also, in the head, but she recovered.

The house I had lived in all my life was in the area in Warsaw that became the ghetto, so we were required to move when they enclosed the ghetto. Friends took us into their large apartment, and mother and I lived in the living room. Then the underground got us a large apartment, four rooms plus a kitchen, and mother and I began working constantly. She was in a shopping network of guns and vegetables. Nobody would ever suspect that a small gray-haired woman would be carrying a gun in her shopping bag.

At first I was a liaison for the underground, relaying orders from one group to another, delivering underground newspapers throughout the provinces. I got involved through social contacts: a friend asked me to join the underground press, and I agreed. I was itching to do something. I was afraid, but I had to do it. I saw the whole Jewish population wearing yellow armbands. I saw beatings on the street of old Jews, of children, shootings, the most horrible sights.

I had always been independent and patriotic, and this was certainly my attitude during the war. It was unthinkable to be anything else. We hid guns and ammunition in our apartment, as well as people. The apartment was divided by curtains, and behind each one there was a different Jewish family. When our house was full, I found hiding places for the Jews with other families because it was too dangerous for them to be where the guns were. Ruth was a friend from school, so of course I didn't turn her away. She stayed only a few weeks, however, until I could help her find a safe place.

Mother and I were in constant danger because to find a gun in a private house meant a death sentence. It was proof that you were in the underground. We were in danger of being raided at any minute, so I had to take the Jews to other houses as fast as I could, even though this hurt me. I didn't like turning them away, even if I was sending them to another house. But I was in touch with the Jewish Committee so that when I had children to hide, they could help me find places.

From the window of our house I could see the ghetto. When the houses were burning during the ghetto uprising in April 1943, I saw people jumping from windows. One family of ten came and stayed for a few weeks until I found other shelter for them. No one was refused in my home. We had at least fifty Jews during the war—friends, strangers, acquaintances, or someone who heard about me from someone else. Anyone was taken in.

I was never interrogated or nearly caught, though I don't know why. Many fellow resistance leaders perished in prison. I was just lucky. Luck, it was only luck, because I kept people and guns in my house from the winter of 1941 until the Polish uprising in August 1944.

At the end of the war Roosevelt sold out Poland. I was arrested by the Russians because I was and still am a Polish patriot. I didn't have to ask for help because my underground friends were there to help me. Until this day I am in touch with my friends from the underground.

My husband and I struggled constantly for a free Poland. We belonged to Solidarity from the beginning, and our home is a meeting place for people to study, kind of like a free university. I am not at all religious today—not since I was eighteen have I been to church regularly—but I do still believe in human beings. There are many people who have saved my belief in humanity, and that is why it is important for people to know about this time, of Poland during the war, and that there were those of us who did try to save Jews. It is necessary for the children to know that there were such people.

Zofia Baniecka (on right).

GERTRUDA BABILINSKA

**Gertruda Babilinska
in Vilna with Mickey
(Michael Stolowitzky), 1943.**

*Gertruda's room in the Gertrud Luckner Home for the Aged in Nahariyya,
with a view of the Mediterranean, is homey and personal. Except for a picture
of the Pope, pictures of Mickey, the Jewish boy she rescued, fill the room:
Catholicism and Mickey are central to her life. A native of Poland, she speaks
Polish and German, never having learned Hebrew since arriving in Israel in
1947 in order to fulfill a promise to raise Mickey as a Jew. Despite her eighty-
five years, she is still a large, imposing woman with an incisive mind. She is
delighted for our company, especially for our lively and caring translator,
Lusia Schimmel, who is herself a concentration-camp survivor from Poland.*

I was born in the North of Poland, near Danzig, in 1902. I had five sisters
and two brothers, and I was the oldest. My father worked in the post
office. We were a good religious family. The proverb in our home was "Love
your neighbor as yourself." My mother was always concerned about everyone else. For instance, when I went into the ghetto to see Mickey I was gone
for several days. When I returned home my mother opened the door, and
instead of saying, "How are you?," she asked me, "How is the child?"

For fifteen years I worked for a very rich Jewish family named Stolowitzky,
taking care of the children, a daughter and a son. [Gertruda is crying as she
talks of the family.] First the father was taken to Auschwitz. When the daughter died Mrs. Stolowitzky thought it would be safer in Warsaw, so I left Danzig
and went with them. Then she heard it was better in Vilna, so we went there.
We got an apartment, but things were very bad. Mickey's mother asked me to
promise her that I would take care of Mickey if anything happened to her.

In Vilna, I rented an apartment which I kept for the four years I was there. The Lithuanians in Vilna were very anti-Semitic and mean. One day one of them hit me. We were having a very difficult time there. The Nazis would give poison candy to the children. I had to teach Mickey never to take anything to eat from anyone.

Then Mickey's mother became sick and died. Mickey came to me and said, "I have no mother. Will you be my mother?" I could not tell him right away. I asked him to wait, and in three days I would give him an answer. I was a single, forty-year-old Catholic woman. How was I going to raise a Jewish child? But I finally told him I would be his mother and he could move into my apartment with me, and he was so happy that he threw his arms around me.

Once Mickey got sick and the only doctor I knew was in the ghetto, so I had to take him to a German doctor. I lied and said that I was his older sister, but I don't think he believed me. After several visits, Mickey was well. When I asked the doctor what I owed him, he wouldn't allow me to pay him. He said to me, "No, you have helped me feel like a man." So he did know Mickey was a Jewish boy.

As soon as the war ended I knew I had to get Mickey to Israel. There was no other way that I could raise a boy to be a Jew. All during the war he had gone to church with me. He learned all the prayers and he even became an altar boy, but I knew I would tell him as soon as I could that he was not Catholic, that he must always be Jewish.

We were on the first ship to Israel, the *Exodus*. The British were so terrible. The ship was crowded and we were not allowed to dock in Palestine. A chef on the ship gave me cookies for Mickey. But we finally arrived, and I tell you, a miracle happened. From the moment Mickey stepped onto the land of Israel he became a Jewish patriot. It was a miracle.

Mickey's mother had told me that her relatives in Israel would help us, so I went to them right away. I will never forgive them for what they did to me. They gave me a little room upstairs, with no water and no toilet. They paid for one-half year for Mickey to go to school. Mickey cried when he came home. They wanted to adopt Mickey and send me back to Poland. They said they would not pay for school for Mickey if I stayed in Israel. Mickey cried and said to me, "You are my mother. I don't want them for parents." And he said to them, "I don't want to be a son of your family. I want to stay with my mother forever. Where she will go, I will go."

So I went to work as a maid to pay for Mickey's schooling. He went to Be'er Shemin to school, to a program especially for children from Europe like him. And for eighteen years I lived in this same room with no water and worked as a maid so I would have money to pay for the room and for things for Mickey. And Mickey grew up to be such a good Jew. I am so proud of him. He is the most wonderful son in the world.

Mickey worked for Copel Tours in Israel, arranging tours, and then they moved him to Miami in 1975. I miss him very much. Now he lives in New York, and brings tours to Israel for another company. He visits Israel often, and he always uses his Israeli passport. It would be easier and cheaper for him to use an American passport, but he believes in being a Jew and an Israeli. And every time he comes to Israel, he comes here to visit me.

If I had known, forty years ago, that after bringing a Jewish boy to Israel I would be living my last years in this old-age home, I would never have done it. There's no one to talk to here. I still speak only Polish, but I would love to discuss things with people. But the intellectual level is very low. To go to church is very important to me, and yet my priest is a converted Jew. Father Daniel will never be a real priest. A Jew who becomes a priest is never a priest. Just as Mickey became Jewish as soon as he stepped onto Israeli soil, so also, for me, the priest is not a real priest.

Mickey doesn't want me to move to the United States because he returns to Israel often and he wants to remain an Israeli, so he wants me here in his homeland. And I don't think I would want to move anyway. I visit him in the United States. He is the best son in the whole world.

From *Tour and Travel News*, March 1989.

RESCUERS

JAN KARSKI

Jan Karski, 1944.

To be in the presence of Jan Karski, Polish spy for the underground, a major fig-
ure in Claude Lanzmann's Shoah, *and professor of Eastern European political*
science at Georgetown University, is a daunting experience. We approach the
interview somewhat in awe of this handsome man, with his regal bearing and
remarkable eloquence. Our insecurity probably stems from the fact that he had
asked for a list of questions before he would make the appointment. He ushers us
solemnly into his house with an accent akin to Bela Lugosi's and sits expec-
tantly for our questions. Our fears are unfounded. Karski is brilliant and severe,
but we quickly discover that he is also playful, boyish, and charming. His stu-
dents are fortunate to have a professor who is not only knowledgeable but pro-
foundly concerned about people. Since our meeting, we have corresponded, and
he remains a helpful, caring friend.

I was born in 1914, in Lodz, Poland, the youngest of eight children. The
oldest was eighteen years older, and all of the other children were out of
the house by the time I was an adolescent. My parents were middle-class. My
father died when I was a child so he did not register much in my heart or in
my mind. My mother—like all mothers, I loved her, I obeyed her. She was
very sensitive, extremely religious. At the age of twelve, I joined a semireli-
gious, semisecret organization. My mentor was a Jesuit Father, so I fell under
the influence of the Jesuits sixty years ago and until today nobody liberated
me from the Jesuits.

I was always a good student. In gymnasium, I became friends with a
group of Jewish students. Jews were always strong in science and I was
strong in history, poetry, literature. So for four years we established the clos-

est relationship. I helped them and they helped me. I remember vividly their names and faces, what each one of them taught me, and what was the particular ambition of each of them. What happened to them all I do not know. Only God knows.

I finished gymnasium in 1931. My mother didn't want me to go to military service, so I went to university. I was the best student in the university. Most of my thinking life I wanted to be a diplomat, an ambassador of Poland. My hero was the foreign minister of Napoleon, Talleyrand. I called him "The Divine Prince of Benevento." For my thesis, I tried to reconstruct every day of his life, which, of course, was impossible.

In 1935, I earned my master's degree in law and diplomatic sciences. Then I went into the military for one year. In 1936, I began an unofficial attachment to the diplomatic service, and went for eight months to Geneva under the League of Nations. Then I went for eleven months to England to learn English, and then in February 1938 I went back to Warsaw to enter training for the Foreign Office, which I completed eleven months later, with the highest grades. In January 1939, I was made the secretary of the Department of Immigration and became the private secretary of the director of personnel in the Foreign Ministry. This was an important position.

On August 23, 1939, the Nazis and Soviets agreed to a nonaggression pact. At the same time Poland semisecretly mobilized. On September 1, the bombs fell. For me the war lasted twenty minutes. I was in the army when the Nazis invaded. I never saw a German, I never fired shots. I saw only chaos and confusion. I was taken as a prisoner of war to the Soviet Union, and I escaped by using my brain and my physical agility.

When I returned and looked for my friends, I found that the underground had already been formed. They knew about my good memory, and that I was familiar with many other parts of Europe, so in December 1939 I did my first job as a courier from Warsaw to France, where the Polish government-in-exile was located. I crossed all of Slovakia and reached Hungary on skis. Once in Budapest, I was provided with false documents and could take the train to France. I was there for four months, and returned by the same route, this time on foot. On my next trip, however, I was arrested in Slovakia. I was tortured and my ribs were broken. I had so much information and I couldn't stand the torture, so I tried to cut my wrists. But I found out it's a very hard thing to do.

The Gestapo sent me back to Poland, where I established contact with the underground, who rescued me. The person who organized my escape was one of my close friends, a prominent rising star of socialism, Józef Cyrankiewicz, the man who was to be the Communist prime minister of Poland for eighteen years. I owe my life to him. In 1974, when I spent six months in Poland under a Fulbright Scholarship to work on my book, I visited with him.

Until that time I had never been hit by anyone, and I had never hit anyone. And then when I saw the ghetto . . . I cannot stand violence. I cannot watch TV when a man and woman argue. I cannot stand loud voices. I have enough of war. War degrades people. War generates hatred. You have to hate. People will do terrible things: derail a train, never mind that innocent people will be killed; throw a grenade, never mind that children will be killed. This I never realized: that war generates such hatred.

As a child I was taught an individual has human dignity, responsibility to society and to our Lord. Everyone has a soul, a human conscience. We have an infinite capacity to choose between evil and good, and God gave us free will. What I did not realize is that only individuals have souls; governments, nations, societies, have no souls. There is no such thing as a collective soul.

What happened to me is this. Two Jewish men from the underground came to me to ask me to help the Jews. They asked me to take the information about the systematic killing of the Jews to the leaders of the Allied governments. "Tell Churchill and Roosevelt that we know the Allies will win the war, but by then it will be too late for the Jews. Tell them we need two things: tell them we can buy Jewish lives, that the Germans can be bribed, so we need money to get Jews out of the country. And we think that the general population in Germany does not know what is happening to the Jews. We want the Allies to drop millions of leaflets all over Germany, informing the population and warning them that if they do not pressure their government to stop, you will bomb their cities." These were the requests they asked me to make on their behalf. But first, they asked me to go into the Warsaw Ghetto and the Belzec death camp, to see for myself. I thought perhaps they were exaggerating, so I agreed. The ghetto was macabre. It was not a world. It was not a part of humanity. I did not belong there. I vomited blood that night. I saw horrible, horrible things I will never forget. So I agreed to do what they asked of me.

In February 1943, I reported to Anthony Eden in London, who said that Great Britain had already done enough by accepting 100,000 refugees. In July I arrived in the United States. Almost every individual was sympathetic to my reports concerning the Jews. But when I reported to the leaders of governments they discarded their conscience, their personal feeling. They provided a rationale which seemed valid. What was the situation? The Jews were totally helpless. The war strategy was the military defeat of Germany and the defeat of Germany's war potential for all eternity. Nothing could interfere with the military crushing of the Third Reich. The Jews had no country, no government. They were fighting but they had no identity. One of my partners in the underground was Jewish. I found out only after the war. It was too dangerous to reveal their identity, even to fellow resistance workers. They had no identity. Helping Jews was no advantage to the Allied war strategy. The highest officials, including Lord Selborne in London, argued that if hard currency were exchanged for Jews, the Allies would be criticized after the war for subsidizing Hitler with gold and silver. They said, "Mr. Karski, this is impossible, we will not do it." Roosevelt gave the underground $12 million, but this was for the army, for fighting, "not charity to save your children," he said. When I hear people say "the Jews were passive," and that "they didn't fight"—this is nonsense. In many concentration camps there were uprisings, escapes, and in the forests they fought with Partisan groups. But they had no identity. The Jews were helpless. If a Jew escaped from the ghetto, where could he go? Abandoned absolutely by all societies, governments, church hierarchies, societal organizations. Only individuals might help and were helping. The help had to come from the powerful Allied leaders, and this help did not come.

Meeting Roosevelt was a great occasion. I was overwhelmed with his majesty. He was a great personality. He was not specific on anything, but you realize, I couldn't ask anything. I didn't come to negotiate, only to report and answer questions. So I said, "I will return to Poland, Mr. President. What shall I tell my people?" He said, "You will tell them we shall win the war and the enemy will be punished for their crimes. Justice will prevail. Tell your nation that they have a friend in this house. This is what you will tell them."

Thirty-five or forty years after the war, I read an interview with John Pehle, who said that my mission had shaken the President and that he had ordered the creation of the American Refugee Board, which was formed only four months after I saw him. Pehle himself was appointed the director of the board but said, "It was too little, too late." Is this true? Pehle says so, but I am skeptical. I read it and it gave me satisfaction, but for myself, I am skeptical.

I know Roosevelt's and Eden's arguments had some logic. Goebbels had propagandized that the Jews had provoked the war, and they made others believe that. And would the French like it, would they say, "Why for the Jews?" And would Poland itself even like it?

At the end of August 1943 I tried to return to Poland, but it was decided it was too dangerous. The Germans believed I was working for "American Bolshevik Jews." So I stayed in the United States, but no longer in secret. Now I was attached to the Polish Embassy; I earned $500 per month, and I wrote articles to every magazine of any importance—*Life*, *The New York Times*, *The Jewish Forward*, *La France Libre* —about what was happening to the Jews. I traveled all over the United States, delivering over two hundred lectures, and by the end of 1944 my book appeared, *Story of a Secret State*. It was a Book-of-the-Month Club selection, and two key chapters were about the Warsaw Ghetto and the Belzec death camp. Nothing seemed to matter. Then the end of the war came and I was a political exile. During those years I was lecturing, I had absolute faith that I was representing Poland and would one day return there. Absolute faith. As the Jews had been abandoned during the war, so Poland and the other Eastern European countries had been abandoned by the Allies.

I stayed in the United States on an entry visa, and five years later I became a citizen. I met my wife here. I had known her by reputation as a great modern dancer in England, but I didn't know her personally. Soon I decided to enter academia. The Jesuits gave me a scholarship to Georgetown University. I earned my Ph.D. in government in two and a half years, and I've been at Georgetown ever since.

After the war I wanted to run away from all my memories. I felt contempt for the hypocrisy of the leaders, great leaders, military men, ministers who went to Germany to see for themselves. They saw, and all of them were shocked. All of them, without exception. They didn't know such things were possible. They were taken by surprise. Hypocrisy. They knew. And if some didn't know, it was because they didn't want to know. Human beings have this capacity to disregard. For over thirty years I never mentioned to anyone that I was in the war. I wanted to bury myself at the university, and I did. And then in 1977, I received a letter from Claude Lanzmann, who made the film *Shoah*. He asked if he could interview me. I didn't answer his letter. I thought nothing would come of it. Then Lanzmann called me and said, "Mr. Karski, look in the mirror. You are an old man. You don't know when you are going to die. It is your duty to appear in my film." I told him, "I saw terrible things in Poland concerning the Jews which I don't want to remember." He replied, "That is why we should not let humanity forget."

So circumstances took me back and broke my silence. I am not happy about it; now I have bad dreams again. But my conscience is telling me that I should speak. But I do not like Lanzmann; I only admire him. He made a great film. He cared only about his work. He cared only about how the Holocaust could happen, what he called "the mechanism of the Holocaust." He was interested only in three kinds of people: the perpetrators, the Jews who were in the camps, and those who actually saw it. He didn't even care about the war. Only about how it could happen. He asked Poles only in those towns near the camps because they saw it with their eyes. So all the Poles looked dumb because they were peasants, little people from little towns. The educated people didn't live near Treblinka and Auschwitz. Intelligent, educated

Poles lived in Warsaw, Cracow, or London. And he insists that the word "shoah" is the only correct one. "Holocaust," he said, "involves also some sense of self-sacrifice, volunteerism of some kind. It is a word for Hollywood which Elie Wiesel made famous. 'Shoah' implies it was planned by humans, executed to the end against the laws of nature and God."

I teach courses today in the government and politics of Eastern Europe. One of them begins with the Versailles Peace Treaty and goes to the present time. My impression is that many of the students, even Jewish students, listen to my lecture about the war and are shocked. They are impressed, but they consider what I tell them as a sort of frightening story, terrible, but still a sort of ancient myth, rather unreal. The point is that it is difficult to visualize what actually happened to the Jews during the war. Their minds cannot absorb that it was real. I have had this feeling often.

I was asked to teach a course on the Holocaust, but I refused. I have no stomach for it. And besides, it's not my specialty. But what teachers of the Holocaust must remember, what must be emphasized, and many Jews do not do it enough, particularly those who teach the Holocaust, particularly to the children—we must be very careful. If the teacher is not qualified, he or she will run a risk of corrupting the young minds. First, that such things were possible, such horrors happened. Corrupting the minds of the young people will cause them to lose faith in humanity, particularly the Jewish children. "Everybody hated us . . . everybody was against us, so I must be only for myself. So I must distrust everybody. Because I am a Jewish girl or a Jewish boy." This is unhealthy. We don't want them to lose faith in humanity.

We should also emphasize that after the war over one-half million Jews survived in Europe. Now, some of them don't owe anything to anybody. They survived in the camps; the Nazis had no time to finish them off. There were others, they don't owe anything to anybody. They survived in the mountains, in the forests, fighting, as Partisans. But most of them were helped, by individuals, by priests, nuns, peasants, some workers, some intelligentsia, whatever they were. In France, in Belgium, in Holland, in Poland, in Romania, in Bulgaria, in Serbia, in Greece. Now, to help a Jew during the war was very dangerous. In France or Belgium you might go to jail if they caught you, in some cases you would be punished or receive a penalty, pay some money. But in Eastern Europe, particularly Poland, instantaneous death! Execution! Sometimes if the family was involved, the entire family shot! There were a few cases, not many, but a few cases where the Gestapo found out that the peasants in the village knew that there was some Jewish family in hiding, they burned the village, the entire village! And still there were people who were helping the Jews!

So children must understand this: do not lose faith in humanity. This is the message to Jewish children. For non-Jews they should understand, "Yesterday Jews, tomorrow maybe Catholics, yellows, or blacks." And secondly, they should know what obedience to our second commandment, "Love your neighbor as yourself," can do. It can save people in such circumstances as this. Lanzmann himself was hidden by a French peasant family for several years.

I worked on my last book for fifteen years. Now I want to retire, and every year I go to the provost and every year he says, "God made you a teacher and a teacher you will stay." So I remain a teacher. At the age of seventy-four. Everyone wants some social recognition, so if competent people tell me, "You are a good teacher, we want you here," then it's easier. Six times in secret ballot the seniors have voted me the single teacher who made the most impact on their lives. And so I teach. And I have another pressure, my wife. She told my dean, "Listen, if I have my husband at home every day, be prepared after a few months I will go mad. Keep him at school!"

So I have become known because of my work during the war. Here is my pride and joy, my medal from Yad Vashem. I was invited to Israel and spent three weeks there. I gave lectures, and I learned that the Israeli people quarrel more than even the Poles. Everybody criticizes everybody. Only when there is an emergency do they come together. And then, after *Shoah*, a British company came to interview me and made a forty-six-minute videotape called *Messenger from Poland* about my wartime work. All of this was not planned. Always people pushed me around. This is what my life consists of.

My life during the war was running everywhere, from this leader to that. My life since the war is hard work. I work all the time. I have enough of it. I am tired. I am tired.

AGNIESZKA BUDNA-WIDERSCHAL

**Agnieszka's wedding
photo. She cut Motl
out of the picture.**

*Much like most Israeli apartments we visited in Bat Yam, Agnieszka Budna-
Widerschal's is on the fourth floor without benefit of an elevator. It is very
warm, the rooms are small, and Agnieszka has provided us with cookies
and soda without ice.*

*Agnieszka's blunt and powerful physiognomy makes it easy to imagine her
rescuing six Jewish men from the ghetto and hiding them for three years, even
in Poland, the most dangerous of countries. Strength exudes from this woman
as she answers the questions fully, though not reflectively: she is clearly a doer.
She enjoys telling the stories of ingenious trickery and brazenness, and a sense
of her courage and natural intelligence isn't lost even in the tedious Polish
translation. All the while her husband, Shimon, watches her with fascination
and love, as if hearing her anecdotes for the first time.*

*Hers is the last interview in Israel and it is the most shocking. With all
the deaths described, the murder of Agnieszka's daughter, Bella, feels the most
tragic, perhaps because it happened after the war, when the world was supposed to be safe again. She tells us about the girl stoically, then goes into the
bedroom to get a framed photograph of her daughter. As a result of Bella's
death, Agnieszka and Shimon immigrated to Israel in 1958.*

I was born in 1909, in a small town in the North of Poland. I'm the youngest of three sisters. Our father did office work; I'd say we were less than middle-class. My parents helped everyone, all the time. They were very religious Catholics, and so was I. I remember my mother being a person who always wanted to give from her heart. There were many Jews in our town but there was never any anti-Semitism in our family. Mother died when I was seven and Father when I was eleven, so I had to move with relatives in Gdynia, a large coastal town near Germany.

Before the war I moved to Przemysl, and I was working in a factory inspecting fruits and vegetables for export. I met a mechanic who was working there, Motl, a Jew, and we got married. When the Nazis took over I got a job in a small office, and my boss was German. They were putting the Jews in ghettos and then moving them to the center of Poland so they'd all be together. I decided I'd better get a big apartment so I could hide Motl and his family. And when the ghetto was closed, the people who worked for German bosses got bigger places to live. So I bought a place on the third floor which had an attic that we could use as a hiding place.

Motl had three brothers. Two of them were in the ghetto. I hid Motl in my new apartment and went to get his brothers. It was just before curfew, and I came up with a plan that I thought might work. I pretended to be drunk while the two brothers walked on either side of me, each of them holding me under my arm. There were Nazis all over the street. I knew we would surely run into one of them, and when we did he just took one look at me and said with disgust, "Ach, that's just like a Pole!" And he walked his way and we went ours!

The third brother escaped from a train taking him to Treblinka—you know that's where they murdered so many Jews. He got to the train station and pretended to be a train worker when I went to pick him up. When we were on the way to my place a Nazi with a huge dog stopped us. I made up some story, and since I could speak to him in German, he let us go, but he said, "The next German won't be as nice as me." And he was right. That one was a real *mensch*. Then two friends of Motl's found their way to my apartment, so now there were six of them to hide. It was a good thing I had the German boss, because I could get extra ration cards just like the Germans got.

As soon as they were all there, in 1942, they built a false wall one foot from the other wall, where they could hide in case of danger. It was all very complicated because, of course, I had no water; the bathroom was on the first floor. And my building was full of nosy neighbors, which meant I had to bring food and water at night when they were asleep, which is also when I had to empty their wastepots. I bought rabbits so that in case the six men made any noise, I could say it was the rabbits. And they were always a good source of food.

One day one of my neighbors told me, "Before the war, Jews lived in your apartment. You know how Jews are; they always have jewels and valuable things. They probably hid them in the attic over your apartment. Let's break through the wall and ceiling to see if there's anything there." I told her, "I work all day and I come home at night very tired. If we break through the wall, who will clean up and repair the hole? After the war we will break through and share whatever we find." That made her happy! [Agnieszka loves telling these stories. She laughs when she talks about getting rabbits. She enjoys remembering how ingenious she was, and her husband, Shimon, looks at her with a wide-mouthed smile, love and amazement all over his face.]

I had many Jewish friends before the war, and we were all very close. During the war I was poor, but I did for all of them whatever I could. It was very dangerous, but I knew that if I decided to help I had to do it without fear. I had to have such a good head on my shoulders, to make up so many stories to get out of so many bad situations. But we all managed to survive.

After the war I was pregnant. Our daughter, Bella, was born in September 1945, but my husband died of diabetes in January 1946. Bella and I went back to Gdynia where I had family. Motl's three brothers stayed in Przemysl, one of the others went to Israel, and one to Canada. I met Shimon and he wanted to marry me. He said he wanted a big, strong woman!

In 1954 there was another big wave of anti-Semitism. One day at the market a Polish woman said to me, "Only the Jews have money to buy food. Look at what you can buy; I can't buy nearly that much." I answered her, "It's because all the Polish husbands are spending their money on liquor and they stay drunk all the time. My husband doesn't drink so I have money to buy food." I know I shouldn't have answered her like that, but I was used to being brave and outspoken during the war, and I couldn't help myself. Shimon asked me not to talk to them like that. He'd say, "They'll bite you back someday."

Bella went to a Polish school, and in the afternoon, Shimon was usually home from work before I was, so he would help her with her schoolwork. But one day when she was nine years old she didn't come home from school. Polish children had come to get her to take a walk with them. These children were a few years older than she. They walked near the train station. The conductor told us later that he saw Bella and then he saw the other children who had been hidden near a wall. They came out from the wall and pushed her very hard in front of the oncoming train. It was such a catastrophe! The mother of one of the thirteen-year-old girls told me at the funeral, "You know, it's a good thing that *our* children are alive."

We came to Israel in 1958. I was honored by Yad Vashem in 1982, and I've been happy in this little town. Shimon hasn't been so well lately. All I want is for him to be healthy.

Agnieszka's daughter, Bella, eight years old, photographed in 1953.

STEFANIA PODGORSKA BURZMINSKI

Helena and Stefania Podgorska.

Stefania Burzminski's face is unlined and her trim figure is enhanced by an erect carriage. A stationary bike takes up a corner of the living room of her spacious apartment in Brookline, Massachusetts, the downstairs of which also serves as her husband's office. Joe Burzminski is a dentist, one of three broth-ers among the thirteen Jews saved by Stefania. He doesn't participate in the interview because we hadn't been aware of his existence, and he phones repeatedly, asking Stefania to come back down to help in the office. But when we meet him on leaving, he is warm and friendly.

Over a year later, Gay returns to photograph the two of them together, and this time Stefania is warmer and slightly less angry. When Gay asks to see and copy additional wartime photographs, more of the story unfolds, including the root of her bitterness.

D o you think it's nice for me to go back and talk about the war? It was a terrible time, and I have to relive it every time I talk about it.

I was born in 1923, in a small village in Poland. I was the third youngest of nine children. I don't know my exact birth date because we all celebrated our birthdays on Easter. My father was forty and my mother was seventeen when they got married. Father taught us, when we fought with other chil-dren, "Fighting will bring nothing good. If you're friends and help each other, that will bring something good." But sometimes the mother of the Jew-ish children would say to them, "Don't play with the *goyim*."

Once I heard my father say to a man with *payes* [earlock curls], "Why do you wear the yarmulke and the long black coat? That is not religion. That's because you used to live in a hot climate where you needed head protection. It announces to everyone that you're a Jew." The man answered, "My friends would give me trouble if I didn't do it. I don't like it either." I know that these are some of the things which caused pogroms, but I never saw a pogrom myself.

I moved to Przemysl when I was fourteen. It was a larger town and my sister was working there, so I thought I could get work, too. I worked in a bakery for one year and lived with my sister, and then I got a job working for a Jewish woman in a small shop. She was Mrs. Diamant, my husband's mother. I lived in her house, went to the market for her, and did the cleaning and cooking. She had four sons; one was a doctor, one went to dentistry school—that was my husband, Joe—and the other two went to gymnasium. After the Nazis came to Przemysl, the four sons went to live in Lvov because they thought it would be safer there since it was near Russia, and they asked me to take care of their parents. When things got worse the four sons returned. Then it was the time the Germans ordered the Jews to wear the David star, and then the Jews were put into the ghetto.

This confused me. Before the war everyone shopped and talked together and everything was fine. But then there was the segregation and the mark of the Jewish star, and that was confusing for me. One day I saw a Jewish boy on the street, about nine years old, and another boy came up to him and said, "You are a Jew!" and he hit him. A man, just an ordinary worker, saw it and said, "Why would you do that? He's a boy just like you. Look at his hands, his face. There's no difference. We have enemies now from another country who say there's a difference, but there isn't." So the boy who hit the Jewish boy looked sad and said, "Oh, all right, I'm sorry."

I listened to him and I came home and I looked at my hands and I said, "No, there is no difference." So, you see, I listened and I learned.

Joe's family had to go to the ghetto. I visited them and they gave me things to exchange for food. After the ghetto was closed I sneaked in through a hole in the fence. It seems like this should have frightened me, but it didn't.

One day I was in the ghetto and I went out through the hole. I looked and I didn't see anybody so I slipped through the hole and then I saw two Gestapo, each with his rifle pointing to my head. Then they moved their rifles and I looked at their faces and like two mummies, they didn't say a word. They hung their rifles on their shoulders and they left. I don't know what happened. Maybe something was in my eyes. What happened? Maybe some invisible man, some force repelled them. I don't know.

Then I decided to get into the ghetto a different way. I made friends with a Polish policeman. I told him to disappear for ten minutes while I go in the ghetto. He said, "Don't be longer than ten minutes." But sometimes I was fifteen minutes and he'd say, "Okay, five kisses." I'd say, "No, three kisses." We all talked together and laughed. This was also not so nice for them to have to stay there and guard. They had Jewish friends, too, and I saw them give bread. I even said once, "I saw you give bread, so if you tell the Gestapo on me, I'll tell on you."

Many things started to happen. My mother and one brother were taken to Germany to work, and that left my six-year-old sister alone. She went to neighbors, but she wanted to come live with me. She begged and begged me until I had to say "yes." It was getting worse in Przemysl, too. There were signs all over the city which said, "Whoever helps Jews will be punished by death."

The ghetto got smaller and smaller. The parents were taken along with two of the brothers. One of them, my present husband, Joe, jumped from the train. He hid in the forest for a time, then he went to the house of someone who was too afraid to keep him, so then he took a chance and came to my apartment. Poor Joe, he was filthy and his clothes were rags. I gave him my nightgown to wear. Joe cried all night, and my sister laughed at him in my nightgown. I explained to my sister who Joe was, that he was a Jew, that Germans wanted to kill him, and that we had to help him.

Whenever my friends came to visit, I hid him under the bed. Joe's brother, Henek, worked on a farm close to the city. I went there to tell him that Joe was safe with me. That night his brother's fiancée, Danuta, showed up at my place. She didn't look Jewish so she could be open, but it was still a dangerous thing to do. After a few days, Henek was sent back to the ghetto. I am still angry with him for what he did next: he sent some stranger, just a street man, with a note telling Danuta to come back to him in the ghetto. This was so dangerous because we didn't know who this man was and it was just an open note. He could be going straight to the Gestapo. So Danuta and Joe said they wouldn't risk my life like that, that they would go back into the ghetto. I went with them, and as soon as I saw his brother I really told him what a miserable coward he had been. He could have come himself, at night, but he was too afraid. So he risked all our lives.

Joe came every two or three days to bring me things to sell for food, and to pick up the food I had for him. Then Joe said to me, "Maybe you'll take a bigger apartment and you'll hide me and a few more Jews." I didn't like the idea, but I decided I would do it anyway.

I thought, "How can I find an apartment? I don't know where to look." So I started walking all around the town, and I went to one area where the Jews used to live, and it was ghostly. Windows and doors had been taken away and used for firewood. Even the floors were gone. We could have taken a place with no floor, but we had to have windows and doors. I didn't know where to go. Just then—you will laugh, maybe not even believe me—but a voice said to me, "Go farther and you will see two women with brooms. Ask them where you can find an apartment. Go." The voice was strong, a woman's voice. So I went to the next block and I saw the two women with brooms. They looked nice, so I asked them if they knew of an apartment. They said, "Yes, go to this place and you will see an empty cottage." They told me the janitor's name, and when I went there, there was a cottage with two rooms and a kitchen and an attic. It was a good apartment. It didn't have electricity, and the bathroom was an outhouse, but it was okay. I just bought a big can with a cover, and they did their business and I emptied it at night. In three days the apartment was ready. My sister and I worked so hard to clean it up, and then Joe moved in.

Then everyone was crying for help. One woman threatened to denounce us if I didn't take her in. She heard about me from Joe's brother in the ghetto. Her children came to me and cried, "I don't want to die." I didn't know what to do. I saw dead here, dead there. "So all right," I said. "Stay with me. We'll try here." Then John Dorlich, the mailman, came to ask me to hide him. He used to take things to and from the ghetto for me, so he knew where I lived. When he came to ask for help, could I refuse? Then came Mr. Shylenger and his daughter, Judy. Then Manek Hirsch and his wife, Sally. One day I went into the ghetto and I told Henek and Danuta that they must come with me. But Henek said, "Why should I go live in a bunker? Here I have my own apartment and fresh air whenever I want." I told him I had heard that the ghetto would soon be finished. During the war my ears were very long and my eyes were very wide. But still Henek refused. I went back home and Joe begged me, "Stefushka"—most of them called me Stefushka—"please, you must find some way to make him come." I went back into the ghetto and somehow I convinced him. Only two weeks later the ghetto was empty.

Soon I had thirteen Jews with me, and we lived there for two winters. It was a hard life, always dangerous. I couldn't bring any of my friends to my house. Once a boy became very attached to me and he would come over for one or two hours at a time. I had to figure out some way to make him mad at me or to scare him so he would stop coming. I liked him very much. He was good and handsome, and if I hadn't had my thirteen . . . So I went to the studio of a photographer friend of mine, and I asked her to give me a picture of a German in his uniform. She found one of a very handsome one, and I took it home and put it on my wall. The next time my friend came over to my apartment he saw the picture and asked, "Well, what is that?" I said, "That is my new boy friend. I am dating him and I will stay with him." He couldn't believe it. He said his heart was broken. I wanted to cry, really, because I loved him. But I had to help my thirteen. I had to save them. I wanted to tell him. But my mind told me not to tell him. He just said, "You and an SS man?" He couldn't believe it. And then he finally left.

One day a German hospital was set up in a building across the street from me. The Germans started to take over all the apartments in the area. They came to my apartment and said I must be out in two hours. I thought, *Where can all thirteen of us go in only two hours?* My thirteen people told me to run away and they would stay and fight the Germans. They say they would not die without a fight. My neighbors told me to run away, but I wouldn't. They all said I was crazy. I started to pray. A woman's voice spoke to me again; it was as clear as your voice. She says, "No one will take this apartment from you. Just send the people up to the attic and tell them to be quiet. Then open all the windows and doors," the voice told me, "and start to clean and be quiet and sing and have your sister sing, too." Of course, they all thought we all would die. I did what the voice told me. The SS man came back and said, "It's good you didn't prepare to move because we only need one room, so you can stay in the other room." And do you know what? They stayed there for seven months with thirteen Jews over their heads!

I think this proves that if you have to do something, you will do it. But if you say, maybe yes, maybe no, then you might not. Some people are old at seventeen, and some are young at seventy. I never regretted what I did. Some people are ugly and miserable, but that's human character.

After the war the Jews still stayed in my apartment for a few days more until they could find a place to live. One day I was fixing lunch because they all came home to eat, but Joe didn't come at two o'clock when he was supposed to. By three o'clock I was worried about him because some people still weren't so nice to Jews, so I went to the market to look for him. I didn't find him but I saw Manek Hirsch and Janek Dorlich, and I asked if they had seen Joe. They said, "No, but don't worry, he's all right." I turned to go and when I was about five yards from them I heard them laughing. I turned to see what was funny and Manek was saying, "Now that the war is over, Joe doesn't need his *goyka* anymore."

At that minute I felt so bad, my heart felt like it was being squeezed. It wasn't that I was in love with Joe and wanted to marry him. I absolutely did not, but it hurt me that they said that about me after they lived in my house for two years. After I walked away, I heard someone say that a Jew had been killed. Violent things were still happening. I was afraid it was Joe.

I went home and at six o'clock Joe finally came home. He was so happy. He had found an apartment for us with water and electricity, and all the things we didn't have before, and he had found furniture, and then when he looked at his watch he couldn't believe how late it was.

About six months later, Joe and I were walking in the park and we saw Manek. He said to me, "Stefushka, are you angry with me? I know you must be." I said, "No, I am not angry. We all make mistakes." He said, "But I said an ugly thing about you that I should not have said. After all, you saved my life. Without you I would not even be alive right now." Then he put his head on my shoulder, and Joe took a picture.

It wasn't long after the war that Joe asked me to marry him. I said, "Go marry a Jewish girl. I'm Catholic and I don't want to marry a Jew." He said, "You fought for my life, now I want to fight for your life."

I fought it, because I had plenty of boy friends, and I hadn't been able to go out with any of them during the war. But Joe asked me and asked me and, well, he agreed to change religions. He became Catholic.

We stayed in Poland until we went to live in Israel for two years in 1958. I didn't like Israel at all, so we came to the United States. We have one daughter and one son, and they live in California.

I wrote my memoirs. I wrote how I struggled to bring food, and everything I did. But publishers refuse. They say they have enough Holocaust books. I said that it is not Holocaust. This is not killing. That was killing but this is saving. You have to show people a good example. Who will teach people humanity if they see only killing and nothing else?

I talked with a rabbi and he said he will give my name to other synagogues. I told him I don't need him to hang my name saying I was good. My story should go to schools to teach youngsters because when there's chaos in a country, it's very easy to be a bad boy or bad girl. But to be good is very difficult. To think separately and not like other people tell you to think, but everyone doesn't think like I do.

I'm sure my book will be published. It took me seven years to write it, and then more years to have it corrected. I had to sit with a person from Boston University and pay her seventeen dollars an hour because my spelling and grammar is so bad that she couldn't know what I wrote. And when I came to the part where the SS man came to live in my apartment, I thought, *I can't finish it.* I went and I lay on the floor and I prayed like I prayed that other time, and this time a man's voice, deep and strong, said to me, "This is no time to pray. You must get up and go finish your writing." And he picked me up and I felt like a feather as I sat down in my chair.

A Christian person helped me to go back to Poland for a visit. A Christian helped me. But where are the Jews? I didn't help Christians. But sometimes I think the Jews are sleeping. I have a medal from Yad Vashem, but I have no tree planted there because I have no money to go to Israel. I think Israel should pay for me to go there to plant the tree.

I work hard all day now, helping Joe in his dentist's practice. Every time I have to do an interview like this, it brings back all the memories and I can't sleep for some nights.

Joe Burzminski's brother, Henek, with his wife, Danuta, and their child, after the war.

Stefania with Sally Hirsch.

Front row: Stefania's sister, Helena, Stefania, and Judy Shylenger, 1947. Judy's father is behind her, next to his wife. Joe Burzminski is on left.

Stefania with Manek Hirsch, after the war. Joe
took these photos as Manek apologized to
Stefania for calling her a *goyka*.

ALEX AND MELA ROSLAN

David and Jacob with Alex Roslan, 1945.

Living in Warsaw, Alex and Mela Roslan were the parents of two young children when the ghetto was created. We interviewed them on the patio outside their comfortable garden apartment in Clearwater, Florida. The sunshine and emerald lawn do not soften Alex's emotional, dramatic story of how he and Mela took the three wealthy Gutgelt brothers, ranging in age from three to eight, into their small Warsaw apartment and kept them hidden for four years. The story is not entirely a happy one; the Roslans' son dies in the Warsaw uprising and the middle Gutgelt boy dies of scarlet fever. Although Mela was full partner with Alex in the rescue, she says little, listening to his every detail, speaking only when he cannot remember something. After two hours he makes us sandwiches, shows us photographs, and continues to share with us what seems to be the most important time of his life.

Today sometimes I don't sleep. I think about how it was and why it happened like that. My story was not possible. My friends said it wasn't possible. "There's not enough food for your own children and certainly not enough for three boys, too." But I thought the war would be finished in two or three months. I wasn't a religious fanatic but I believed all the time that somebody watched over me.

Mela and I were both born in a small village twelve kilometers from Bialystok, in Poland. Mela was born in 1907, and I was born two years later, in a house just two blocks from hers. There were maybe 100 people in the village, but Bialystok had about 200,000 people. Mela's father was a shoemaker in Bialystok, and he made a study of Jewish people. He spoke Yiddish like he was a Jew.

My grandmother was very religious, but not my grandfather. My father went to the army when I was six years old and never came back, but he had taught me to fight for what I thought was right, and that those who follow like sheep are led to the slaughter. My mother was thirty-six years old then, and she married a man twenty-four years old. He married her because she had a good farm, but he was not a farmer. I was twelve years old and they thought I was a troublemaker because I was always angry that he was letting our farm run down. So they sent me away to Bialystok to become a shoemaker, but I left there and didn't come home. I went to another village and got a job, and three years later I went back home. But I still argued with my mother that her husband isn't a good farmer, so I sold my part of the farm and left for good. I cried when I had to leave home. [Alex cries here, remembering the pain of leaving his mother.]

Mela and I were married in 1928, and we moved to Bialystok. Our son, Yurek, was born in 1931, and our daughter, Mary, in 1934. I was working as a textile merchant and I made a lot of money. Most of my customers were Jews, but overnight, when they put the Jews in the ghetto, I lost everything. I wanted to know what had happened to my friends and customers because I heard terrible stories. I got a Jewish friend to bring me into the ghetto through a tunnel. It was dangerous for a non-Jew to be inside the ghetto so I wore a Jewish star. I saw so many children, hungry and starving. They were so skinny. The parents had been taken to "farms," but we knew what that meant. The children came around and begged for a penny to buy some bread. My Jewish friend stopped me. He said it wouldn't make any difference, that they would die anyway. I came home and told Mela we had to do something. We decided to go to Warsaw.

You know, I think I cry a lot. I cried when I had to leave my mother's house; I cried when I went into the ghetto and the little children clamored after me and kissed my coat and cried for help. I'm very sensitive to the poor. My grandmother was like that.

We got a nice one-room apartment in Warsaw, and one day I met my friend Stanley, from the next village from mine. Stanley told me he had been working for the Gutgelt family before the war; he was the chauffeur for the grandfather. He said they were wonderful people, and very rich, but now they are in the ghetto. He told me that the grandfather had taken the three sons and the son-in-law, and almost all the money, and they had left Warsaw, hoping to get to Palestine. They believed the Germans were only interested in killing men, and thought they would leave the women and children alone. So in the ghetto were the grandmother, two aunts named Janke and Devora, and three children, Jacob, Sholom, and David. The boys' mother had died when David was born. I told Stanley he should help them, that he should take the children, but he says it's too hard. I say maybe they can come to my house. I have two children, no one will notice one more. Stanley made a connection with Janke and told her that he was considering taking the children, but before anything could happen, Stanley had to go one day to the next town to buy some tobacco to sell. He asked me to go with him, but something told me not to go. The next day I found out that Stanley and all the people he was with were killed.

A couple of days later a man dressed like a German civilian knocked on my door. He was looking for Stanley, and I told him what had happened. He cried out, "Oh, now everything is finished." I asked him what he meant, and he said, "Do you know Janke?" This man was Dr. Kowalski, the brother-in-law of Janke's husband. His real name was Avraham Galer, but Kowalski was the name on his fake I.D. I told him I knew Stanley was making plans, and he asks me if I will take one boy. I tell him I will try.

I met with Janke at my house. She explained that she doesn't have any money, and that she would like to give me some of the family's real-estate holdings. I tell her, "This is still war. If after the war you can pay me, maybe, okay." She asks me, "How do I know I can trust you? I don't know you." I say, "Trust me." She cries and kisses me. I want to take her and the rest of the family, but they want to stay in the ghetto until after Passover. So two days later I meet her and take Jacob.

Jacob told Janke goodbye and right away I told him, "Jacob, from now on you're not Jacob anymore. You look just like my brother's son. Your name is now Genek. I will make you two promises right now. No matter how bad things get, we will live through it. And you will remain Jewish." I don't know how I could promise him that, but I did.

Jacob was about nine or ten years old, and so smart and clever. I told him he had to stay in his room and not look out the window. We had to be careful that the neighbors shouldn't see him. Our children liked him so much. We always divided everything fairly between all four children. I tried to make sure that the children didn't understand they were strange because Janke had told me, "Try to make sure Jacob doesn't know he's different. Try to make sure that he doesn't know what danger is. If there is danger, don't talk about it."

We built a false floor in the kitchen cupboard; Jacob was skinny so he could fit in. But about two weeks later the Gestapo came because a neighbor thought she had seen Jacob. They looked everywhere, but they didn't find him. Then one day that same SS man came again, but that time my brother-in-law was visiting and he knew this man. Jacob was hiding under the sink, and we started giving the Nazi whiskey. They drank and they ate so much, and my brother-in-law convinced him his sister would never hide a Jew, so we escaped that time. But I knew I had to go looking for another apartment.

I found a nice big apartment in a quiet neighborhood. I put Jacob inside the couch, and that's how we moved across town, right under the noses of the Germans. A couple of days later Dr. Kowalski came to see me and he says, "Mr.

RESCUERS

Roslan, I want to bring you another boy. He's in a place now where he has to stay in the attic laying down all the time. He's so skinny and sickly."

So I asked my wife what she thinks. We talked. But I said, "Mela, if they catch us for one, it's the same if we have two." So Sholom came, and we changed his name to Orish. He was so hungry, but so sweet. I think he was here only two months when my Mary and Yurek, and Jacob got scarlet fever. The doctor said it is very bad. Yurek was in the hospital and he gave Mela half his medicine every night for Jacob. Then Sholom got sick, and he was too weak. Mary, Yurek, and Jacob got well, but Sholom was too sick. Dr. Kowalski came every day, but then he didn't come for a few days. One night in the middle of the night I went to Sholom and he says he feels so bad. He says, "I would feel better if you would hold me." I picked him up, and he died in my arms. We buried him in the basement, sitting up, because someone told me that was the way to bury a Jew.

Then Jacob got sick again and he had to have an operation. My brother-in-law knew a doctor who had a clinic and would do the surgery, but I had to find 10,000 zlotys. This wasn't so much money but if you had none it was too much money. I decided to go out and sell our nice big apartment and get a smaller one, and I did it. Somebody watched over me. I got 60,000 zlotys, but when I told Mela I sold the apartment she cried and cried. She said, "Orish died, Genek will die, and now we don't even have an apartment." I said, "Mela, don't worry, I bought a one-room apartment and I'll make more money so we can get a bigger one soon. Don't worry."

The next day I bandaged Jacob's head and took him to the hospital on a horse. His operation was a success, and everyone cried. Then David came to us. He was about four or five, and so cute, so cute. He had been at my brother-in-law's but it didn't work out, so we took him.

I had to keep doing everything I could think of to make money. I did a lot of tricks, but Mela, she had her tricks, too. When we moved she knew the Gestapo was looking for me so she took all my clothes to a friend's house so she could say I was gone for good. I was arrested near the end of the war, and Mela came every day to a different gate with money for me to use to buy my way out. We never would have survived without Mela. I was in jail for six weeks and Mela took care of everything, of the children and of getting me out. Until that time I was worried because she was always weak. But from that time when she had to do it on her own, she was strong. I know I couldn't have done it by myself.

Then came the Warsaw Uprising, when everyone thought the Soviet troops were just outside the city and about to liberate us. Our son, Yurek, was killed on the street by a Nazi sniper. He told Jacob that he was helping the Partisans, but he never told us that. It was a terrible time.

As I said, I thought the war would be finished in two or three months.

We got the underground paper and it seemed good. But '43, '44, beginning of '45 were very tough years. You know it was terrible that the boys' aunts and grandmother wouldn't come with us, too. Three weeks after we took Jacob, the ghetto was liquidated and they went to Auschwitz.

So after the war we went to Berlin looking for Jacob and David's father. We found out they made it to Palestine, so we all wanted to go. But the British wouldn't let us go, only the boys. It was so hard to say goodbye to them. They had been with us for four and a half years, and two and a half of these had been so hard. So, in 1947, I had fine suits made for them, and they left.

Mela and I and our daughter, Mary, came to the United States. We wrote letters, so many letters, to David and Jacob, but we didn't get answers. I couldn't believe it! I said, "They were like our own sons, and they forget us!" But I think their father threw all our letters away. Then one day in about 1963, we were living in Queens and got a phone call from someone in Forest Hills, New York. He asked me, "Do you have a relative in Israel?" I was so excited I said, "Yes, Gutgelt, but they changed their names to Gilat." He said, "Maybe we'll see you tomorrow." And the next day, Jacob came. He was in California, studying for his Ph.D. at Berkeley. We talked and talked; he remembers everything.

He told us some old secrets: "You know, Uncle, when I went to you, Grandma said, 'Don't become a goy. Die with us together, because you will eat pork with the goys and die. Do not speak like the goy; they're different. Don't try to speak perfect.'" You know, the Jews spoke Polish with a Yiddish accent. "But then my Aunt Janke said, 'Jacob, don't listen to Grandma. She's old-fashioned.' And that was that."

A few years later David came to study for his doctorate, and we saw him. At first I didn't recognize him. I hadn't seen him in so long, and he had a beard. But then he threw his arms around me. That was in 1980. David is a mathematician and Jacob is a nuclear scientist. We didn't all get together again until 1981. Jacob and David asked us to come to Israel for Passover, and to get our medal from Yad Vashem, and plant a tree there. I was so happy that I had been able to keep my promise to Jacob.

It was a wonderful reunion. We all had Passover together, even the boys' father. We were there for twenty-one days. David took us to the north and Jacob took us to the south. I know Israel better than Poland. Israel is like a magnet. I like Israel ten times better than the United States.

You know, Rabbi Schulweis has been wonderful to me. People like him in the world maybe you can count on one hand. He invited us to California, he sent us a ticket to go to Israel, he got us $2,000 from Buffalo, and now we get $250 every month from the foundation in New York.

The man who owns this building where we live gives us our apartment for less rent. So I told my wife—this is no joke—"Schulweis is like mother and this man is like father. I have two support people." I play the lottery, and if I win I will split it with Schulweis. Sometimes he calls me and I cry when I hear his voice on the phone.

When I look back on those times I think that maybe there were so many anti-Semites in Poland because there were so many Jews who did well in business and the Poles were jealous. In this country, if something happens, nobody helps you. In my building everybody has a car, but many people are very old and can't drive anymore, but no one gives them a ride to go shopping. I never go shopping without taking someone with me.

The best years of my life were when I first came to Warsaw and became successful in business. And then I was so happy when I brought Jacob home. No one was paying me, but I felt I was doing something great. I thought, *If I survive this, I've done something great.*

Aunt Janke with Jacob, David, and Sholom Gutgelt, in the ghetto, 1942.

Jacob in 1940.

Jacob in 1940.

Jacob and David in the suits Alex and Mela had made for them, with their father, just after the boys' arrival in Israel, 1947.

Alex during the interview, 1988.

IRENE GUT OPDYKE

**Irene Gut Opdyke as a
nursing student at the age
of eighteen.**

*Irene Gut Opdyke was once an interior decorator, and her stylish townhouse
in Yorba Linda, California, reflects her attention to her surroundings. Her
attractive appearance, Zsa Zsa Gabor accent, and sense of drama make her a
popular and compelling speaker about the Holocaust. Furthermore, her story
of rescue in Warsaw would make a riveting film, and the ending, where she
saved all eighteen Jews, is one of success. Unlike some rescuers, she is not shy
about talking about her deeds, feeling it is her responsibility to tell children
about the price of hate and the courage of a few.*

I never talked about what I did during the war, and I still wouldn't be talking about it if I hadn't read that article in the newspaper in the early seventies that said the Holocaust didn't happen. That started my Polish blood
cooking and I said, "Well, I have to speak out." And that's the reason I put
my time, my heart, and my feelings into speaking about the war, to so many
groups, all over the country.

If someone would say I had to go back to do the same things to be able to
help people, I'd do it without question. I was born in Poland in 1922. My family was Catholic, and my mother was such a strong influence. She didn't have
much schooling but she was smart, and she never turned away anyone from
her doorstep. We five girls were always bringing in animals which needed help!

I always wanted to be a nurse, to help people. In 1939, when I was seventeen years old, I was 200 miles from home in central Poland in nursing
school. I joined the Polish army with other nurses. One night we were cap-

tured by Russian soldiers who had also invaded Poland. Three soldiers beat me and the next thing I knew I was on a truck to a Russian hospital. Later I was able to return to Poland on an exchange between Russia and Germany, and I began working in a munitions factory that supplied the German front. One day, because of the fumes, I fainted at the feet of a German major. I looked German because I was blond and blue-eyed, but when he asked me if I was German, I said I wasn't. He liked that I was honest, so he gave me a job serving meals to German officers.

One day I was running an errand and I found myself in the ghetto. There were all kinds of people, pregnant women, children screaming "Mama, Mama!" Then I saw a woman with an infant in her arms. With one movement of his hand, the SS man pulled the baby away and threw it to the ground. I could not understand. But later on I realized that God gave us free will to be good or bad. So I asked God for forgiveness and said if the opportunity arrived I would help these people.

Soon the German major was transferred to another Polish town, Ternapol, and he took me with him. There I met twelve Jewish people who worked in the Gestapo laundry room. We became friends. They had been people of means, businessmen and women, a medical student, a lawyer, a nurse. I thought we were all the same: we were all in trouble and the Germans were our enemy. One night when I was serving dinner I heard the German officers making plans to raid the ghetto. The Gestapo man said, "Herr Major, Thursday or Friday don't count on the Jews to come to work." I realized that was the day they would make the raid on the barracks. I started getting the message to the laundry room and they got the word around. Many people were able to escape.

Then one day I heard them making plans to wipe out the whole ghetto in Ternapol, and I knew this meant my friends in the laundry room would be killed. I didn't know what to do. Then a miracle happened. About three days later the major called me and said, "I have a villa and I want you to be my housekeeper." I knew then that could be the place I would hide the Jews.

They stayed in the attic when the major was downstairs and in the cellar when he was upstairs. Then we had a real problem to deal with. One couple was expecting a baby and we knew the child would cry and make too much noise. They said they'd give up the child, but I said, "Ida, please, wait, don't do anything. We'll see—you'll be free." Then one day in the middle of the marketplace they hanged a Polish couple with their two children and a Jewish couple with their little child. They forced us to stay and watch to see what happened because there were signs on every street corner saying they would do that if you helped Jews. I ran home to my friends. Three of my friends were in the kitchen and I was so shaken that I forgot to leave my key in the lock after I locked the door. This was the way I would protect us from the major coming in unexpectedly. We were talking and all of a sudden the major was standing in the kitchen. He was looking from one to another, trembling, and he didn't say one word. He went to his library.

I ran out after him and he was screaming at me, "I trusted you. How could you do this behind my back, in my own house? How? Why?" I cried. I said, "They are my friends." I was kissing his hands, holding his knees. He said, "No! I am an old man. I have to go now. I'll give you my decision when I return." After a few hours he returned and said he'd help me for a price. He would keep my secret but I had to be his—and willingly, too. There was no other way. I won't tell you it was easy. Not only because he was an old man, but I still remembered the Russians raping me. But I knew there were twelve lives depending on me. This went on for several months until the Germans started losing.

Everyone left the villa and we fled into the forest. We had a radio and we knew the front was coming. Then the Russians came and we were all free. And on May 4, 1944, a little boy was born in freedom! That was my payment for whatever hell I went through—seeing that little boy. His name was Roman Heller.

After the war I joined the Polish Partisans hoping to find my family, but instead I was arrested by the Russians. Some Jewish friends helped me escape to Germany. I went to a Jewish displaced-persons camp with all the Jews who were homeless after the war. From that camp they helped people settle in Allied countries. A group of men came from the United Nations to the camp. One was American and he interviewed me and said America would be proud to have me. So I came here in 1949, to the United States, alone. I didn't know a word of English. I worked in a union shop, sewing, and then I met a Polish-Jewish woman who gave me a job, and we've been friends ever since. One day in New York, a man came up to me on the street and he said, "Irene, you don't remember me, but you brought me shoes in the forest." There were so many of these people I didn't really know.

So for five years I lived alone, working. Then one day I went to the U.N. to have lunch in the cafeteria and I started talking with a man and all of a sudden I realized he was the man who had interviewed me. At that time he was a widower. He asked me to go out to dinner, six weeks later we were married, and two years later, in 1957, we had a daughter.

I was busy working as an interior designer, and raising my daughter, and traveling a lot with my husband, but I still missed my family in Poland. One night my husband brought a woman home for dinner and she stayed for fourteen years. Her name was Vivian Bennett. She was a wonderful lady and she was going blind. She had no one to help her through eye surgery so I told her she could stay with me. She spent her last $1,500 on the surgery, and from then on I took care of her. She was so intelligent; there wasn't a subject she didn't know about. She was like my mother. I learned so much from her. Yes, she needed me, but I needed her, too. She helped me start my book. I never told her anything about what I did until I returned from Israel in 1982, and then she helped me write speeches. But she didn't finish the book. I could see at the end she was clinging to life so she could finish it. She was in such agony. Finally I told her, "Vivian, you don't owe me anything. Please, rest in peace." And she died that day. I still miss her.

But I always thought of my family in Poland. What had happened to them? In 1982 I was honored by Yad Vashem. I went to Israel and planted my tree on the Avenue of the Righteous. There was a lot of publicity, and my family in Poland found out that I was still alive. In 1985 I went back to Poland to see my sisters. We went to Auschwitz, and even after so many years there is still a smell of death. I never saw the ovens at Auschwitz. I was like a mother hen sitting on her eggs all during the war. But I was so ashamed for the human nation that genocide of this proportion could happen.

In 1975 I heard a neo-Nazi say that the Holocaust was a hoax, and I decided I had to start talking. I think another Holocaust could happen if we don't mingle together to try to understand one another and not be ignorant. It's my duty to tell the truth about what I saw. So for the last ten years I've been telling my experiences to many groups all over the country, and now I do it so much that I'm only at home about five days each month. My favorite groups are the children. They give me standing ovations, and then the big, macho boys come and give me a big hug and kiss. This is the most important thing for me now, to reach the young people. I tell them, "You can do what I did! Right now! Stand up when you hear name-calling, when you see skinheads. You are the future of the nation." I don't tell them what to do; I tell them I believe in them, that they can do it. They're the last generation that will hear firsthand accounts of the Holocaust. They are the future. We all have to reach out to know we're not alone in the world. You have to give not just money, but you must give of yourself.

Irene with some of the Jews who worked in the Gestapo laundry room.

Clara Bauer, Same Rosen, and Agie Marx with Irene in Cracow, 1947.

From left: Irene, Harry Marks (a tailor), and Pola Marks, 1946.

STEFAN RACZYNSKI
WITH SHOSHANA RACZYNSKI

Stefan Raczynski, 1940.

When we arrive at the dilapidated, two-room house of Stefan and Shoshana Raczynski, in Be'er Ya'akov near Tel Aviv, they introduce us to Danny Rogovsky, a young bus driver who isn't just paying the couple a social call. He has something to tell us. A year and a half before, he had seen a television program describing how the Christian rescuers had been ignored and mistreated in Israel. Danny explained the situation: "Because they weren't Jewish, they had never been entitled to the same rights as citizens, and now they were being denied their pensions. And really, these people are the 'flowers' of our society. We must remember them because a nation which doesn't honor its past will never have a future. These rescuers saved the people who helped build Israel. Here they are called 'The Righteous Among the Nations' and yet we have neglected them all these years. These people are not looking for publicity. They're modest. They're not talking about money, either. It's only about attention, you know, tenderness, not more than that."

Danny became connected with Shoshana, who had begun a lobbying network of the forty rescuers in Israel. To get them to meet one another, Danny took them on his bus to Herzlia for a picnic at the seashore; he has continued these outings as regular social occasions. "A lot of them are very old and sick," says Danny. "Now, since this was made public, they're finally getting an extra pension, an honor pension. But it's just been a year and it's a little late. They've been living in very, very terrible conditions."

STEFAN: I was born in 1921 on a farm near Vilna. I had a brother and two sisters, and my parents were farmers. Our family was Catholic, and deeply religious. You know, when six people live together they always help one another, and that's what it was like in my family. It was considered natural. In a nearby town lived 800 Jews. My father loved his fellow man; he would take me to meet the merchants, and he taught me to respect the Jews.

SHOSHANA: I was in the Vilna ghetto, and when I was twenty years old my parents were killed and I escaped. I got to a nearby village and started caring for an old woman who had tuberculosis, and Stefan found me there. When the woman died, Stefan's mother invited me, through Stefan, to come to their home, to stay there, and she even offered to be my mother. And once I was there I met a lot of Jews there.

STEFAN: Our farm was seven kilometers from a forest where the Nazis took all the Jews from the nearby town and shot them. They dumped their bodies into a ditch and covered it with sand. I remember seeing them falling like matches. Now some of the people at different stages managed to escape, and they knew about this farm and that the owners were good people who would take them in. Some who were shot but not killed managed to get out of the forest and make their way to the farm.

It was a natural thing to do, like when you see a cat on the street, hungry, you give it food. When the Jews started coming from the forests and they were hungry, we gave them food and we didn't think anything of it.

The first man to come was a friend of mine from that town who had escaped before they were taken to the forest. After that others came that I didn't know. We had one Jew who used to pray so loud that you could hear him two kilometers away. All the neighbors knew he was there. We had three religious Jews who would eat only dairy, and we had to bring in special plates for them. Altogether we took in about forty people, but we would have only between four and ten at any one time. The neighbor kept four people, and that neighbor was also giving the Jews a place to work besides a place to stay.

SHOSHANA: When I was there you had twenty people in your house, all at the same time. I think you're trying to be modest. I remember the time when Stefan's mother prepared for us a ceremonial dinner for Chanukah. She put colored carpets on the floor, and we all sat together, twenty Jews, and ate, drank, and sang in Polish, Yiddish, and Hebrew. And Stefan guarded in the yard so no stranger would approach the house.

Stefan's father would say to each Jew, "Everything that we own belongs to you as well." And Stefan himself slept in the barn with a few of the Jews hiding there.

STEFAN: We all felt terrible anxiety that cannot be described. We were scared that the Nazis would come and kill us and burn us. In fact, it was hard for us to believe that it would not happen. Everybody was scared the same way that today Israelis are frightened of terrorists in certain areas.

Every month about twenty or thirty soldiers came looking for Jews. They broke down doors, tore things apart, did everything to find Jews. I stood guard and when the Nazi soldiers approached I hid the Jews in the forest because we knew the Nazis were afraid to go more than a short distance into the forest. Each of the Jews had a special place to hide; some dug bunkers, or holes which they covered with trees and leaves. They spent a lot of time in these hiding places during the day.

People ask me why I didn't join the Polish Partisan Army, but everyone was fighting everyone else. I didn't want to take part in that. I only wanted to clean the land of the murderers. I was ready to do everything to remove from the neighborhood people who were denouncing the Jews to Lithuanians and Germans. Then a Lithuanian officer told my father he knew they were hiding Jews and we'd be killed if they were found. My father and the officer made a deal: he let the officer live in my uncle's house for free, and gave him all the vodka he wanted, in exchange for becoming our informer. He began telling us whenever the Germans were coming so we could make sure the Jews went to their hiding places. After that we all felt a little freer, and because we weren't so scared, the Germans didn't really search the house so much. They would just come to sit and drink. One day Germans came to the house and got drunk, but one who was sober found one of the Jews hiding in the barn. He shot him and arrested my father. My mother went to the Lithuanian officer and asked what we should do; this was a jail from which no one ever returned. We had to pay his way out of jail. When he came home he told us about how they had begun to torture him when the call came from the officer telling them to release him. After that they left us mostly alone. The police acted as if they were scared or ashamed, or maybe they thought we had only the one Jew here.

The world was crazy; it was like a comedy. Really, there was a lot of humor involved. It was like a game—we wouldn't let ourselves think that. . . .

SHOSHANA: We wouldn't agree with the world being run that way. And the harder the Germans worked, the harder we worked, because we couldn't accept that way of living.

STEFAN: It was like gambling for us. That's how we felt about it. Risking our lives. We only lived until tomorrow.

SHOSHANA: We ended up being addicted to it.

STEFAN: And we were all together.

SHOSHANA: After the war, Stefan and I married and lived in Vilna, which was then part of Russia. He was almost sent to Siberia, so we returned to

Poland under the repatriation laws which said that any Pole then living in Russia may return to Poland. In 1958, we began trying to get a visa to come to Israel, which was refused us because Stefan wasn't Jewish. It was only through my brother that we got permission to come.

STEFAN: Jews lived in Poland for one thousand years, but Poles were not allowed in Israel even for a peek. In my passport it said that I am a Jew, but later I hired a lawyer to rewrite it, because I didn't want to lie.

SHOSHANA: I was a Zionist so I had always wanted to come to Israel, and my only brother had already come here.

STEFAN: We finally came to Israel in 1960. All the rest of my family stayed in Poland. My father is now dead, and my mother is very old. Just before we left for Israel, my father told me, "In Israel, Jews will dote upon you for what you did for them during the war." I was convinced this would be so.

SHOSHANA: Stefan has changed a great deal since we came to Israel. They injured him; he felt humiliated and he became cynical. When our son went to the army he wanted to be a pilot. They told him, "Your father is a Polish Catholic; you won't be a pilot." Stefan went there and told them, "My son wants to be a pilot, and he will be one." Of course, today our son is already an ex-pilot, and we're very proud of him.

STEFAN: He's a great pilot. He gave a lot for Israel. Our daughter got married and lives here.

SHOSHANA: One day a few religious Jews were throwing stones at our house, screaming, "Go away, goy."

STEFAN: I was a Catholic and I will stay a Catholic. Things have been very hard for me here in Israel, but I don't regret what I did during the war. I was honored by Yad Vashem as one of the "Righteous," and in 1985 I was quoted in a newspaper as saying, "I will yet one day hang myself from the tree in the Avenue of the Righteous Among the Nations. Maybe this will move something." But I've become a little less angry now. I'm sure none of us who are living in Israel regret what we did. Now the country is trying to make amends for the way they wronged me.

Stefan and Shoshana Raczynski.

Shoshana with Adolf, Stefan's father, immediately after the war.

Shoshana (right) with her parents, Chava and Nissan, 1939.

The Yakob Gtoch (now Gal) family, who were hidden in the Raczynski home. This photo was taken when they arrived in Israel.

CZECHOSLOVAKIA

C zechoslovakia was created after World War I from the Austro-Hungarian territories of Bohemia, Moravia, and Slovakia. The 150,000 Jews of Bohemia and Moravia, largely German speakers, were part of the middle class. Anti-Semitism existed, of course, but had not yet become politicized. The new nation-state gave Jews full social and political freedom.

Slovakia, once part of Hungary, was poorer than Bohemia and Moravia, and the 200,000 Jews who lived there were largely excluded from the community. The assimilated Jews spoke Hungarian, but most of the others kept themselves apart by dressing differently and speaking only Yiddish. Both the churches and the political parties in Slovakia characterized Jews as the enemy.

Hitler invaded Czechoslovakia in March 1939, and the Czech Resistance produced brutal German retaliation. Political dissidents such as Antonín Kalina, a Communist, were arrested immediately. When the Nazi official and Hitler protégé Reinhard Heydrich was blown up by a Czech underground group, the Nazis retaliated by destroying the village of Lidice and killing all its male inhabitants.

Most resistance came from Bohemia-Moravia. To appeal to Slovak nationalist feelings and gain an ally, the Germans designated Slovakia as an "independent" state rather than an occupied territory. Slovakia resisted Hitler's policies much less, because at first the new "nation" benefited from increased trade. Slovakia was the first state to agree to deport its Jews.

The deportations of Jews to Poland began in 1939. Theresienstadt was built in 1941 as a model concentration camp. Libuse Fries describes her visits to her Jewish friend, Egon, when he took part in one of the earliest work details there. It was not a death camp, but most people sent there were deported to Auschwitz, Buchenwald, or Birkenau for extermination. In Slovakia, the Nazis designated five assembly points for deportation.

The Jewish community tried to stop the exodus by appealing to the authorities and to the Church, to no avail. From March to August 1942, 75 percent of the Jews were deported, primarily to Auschwitz. By the war's end, 11 percent, or approximately 35,000, Czech Jews survived, with 5,000 in hiding and the rest returning from deportation. When Hitler was defeated at Stalingrad in 1943, the Slovaks began to participate in the Resistance. Soviet troops entered Prague in April 1945.

ANTONIN KALINA
WITH JINDRICH FLUSSER

Tony Kalina just after the war.

*Despite the odor of decaying food left on the patio for a stray cat, Tony Kalina's
dacha a half-hour from Prague is charming and bursting with fecundity in middle summer. A fruit orchard, barrels of cherries fermenting into wine, and long
rows of vegetable plants reveal the labor of this eighty-six-year-old man, who
has been gardening since he could walk. He lives as a young boy or an old man,
with cheerful indifference to hygiene or order. Jindrich Flusser, a Jew who helped
Tony save 1,300 children in Buchenwald, has brought us to Tony. He translates
Tony's Czech and adds some of his own story, never taking his hand off Tony's
knee. He says Tony is the only hero he's ever touched.*

ANTONIN: I was born in Sebiche, in Moravia, in 1902, the second of
twelve children. My father was a shoemaker for the ballet, and my
mother took care of us at home. When there are twelve children, everyone
has to help, so I worked in the garden and learned to grow fruits and vegetables. I still do it now. These are grapes over your head, those are cherries
from that tree fermenting for liqueur, and my vegetable garden produces
plenty this time of year. Anyway, my parents were Social Democrats, and I
joined the Communist party in 1923. There was a Jewish community in our
town, but there wasn't much anti-Semitism.

Because I was a Communist the Nazis arrested me in 1939, just after
they invaded Czechoslovakia. I was taken as a political prisoner and
remained in concentration camps until Liberation in 1945. From the beginning I risked my life thousands of times to save adults and children. My
father was the kind of man who would have done the same thing. When I
was arrested in 1939, my father had a stroke, but he lived until 1948.

234

I was in many camps before Buchenwald. One of them was Dachau, and there I met another prisoner who was also a Communist, but from Germany. He had the duty of telling new prisoners the rules, but some of the Czech prisoners didn't understand what he was saying. This made him angry, so he took a chair and threw it at all the people. This was my first day in Dachau, and I couldn't believe my eyes. I stood up and jumped on him, put my hands around his neck, and said, "You are a Communist and you throw things on people who don't understand?" His answer was, "Just wait until you are in a camp for years, as I have been, and all you've learned from your parents and in school has been forgotten." I told him, "If we survive this time they will ask you how many people you have killed!" Well, it happened that this man and I both ended up in Buchenwald, and he was the head of the store. Whatever I needed for the children in my block, he got for me.

From the summer of 1944, I was the leader of Lager 66 in Buchenwald. The Nazis used the political prisoners to help run the camp. As the Russians advanced westward, camps to the east were being emptied and the prisoners began arriving on transports every day in Buchenwald. With each transport I noticed twenty to fifty children would arrive from all over Europe. I told the chief that I wanted to put the children all together, and he agreed. But the Czech National Committee disagreed because they thought that if the Jewish children were all together they would be easier to round up and send to the gas chambers. But I told them I would put a sign on the door which said there was typhus among them, and you know how afraid of diseases the Nazis were. I knew they wouldn't come near my lager.

Finally I had 1,300 children in my block. Twelve hundred were Jewish. I knew all the languages of the children except French, and someone told me that in another block there was a prisoner who read Flaubert. That was Dr. Flusser here, and I enlisted him to help me. First we moved children to Lager 66, and at the same time moved out the adults to make room for them. Then we had to build beds and get blankets and shoes. But how to do this for 1,300 children who ranged in age from three and a half to sixteen years old? This is where my German Communist friend from Dachau came in.

Flusser helped me make two lists of the children, one with their real names and one with all the Jewish names changed to Christian ones. I told the children that if anyone asked if they were Jewish, they had to tell them "No!" or I would hit them! We practiced this many times. I wanted to keep the children amused but it was impossible to teach them to laugh and play. They had seen their parents go to the gas chambers. Flusser taught them about the French Revolution, and I remember how they listened. It was very interesting for them because they could feel it.

This late in the war, 1944, after the bombardments had begun, there was no longer a central list of prisoners. If a prisoner was sentenced to death, for instance, it was possible to change his file for someone who was already dead. We did this often. One day I received a notice from the leader of prisoners that six of my students must immediately disappear. I knew this was a warning that they would be called to the gas chambers. The next morning I sent them to work with different names and numbers. I told these boys that their families would be notified that they were dead and that after the war it would be very difficult to get proper papers. After a few days, the SS called the numbers of those six. The commander called on me, took me to the SS, and asked me, "Where are the six Belgians?" I said, "Mine is a transport block. The people change each day. In my block, twenty people die every day. Give me the numbers and I will look in my book to see what happened to those six." I made up a different thing for each of their deaths—one pneumonia, one typhus, and so forth. In 1948 I went to a celebration of the liberation of the camp. They told me some men from Belgium were looking for me. There were five boys there—now men—big! They picked me up in the air and almost broke my ribs!

Toward the end, near Liberation, a high SS came to me and asked, "Where are your Jews?" I said, "I have no Jews here. The Jews I had yesterday went out on a transport. Here I have only children." One of my fellow prisoners asked how I could be so brave. I told him, "My life is past, but the children, they have their life before them." We saved all 1,300 boys. We all marched out of the camp after Liberation.

You know, I'm an optimist. If I would not be, I would not exist. I believe in people. It was necessary to believe in oneself, and those who lost that belief were lost. All the children lost their parents, their whole families. They are now old men. I wouldn't wish that same experience on those you write this book for, but that's why you should write the book.

After the war, when I saw my sister, she fainted. She was sure I was dead. She said she would go see our mother and slowly, slowly tell her I was alive.

JINDRICH FLUSSER: The war changed me. If I am an optimist, it's because of what I saw—that in the worst situation, people are able to surmount the bad if they stay together. Tony is the only hero I ever touched.

Antonín Kalina died in November 1990. He was still a Communist and lived in Prague.

"Some of the healthier of the liberated children."

The back of the photo reads, "To the outstanding memory of our dear unforgotten 'Chief of the Block,' Tony Kalina, we send this picture made of the children marching through the gate of Buchenwald camp to the SS barracks."

From Fience-Le Vesinet
12/12/1945

LIBUSE FRIES
WITH ERNA SEYKOROVA

**Libuse Fries (right) with Erna
Seykorova.**

*Because of Libuse, at least two people survived the Holocaust. They are her
husband, Egon, and his sister, Erna Seykorova, who is the translator and second voice in the interview. We weren't sure until an hour before that this
appointment would take place because Libuse lives in a town two hours from
Prague and, although she had told Erna she thought she could come in for the
weekend, she has no phone at home so we could never get confirmation. We
meet in our small hotel room, so this is the only interview which did not take
place in the rescuer's home. Libuse is gentle and compassionate, and she cries
when she tells us that no one has ever asked her about this time before today,
that no one has been interested.*

L IBUSE: I was born in a small village of only about 250 families, near
Prague, in 1923. My father had been wounded in World War I, so he was
an invalid when my mother married him. He had a funeral parlor and was a
tobacconist. We were three girls and two boys, but one of the boys died as a
child. I went to a Catholic school, but after World War II I left the Church. I
was educated to be modest and to love nature and all human beings. In sec-
ondary school when I was about fourteen, I had a good teacher who taught us
to be useful and good to others. He did more than his duty as a teacher; he
took us on excursions to visit important people. My father was interested in
culture, especially music, and he taught us these things.

Less than ten Jewish families lived in the village but there was a synagogue. The Jews were doctors or scientists, intelligent people. Before my parents married, my mother had worked as a maid for a Jewish family and she had a very good feeling about them. There were always normal relations between the Jews and the other families in our village.

In 1941 I got a job in a small electrical shop in Prague. Egon and about twenty other Jewish boys were working there with about four or five non-Jewish boys. We knew one another for about three months before all the Jews were transported to Theresienstadt. This was the first transport, and they took only young men to help build the camp. There were fifty of these boys and only about five or six survived. But we weren't worried yet; we thought the war would end soon. When Egon left he said, "It is not your duty to wait for me."

I thought it was inhuman to take young people from their families for no reason and take away their freedom and make them live in such bad conditions. I thought all the laws about the annihilation of Jews and Gypsies were very bad; it was hard to believe it would be possible to realize these plans.

At first Theresienstadt was not yet a prison, but the men were separated from us and not free. Egon lived in a house that no one was allowed to enter, but I did it anyway. I climbed over the wall and hid under the house in the evening until it was safe to go inside. Once a Czech policeman came in and shone a flashlight on us, but he left us alone. I went to see Egon during the day several times. We couldn't talk but I could see him going to and from work. Erna went with me one time. Then they lived in the new barracks and I would go to his window wearing a yellow star so I wouldn't be recognized.

I became friends with Erna through Egon, and I knew that what had happened to her brother was waiting for her also. In April 1942 she was ordered to go on a transport to Theresienstadt, but we discussed it and she decided not to go. I gave her my identity card without changing the photo, and I got a new one. We decided Erna should go to Vienna to work since it was dangerous for her to live in Prague under my name.

It was especially dangerous for me to go see Egon, but I continued to do it anyway. I took letters and packages, and sometimes people were shot if they were caught bringing a letter, but I was young and I hated the Nazis. This was my resistance.

Once I even got an identity card for Egon, but he refused to leave because he was afraid others would be punished for it.

ERNA: Before I went to Vienna we changed the photo and a few letters in the name on the identity card, but we did it in a primitive way. The Nazis sent word back to her village about it.

LIBUSE: They called me into the office and asked me if I had been in Vienna. I had to tell them that I didn't know who it was, that I had lost my card a few months before. I wired Erna in the code we had agreed on: "Charles is ill."

ERNA: I had been there only two months and I was working in a small restaurant. When I got the wire I knew something was wrong but I didn't know what to do. I went away for three weeks but I returned and still didn't know what to do. A man came into the restaurant and told me he had friends in Switzerland, so I thought he could help me escape. I didn't say I was Jewish, just that my parents had been arrested during martial law, and that was why I had escaped Prague. He promised to help, but in two hours he came with a policeman. I was arrested but I didn't give my real name. I was transported to a prison in Prague. Libuse had been arrested, too, so we met again in Gestapo headquarters. We laughed when we saw each other. They asked her why she had helped me and she said because we're friends. They said it wasn't possible to do this only for love.

LIBUSE: I was sentenced to nine months because I was only nineteen. If I had been twenty-one I would have been shot.

ERNA: I was "liberated" to Theresienstadt, then my journey continued to Auschwitz and Christianstaad.

LIBUSE: I was sent to another prison, and to make me afraid I was put in a death cell before I was released in 1943. When I returned, I contacted Egon again in Theresienstadt before he was sent to Auschwitz in December 1943. I continued to receive letters from him and from his parents, who were in Theresienstadt at this point. I always told their parents that Egon and Erna would return. I was young and optimistic.

ERNA: My parents were on the last transport to Auschwitz on October 28, 1944, and they died in the gas chambers. I left Auschwitz in July 1944 for Christianstaad, where I worked on con-struction. Two German guards who were our chiefs helped me send letters to Libuse, and she sent me packages in the German men's names. I even sent Egon a package to Auschwitz with some bread and a piece of garlic inside. This was already 1944, and they knew the war was lost.

During the hunger march in February 1945, I escaped with three others and returned to Prague. I contacted Libuse right away and we arranged to meet.

LIBUSE: My sister was a farmer so I had some food to give to Erna and a little money. I helped her find a place to live, and we met every day. Another friend helped me get an identity card with another name.

Egon returned on May 11, 1945, two days after Liberation. There were many dead people on his transport. He told me that he was able to survive because he knew I was waiting for him. He felt that his hatred for the Nazis and belief that they could be suppressed, that his time would end, also kept him alive.

ERNA: My brother and I were Communists during and since the war; we supported Dubcek. During the war you had to believe in something, an idea, the future, that someone was waiting for you, in God, in anything. Without belief it was the end.

LIBUSE: Egon and I lived together from the day he returned, and I cared for him. It took nearly a year to get all the documents in order for us to get married.

Egon and I lived in Prague in the beginning, but in the fifties because of anti-Semitism and our political beliefs we were forced to leave Prague and live in a small town. Egon was a journalist and wrote for the newspapers, but in 1969, because he was a Dubcek supporter, he was expelled from the party, lost his job, and wasn't allowed to publish anything. Now he works in a factory but he is heavily guarded.

We have two daughters and they each have two children. You are the first to be interested in this; no one else has asked since that time about the things I did then.

ERNA: There would be no way for her to receive a medal from Yad Vashem. We have no diplomatic relations with Israel. In fact, I once talked about the kibbutzim in the fifties and I was arrested for propagandizing for Israel.

Libuse Fries at her marriage to Egon. Erna is on the left.

HUNGARY

Without full cooperation and the Hungarian gendarmerie of 20,000 men,
Veesenmeyer, the German Ambassador, testified after the war, the deportations
would not have been possible.

—Helen Fein, *Accounting for Genocide*

At the turn of the century, Hungarian Jews enjoyed more freedom and acceptance than Jews in any other Eastern European country. The sciences, government, and the arts all welcomed them, and in Budapest, where half of Hungary's 450,000 Jews lived, exclusive clubs held no barriers to Jewish membership. Twenty-eight Jews were barons and 350 families belonged to the nobility. Jewish culture flourished and the Jewish community enriched Hungary by its presence.

Why this previously anti-Semitic country offered such freedom to its Jews was for an entirely pragmatic reason. Hungary had always been an amalgam of peoples: Slovaks, Serbs, Czechs, and Germans were among the eleven different cultures represented. Magyars, the original settlers of Hungary, made up only 51.4 percent of the people in 1900. To increase their slender majority, the Magyars eagerly claimed anyone who wanted to identify as Hungarian and who spoke its unique and difficult language. Jews, who had never been offered such an opportunity before, leaped into Hungarian society. Assimilation, intermarriage, and baptism were natural consequences, but many in the Jewish community preferred those problems to pogroms. Gustav Mikulai grew up with Jewish neighbors and friends in Budapest during this peaceful time. The music school he attended had many Jewish professors and students.

After World War I, the Allies reduced Hungary to 40 percent of its previous size, eliminating most of its ethnic diversity. The Magyars made up 90 percent of the new Hungary, and the Jews were suddenly left in a dangerous climate of rising nationalism. Blamed for postwar economic problems and an unsuccessful Jewish-led Communist dictatorship, Jews found themselves once again the target of discrimination.

Hungary looked to Germany's rise and wanted an alliance that promised a Greater Hungary. In 1930 Hungary enacted anti-Jewish laws, defining the status of Jews and establishing quotas in the universities and certain professions. The next year, Jews could no longer work in the media or obtain trade licenses. The state took their land with minimal compensation. Hungary joined forces with the Nazis in 1939 in dismembering Czechoslovakia and taking some Slovakian territory as spoils. Hungary also took part in the invasions of

Romania, Yugoslavia, and the Soviet Union, each time increasing its borders. By now Greater Hungary contained 650,000 Jews.

Despite Hungary's early enthusiasm for the Third Reich, war losses caused Regent Miklós Horthy to doubt the wisdom of continuing to fight on the German side. In 1943, when Hitler asked Horthy to give Germany jurisdiction over Hungarian Jews, Horthy refused and would not yield until he knew what "resettlement" actually meant. "The Jews cannot be exterminated or beaten to death," he said. Jews from Austria and Poland found refuge in Hungary, where Jews did not have to wear the yellow star and were relatively free.

Hitler accused Hungary of no longer being an ally. By 1944, the Germans had lost patience with Hungary and wanted quick deportation of its nearly 750,000 Jews. In March, Horthy was called to Vienna, and agreed to allow the Nazis to deport 100,000 Jews. But before he returned to Budapest, Adolf Eichmann had invaded Hungary, replacing government positions with Hungarian Nazis and members of the Hungarian Fascist Arrow Cross. Eichmann divided Hungary into six sections, putting the Jews in ghettos to expedite deportations. To avoid resistance, the Germans told the Jews that they would not be harmed. Their property would be taken, but after the war they could do as they pleased. From one of these ghettos Malka Csizmadia was able to rescue twenty-five men. By July more than 437,000 Jews had been deported.

In the midst of this rapid destruction of Hungarian Jewry, the best-known and one of the most amazing stories of rescue took place. As news of Hungarian deportations reached the free world, the U.S. War Refugee Board began to look to neutral countries to help stop the deportations. Sweden offered Raoul Wallenberg as a special envoy to Hungary. With money from Jewish sources and diplomatic immunity, Wallenberg issued false Swedish passports, which he had designed himself. Belonging to another country restored rights to Jews, because Sweden demanded that their "citizens" not be deported. Every day Wallenberg went to the train station and saved hundreds with these passports, taking Jews to apartments in Budapest which were under Swedish protection. Gustav Mikulai received one of Wallenberg's visas for a Jewish family he was rescuing. They never met personally, however. Wallenberg managed to save more than 100,000 Jews before Eichmann fled the advancing Russians in January 1945. When Wallenberg asked the Russians to help in saving additional Jews, they arrested him. His fate is still unknown.

Raoul Wallenberg.

Despite the courageous position taken by Horthy against the Nazis, 70 percent of Greater Hungary's Jews were killed in only a few months, and most of those met their deaths in Auschwitz. Eichmann's force of eight men and forty soldiers succeeded without Hungary's full collaboration. After the war Eichmann said, "It was clear to me that I, as a German, could not demand the Jews from the Hungarians. We had had too much trouble with that in Denmark. So I left the entire matter to the Hungarian authorities."

MALKA CSIZMADIA

Malka Csizmadia, 1947.

Malka Csizmadia's front door has a peephole four feet off the ground. A shade over four and a half feet tall, she ushers us into a sunlit apartment in a low-cost housing project in Nahariyya, Israel. It is populated mostly by Moroccan Jews. She knows her neighbors well and they know her. They call her "the sun," and it's easy to see why.

She begins to answer our questions matter-of-factly. Then she talks non-stop for twenty minutes. She doesn't want to be interrupted because she is reliving that time, telling her story as if it were a movie, scene by scene. Her words, spoken in slow, carefully enunciated Hebrew, quickly transport us to Satoraljaujhelyen, where her family of women—she with her two sisters and mother—saved more than twenty-five Jewish men from a nearby work camp.

My mother always reached out to others and she taught all of us to do that, too. She especially helped old people; I think it's in our blood.

We heard about the Nazi occupation of other countries but we didn't think it would reach Hungary. But beginning in 1944, they began closing the schools—that's the first thing I remember; I could never finish school after that. Then they started to do things to Jews, like closing their shops, and rounding them up and putting them in ghettos. We would hear that a certain street was closed and we wouldn't know why—just that it was where Jews lived. I was only seventeen, and my sisters were twenty-one and fourteen.

I was born in 1927, in a small village, Satoraljaujhely, which went back and forth between Czechoslovakia and Hungary. We were Protestant, but simple people, not fanatic. I was the middle one of three sisters, and we lived with our mother because our father had left when I was very young. All my life we had Jewish friends.

We were living in an apartment building with eight other families, and one morning I woke up and saw a barbed-wire fence on the other side of our garden. They had put it there during the night. That day I walked around the neighborhood and saw an abandoned house; it was an image I'll never forget. There were things all over, food left on the table, spilled, a heater turned over on the floor, a little girl's dolls, and even dough left in a baking pan turning green with mold. Later I found out this was a house in the ghetto where children and old people had lived. The ghetto had been closed and the people were taken. I sat by the window and cried to think of how these people had had to leave their home and all their things. It's the clearest picture that still sticks in my mind and is always there. If a painter had been there, the painter could have captured the sadness of it. Whenever I think of it, I cry.

Later that day, I wanted to see what was on the other side of the barbed-wire fence, so I climbed a tree in our garden and spotted a man in civilian clothes but with a Hungarian army hat, standing outside over a big pot, cooking something. I asked him, "Who are you?" He answered, "I am a Jew, but it's very dangerous here. Who are you? What are you doing here?" I told him, "I live here, and I'm not afraid of you; I want to talk to you." I was seventeen, but because I was so small, I looked about thirteen, which was always to my advantage during the war. I kept talking to him from my place in the tree, and I even talked to the guard who was walking back and forth. He also asked me who I was and what I wanted. I told him I was just curious, and he told me, "It's too dangerous; I think you should leave." I climbed down, but when he was out of sight, I climbed back up again and asked the Jewish man if there was anything I could do to help him. He said, "You could take letters out for me." So this is how it began.

Anything he asked for, like newspapers, or paper and envelopes, we passed through the fence when no one was looking. He gave me his letters and I put my return address on them so the people could send their answers to me; then I gave them to him. I listened to the radio and kept him informed of the news about the war. I found out there were about three hundred men in this work camp—women and children had been taken to a different place—and Szarany, the man I was talking to, was the cook for the camp. These men were from all over Hungary, and they knew they would one day be deported to a death camp.

I didn't realize how dangerous it was until I began hearing stories about how people who were helping Jews were killed immediately or put into prison. But I continued even after I knew the dangers. And I didn't tell anyone about what I was doing. But one day Mother asked me, "Why are you spending so much time in the garden? You never used to like the garden." I didn't really answer her, but one day she saw me in the tree and asked what

I was doing up there. I told her, "Look across the fence; I'm looking at that man." Then I whispered to her, "Mother, don't you understand? These are Jews and I'm helping this man by passing his letters back and forth." Mother and I discussed it and she agreed to help them, too. She said, "Who knows what will happen tomorrow. It's the middle of a war and today we'll do what we can."

With my whole family helping, we became even more involved. We took other men's letters, which were mostly to relatives in Budapest, so they'd send return letters and packages. All of a sudden I was getting so much more mail that the postman became suspicious. Then we dug a hole under the fence so the men could come to our house and listen to the radio. We paid off the guard, and he was happy as long as they returned that night. One night when a Jewish man named Friedman was at our house, our village was under attack so we all had to go to the shelter. I told Friedman that he'd better leave, but it happened that one of the German officers in the shelter understood Hungarian.

The next day, Mother said we had to stop, that it was becoming too dangerous. But then this German called me into his office and said, "You're small in size, but not up here," pointing to his head. "War is terrible. I haven't seen my children for five years. You should keep helping people." He gave me cologne and cake. I asked if there was anything I could do for him, but he said, "No, nothing."

Sometimes the men's relatives came from Budapest to stay in our house. They brought false I.D.'s and visited them through the fence or in our house. I'd go to the store and buy cake and ice cream. When the clerk started asking me why I was buying so much ice cream, I told her it was someone's birthday, and then somebody else's. They never really suspected because I looked so young.

In late summer we knew the war would soon be over because the Russian army was advancing quickly. We were afraid they'd kill everyone or take them to a concentration camp in Germany. Szarany said he would not go, so we decided we'd make plans to hide as many as we could when the time came.

One day in mid-November, very early in the morning, Szarany came to me and my mother—he always called her "Mother"—and said that at 10 A.M. there would be a lineup and they'd all have to report for it because they were moving all the men out. We had plans to take as many men as we could to nearby farms where people had agreed to hide them in their wheat. The first man we took had such Jewish features that we had to dress him as a woman and put a bandage on his face as if he'd just had a tooth pulled, to hide his beard. Mother took him and I took Szarany. The plan was for

Mother to go first and I would come five minutes later, but by the time I got Szarany, Mother was nowhere in sight, so we had to make our way alone.

I found out later that she knew a way to go through the fields. The only way I knew was by the roads which were full of German and Hungarian soldiers. It was a very cold, rainy day, and Szarany had on a winter coat; his pockets were filled with cigarettes to give as bribes. He was so afraid that his teeth were chattering. I took his hand and gave him a cigarette, and tried to get him to relax. We decided to walk separately because it was safer. When a soldier stopped me to ask where I was going, I said, "To the village to get bread." I would distract them by giving them cigarettes so Szarany could sneak by. We finally reached the farm. My mother wasn't there yet, but she came in half an hour. My mother and I went back and forth bringing food, and my sister and mother brought about twenty more men; we just kept moving the men from hiding place to hiding place. We continued this for five weeks until the Russians liberated our area.

The Russians liberated Hungary on January 7, 1945, and all twenty-five of the young men came back to our apartment because they had nowhere else to go. Slowly they rented apartments and six months later my older sister married one of these men. Szarany said he'd never leave this family again. He married my younger sister and we all stayed in the same house. They had a son, and in 1949 Szarany wanted to come to Israel. He came first, then my sister and the baby. I wanted to be with them, and so did my mother, so we all followed him. We were real pioneers; Israel was a very difficult place in those days.

In 1950, I married a Jew from Morocco and we had one son. My older sister had converted to Judaism in Hungary; her husband is a religious Jew and they moved to Israel in 1955. They live in Akko, but Szarany and my younger sister live across the street here in Nahariyya; we're very close. Sometimes I talk with him about this time, but it's very painful. I told him I'd rather have a bullet in my head than do it again.

I live in this neighborhood full of Moroccan Jews, many of whom don't know anything about the Holocaust. Most of them don't know that I'm not Jewish, so they certainly don't know what I did during the war. I received the Yad Vashem medal in 1966. Neither of my sisters would accept the medal; they didn't want to talk about the war. They say they didn't do it for publicity or reward or money. But I was divorced in 1964, and in a very bad financial position, alone with a young child, and I wasn't well. My son had been born in 1954, by cesarean, and three days later I had a heart attack. I thought I would get some money if I got the medal, which wasn't the case. The International Jewish Congress started giving me a small amount of money in 1966, but things didn't really improve until the Israeli government recognized the needs of the Righteous last year and began giving us an honor pension. That was when I was able to buy furniture for my living room; before that I had only a cabinet and one chair.

My son had to have a formal conversion because I'm not Jewish, but even before that he was a Jew in every way. He's the vice president of a bank, he's married to a wonderful woman who's Moroccan, an English teacher, and they have three children.

I went to a kibbutz to tell the children about the war and what I did. Many reporters have visited me to hear my story. I do this because I believe in educating and teaching, especially the children, so it should never happen again. I'm sorry to come up against the Israeli youth attitude of not wanting to hear about the Holocaust anymore, but I keep my mind open about what everyone says.

I'm very idealistic. I love this country so much; you can be one people here. I often talk with soldiers to try to talk them out of leaving Israel. It's important to live here. I haven't had any problems not being Jewish. I've always identified with Jews, and from the very beginning I felt at home in Israel. I don't make a distinction between religions, but between people.

Poster advertisement for Gustav Mikulai's all-women orchestra, 1938–40.

GUSTAV MIKULAI

*Gustav Mikulai surprises us the first time we arrive at his apartment in Bonn.
He takes one look at our translator and announces he will not speak to her.
"You're German," he tells her. "I'm a Judeophile, and you cannot understand
anything, and, because you're not Jewish, you must be an anti-Semite." We
apologize to the translator, who assures us that because she is not an anti-
Semite, his accusations were not wounding. Mikulai tells us to return that
evening, when he will provide his own translator.*

*We arrive to meet Miriam, a beautiful sixteen-year-old girl, one of his vio-
lin students. Of course, she is Jewish. He is a different man, relaxed, charming,
and fully cooperative. After the interview he pours us sherry, all the while
beaming at his protégée.*

My whole life I have had three passions: music, women, and Jews. The
Jews were capable and everyone was envious; I understood that from
the beginning. I couldn't be anti-Semitic, first because I thought it would be
immoral, and second because I thought well enough of myself that I didn't
need to be envious of them.

I was born in 1905 in Budapest. My father was a stage technician at the
theater. He wasn't intellectual but he was clever and politically left, a Social
Democrat. My parents were Catholics, but not devout. We had many Jewish
neighbors who were friends of ours and we really didn't see any differences.

By the time I was ten years old, I knew I would be a violinist. It was my
father's idea because he saw that the musicians were better paid than others in
the theater. My mother taught me piano for about eight years. Just after World
War I, I started thinking about politics. There was a sort of offensive against
the right wing at that time, and I could see poverty and injustice all around me.
I was going through a period of general insecurity and curiosity. Friends influenced me to become a Social Democrat. So I learned about Marxism.

At sixteen I entered a private music school where one-third of my class was
Jewish. There were quite a few Jewish professors at this school because they
weren't allowed to teach at the university. The Jews appeared more intelligent
and talented than the rest of the students, and everyone was envious.

By the time I was twenty-five, I had been in love with about twenty-five
Jewish girls. In 1930 I got my music diploma and married a Jewish woman,
Clara Hirschman. She was a pianist, and very poor. I founded an orchestra
of fourteen women musicians, and all but three were Jewish. An all-female
orchestra was a great novelty at that time.

Hungary wasn't occupied until March 1944, but the minute the Nazis invaded, I hid my in-laws and my wife. I had money and I knew the city very well, so it wasn't difficult. I had false identity cards made for them and for myself because I had changed my name to avoid being arrested. I was in danger not because I was particularly important but because there were so many posters all over town with my name and picture on them, advertising the orchestra, and I was known to be a Social Democrat. I think I lived in twenty-four hideouts altogether.

All my friends knew that if they needed help for a Jew, I was the one to do it. The Jews called me the "Scarlet Pimpernel of Budapest." For the next eight months, my friend Donny and I were busy hiding all the Jews we could. The Germans put the Jews into one area in Budapest, and Donny and I walked up and down the streets of the ghetto, knocking on doors and handing out false papers to the Jews and giving them another place to live. I found during this time of the Holocaust that I could kill anyone who was suspicious to me. It was a terrible time for humanity.

Even though I was in many life-threatening situations, I was never afraid. I was frankly sort of drunk with my rebellion against the horrible injustice to the Jews. Donny and I would go into a camp where the Jews were being held just before deportation, and we would take some out and put them in hiding places. I'd like to tell you one of these stories.

There was one family related to my wife who were in a camp of about 9,000 Jews just outside Budapest. It was a very hot day in July 1944, and I went there to find these people. There were guards on horseback all over the place. There was no water in the camp, so they released about fifty people at a time to go to the well. I saw a young man from this family, so I threw down a note warning him that they would be sent to Auschwitz the next day and that I would be there to try to get them out. I had false documents ready for them.

The next day I went there, dressed in the same clothes as the prisoners. There were 9,000 prisoners, 200 guards on horses, and one commander. I found the old couple easily, because he was pushing a wheelbarrow, but they were too weak to go with me. But I found their daughter and son-in-law and their one-year-old child, and they were willing to try to escape. I just began walking with them. A forest bordered the train station, and as soon as we weren't being watched I took them out. We met my brother at a pub as we had planned, and he took them to his house. The next day I went to my mother's house and she told me that during the night the Gestapo had come and taken the family as well as my brother. The taxi driver who had taken my brother and the others just happened to be from the same village as the family, and he denounced them. The Hungarian Fascist party, the Arrow Cross, was very strong in Hungary and had many supporters.

It happened that my father knew about Raoul Wallenberg, and he sent a note to him to ask for help for this family and my brother. I never met Wallenberg, but he was able to get them all released. Today they live in Zurich, and the little girl is now married to a professor of medicine, and they have two daughters and live in Canada. The parents also had another child after the war, and they also have two children. So, even though 600,000 Jews were killed in Hungary, I helped preserve a small part of them. I think in all I was able to save at least fifty people, and maybe eighty or a hundred. I'm happy about the times I was able to rescue children who, now married and with children of their own, would not have had such a life without my help. It isn't just a matter of 6 million who were murdered. It's the children and grandchildren they would have had. All of these lives have been prevented.

After the war I was able to get out of Hungary because I was a good Communist. I formed another all-women's orchestra, and since the best place for an orchestra leader was Germany, I came here. At first I thought it was a mistake because of their history, but I've met some great people here.

I am abnormal in three respects: I'm never afraid, I don't really know what age means, and I don't care if a woman is sixteen or sixty—I like them all.

YUGOSLAVIA

Yugoslavia attempted to remain neutral when war broke out, but in March 1941, perhaps to avoid invasion, it joined the Tripartite Pact of Germany, Italy, and Japan. The next day the government was overthrown and declared itself neutral. Within a month, on Palm Sunday, Hitler invaded Yugoslavia and divided the country into Serbia and Croatia. The Germans ruled Orthodox Serbia, while Catholic Croatia became an Italian satellite. Despite its proximity to Italy, Anton Pavelic, leader of the Croat Fascist Ustase and newly appointed head of the province, wanted a closer alliance with Hitler. Both leaders shared an enthusiasm for genocide. Croatians had long been anti-Semitic, but most of their massacres had been aimed at Serbs, who were politically threatening to them, and at Gypsies. The Croats were unconflicted about Hitler's Jewish policy; within months of the invasion they murdered thousands of Jews.

More than 70,000 Jews lived in Yugoslavia in 1941, as well as 6,000 refugees from Poland, Germany, Austria, and Czechoslovakia. The vibrant Jewish community of Yugoslavia dated back to the fifteenth century, when the first Jews from Spain settled primarily in Belgrade. Without legal restrictions, Jews became part of the middle class in the largely agricultural country by selling goods to farmers, and experienced no anti-Semitism in Serbia.

When Hitler invaded Yugoslavia, thousands of Jews served in the army, making up a significant part of the high casualties. Within weeks the Germans had set up camps near Belgrade, first interning Jews and then shooting them. Despite the brutality of the Germans and the well-known danger of the Croatians, a few tried to help Jews. Mustafa Hardaga, a Muslim, was the landlord of a steel factory owned by Josef Cavilio, a Jew. In spite of posters warning citizens not to hide Jews, Hardaga sheltered Cavilio and his family for six weeks, until they could escape to Italy. Ivan Vranetic was just fifteen when he met a young Jewish man whose entire family had been killed and who was desperate. He was the first of many Jews Ivan hid.

By the end of 1942, the centuries-old Yugoslavian Jewish community had disappeared, with 30,000 dead or deported. Some 4,500 Jews joined Tito's Partisans. By 1944, 60,000 Yugoslavian Jews had been killed, at least 24,000 of them by "knife or hatchet or by torture, rape, epidemics, and starvation in Croatian camps," according to Helen Fein in *Accounting for Genocide*. The Croats had also slaughtered more than 28,000 Gypsies and 570,000 Serbs. Despite repeated reports to the Vatican of the massacres, the Pope never reprimanded the Ustase, and, in fact, commended Pavelic for ridding the state of abortion and pornography, two evils he claimed were practiced by Jews and Serbs.

IVAN VRANETIC
WITH ERNA MONTILIO AND ELLA SCHNITZER

Ivan Vranetic, 1946.

*The interview takes place at the home of Ivan Vranetic and Erna Montilio, one
of the people he rescued in his native Topusto. They live in a new apartment
in Holon, a suburb of Tel Aviv, near the home of Erna's daughter, Ella
Schnitzer, who is also present. Ivan was only seventeen when he helped many
Jews escape the Nazis. He has the persona of an adored son who had all the
family support he needed, as well as the freedom to do as he pleased. Erna is
more serious, even agitated, and talking about the war is more difficult for her.
Ella is totally loving and respectful of these two people, both of whom she con-
siders her parents. Ivan is warm, and generously offers to translate from Bulgarian at our next interview.*

IVAN: I was born in 1927 in Vrbas, but a year later our family moved to
Topusko on the border of Bosnia. My father had a general store and he
liked people no matter what religion they were. We were religious Catholics
and financially comfortable. My mother was a good woman. My sister was
four years younger, and we were brought up to love humankind.

At the beginning of the war the Germans occupied our town but they
didn't seem to be any more concerned with catching Jews than Catholics. Of
course, later they started looking for the Jews. In 1943, Topusko was liberated by the Partisans, but since the border was only about six kilometers
away, the Germans continued to come to our village looking for Jews and
Communists. My father was a member of the Partisan army.

ERNA: I lived with my family in Sarajevo. When the Germans occupied
in 1941, they took all the Jews and killed most of my family. I had managed

254

to get out with my baby daughter, Ella. We joined my mother and sister, who was twelve years old, in an area of Yugoslavia which wasn't too bad for Jews because it was regulated by the Italians. But when the Germans invaded this area they rounded up all the Jews and put us in a concentration camp on an island in the Adriatic Sea. There the conditions were very bad, not enough to eat, and we suffered quite a lot.

IVAN: I began hiding Jews in 1942. The first was a twenty-year-old man from Sarajevo who was hiding from the Germans and the Partisans because he didn't want to be drafted. His entire family had been killed, and he was weak and sick and he didn't want to be killed, too. He had no shoes, nothing, and when he started to tell me his story I had to help him. I think it must be in my upbringing, because I had seen people who were homeless and I had feelings in my heart that I had to help.

ERNA: In 1943 the Partisans liberated the camp and put us on boats and took us to the mainland. They left us on the beach and told us to escape, to hide from the Germans as best we could. Ella and I, my mother, and my sister stayed together and walked for five months, through forests and fields, until we reached Topusko, in August or September 1943. I looked around the village and I kept seeing other Jews I had known in the camp walking around. They looked so well that I asked what they were doing there. They all told me, "There's this young man here named Ivan, and he helps everybody. He gives us a place to stay, helps us find food . . . " And at that moment Ivan passed by on his bicycle. I said, "He's so young; he doesn't look like the kind of person who could help so many people." I was only twenty-two, but he was just seventeen.

IVAN: Erna asked me to find them a place. I had already found a place for three other women—it had no window, but it was a place to stay. I knew Erna was with her mother, her sister, and her two-year-old baby, and I didn't know what to do, so I offered them my home until I could find something else. My father was already away with the Partisans, and only my mother and sister were at home, so they stayed with me. Erna helped my mother cook and clean in exchange for food and a place to stay.

The German border was very near so they frequently came looking for Jews. Whenever I knew about it, I'd warn all the Jews I was hiding in farms and other villages, and they all went to hide in the forest for a few days. Sometimes they'd have to stay there for two weeks.

ERNA: When we were told to escape we had to move in minutes. We had no time to do or take anything.

IVAN: Yes, one time I didn't have time to give them directions about which way to go, and they started going the wrong way, toward the village occupied by the Germans. I asked people if they'd seen them and they told me, "Go that way," so I finally caught up with them just at the very edge of the forest, just before they were about to enter the occupied village. I brought them back into the forest and we stayed there all night and the next day. There was snow everywhere, and we had no food, and Ella didn't have shoes. The next day I took them to another village and left them with a family I knew. I knew many people in the area and they took the Jews into their homes as a personal favor to me.

You know, it's impossible to describe the conditions of life in those times. It's not something you can understand. Several times I had to escape with all the Jews I was hiding, and we would have to stay in the forest sometimes for as long as two weeks. No one had anything: they carried anything they had on their backs and they covered themselves with newspapers while they were in the forest. It was a frightening time. Every time we returned from the forest, I had to find new hiding places for the families because the Germans wrecked empty houses. It's difficult after forty years to tell you these stories, especially with the language barrier.

ELLA: Every time he sees me he thinks of this time because he looks at my feet.

IVAN: Many times when we ran to the forest I held Ella on my shoulders. [Ivan begins to cry as he recounts this story.] The winter of '43–'44 was very cold and we were running in snow up to my chest. As I carried her, I would rub her toes all the time because she didn't have shoes, but still two of her toes froze. At the end of the war I went with them to Sarajevo. One of Erna's brothers who had joined the Partisans was still alive. I wanted to stay with them; Erna and I wanted to marry, but her mother said I wasn't Jewish, and I was so much younger . . .

We became separated because my father had been injured in the war and I received a telegram that he was dying. I went home and when he died I had to stay to take care of my mother. Erna left with Ella for Israel in 1948. Erna's mother stayed in Sarajevo so I was able to keep in contact with them through her.

In January 1963 I came to Israel just to see the families I had saved. I stayed with Erna, and I liked it so much that I stayed nine months. I knew many people and they all treated me so nicely and wanted me to stay. I returned to Yugoslavia for a short time, but in 1964 I came back to stay.

ELLA: He's like a father to me. I have four children—in 1964, I had only two—and I think it was I who convinced Ivan to stay. He's the grandfather of my children. You know, he's not my father but he's not less than a father. I think maybe he's more.

IVAN: It's been good here for me. When I received my medal and planted my tree at Yad Vashem, twelve families gave testimony about what I did for them. And many people had already died.

I had a job cleaning in a bank but then I had two heart attacks and I couldn't work but four hours a day. But even though it's been hard, Erna has always been happy with what she's had.

ELLA: It's too bad they decided to raise the pensions for the Righteous so late because he worked very hard and they lived for a long time in a hole in Jaffa. They had no money, and when they began getting sick I decided I had to have my parents near me. My husband retired from the police and got some money and we used it to buy them this apartment. We're still paying for it, but it's okay because I have them nearby. He did everything for all of those families because his heart is so pure. He still does a lot for people in the area and for other Righteous.

ERNA: I planned not to be here today but Shoshana [the wife of another rescuer] told me Ivan needed me and I should be here.

IVAN: Every time I talk about this time, it's like opening up old scars.

ERNA: It's hard to have these pictures in my mind again.

IVAN: I'm glad you're doing this book because I want people to learn about the Righteous in general, about what they did. I see racism here in Israel, and I know it exists everywhere in the world. Here some people think Gentiles are bad, and they're the ones who need to know about us.

Erna Montilio, 1935.

BULGARIA

Bulgaria, the only Eastern European country without strong anti-Semitism, holds the honor of having saved its 48,000 Jews. Like the Netherlands, its Jewish population was small (1 percent) and a well-established Sephardic community. The Bulgarian government paid for its chief rabbi, who represented the Jews in government. Although Bulgarian Jews possessed full social and political freedom in the twentieth century, they didn't intermarry or assimilate as did Hungarian Jews. Instead they continued to educate their children in Jewish schools and chose a cordial separation from Bulgarian society.

Bulgaria was neutral at the outbreak of the war, but because the premier in 1940 was pro-German, anti-Jewish legislation was passed. The so-called Law for the Defense of the Nation required Jews to register, pay special taxes, and keep a curfew, and prevented them from serving in the military. Bulgaria became part of the Axis in 1941, allowing Hitler to march through Bulgaria to help Mussolini with Greece. In exchange, Hitler gave Bulgaria parts of Romania, Yugoslavia, and Greece, thus restoring its pre–World War I borders; yet Bulgaria itself never actively took part in any of these invasions.

Although 600,000 German troops occupied Bulgaria, the government remained Bulgarian; those who would collaborate met fierce opposition from the Orthodox clergy, professional organizations, and prominent politicians-in-exile. Therefore, the Law for the Defense of the Nation was weakly enforced. When the wearing of the yellow star became law, only a few Jews wore it. The Bulgarians rescinded the law after a year, telling the Germans it was because they didn't have enough sewing machines.

In 1943, the Bulgarian government agreed to deport 20,000 Jews, most of whom were living in the newly acquired parts of Yugoslavia and Greece. This was done covertly and far away from Bulgaria's original borders. But when the Germans began deporting native-born Bulgarian Jews, great protests erupted. Farmers threatened to lie on the train tracks that carried Jews to the east. The Church and the people kept the government from further compliance with the Germans.

King Boris of Bulgaria agreed to move Jews from the capital city, Sofia, where most Jews lived, and put them in internment camps in the country, but he would not allow further deportation. It was to one of these camps that Mihael Michaelov, a young accountant in Sofia, brought food and provisions to imprisoned Jews.

Boris knew that Germany was losing the war and he no longer needed to collaborate. Furthermore, if he wanted to save his kingdom, he had to save his Jews: the clergy, the intelligentsia, and the democratic parties demanded it. Bulgaria had always been proud of its relative absence of anti-Semitism. The German minister to Bulgaria understood the phenomenon in this way: "The Bulgarians had been living with people like Armenians, Greeks, and Gypsies for so long that they simply could not appreciate the Jewish problem."* Without their "appreciation" and therefore, cooperation, Germany could not deport Bulgaria's Jews. By September 1944 all anti-Jewish legislation had been rescinded. A few days later, when the Russians invaded Bulgaria, the Bulgarians asked for an armistice, and then declared war against Germany.

*Lucy Dawidowicz, *The War Against the Jews, 1933–1945.*

MIHAEL MICHAELOV

*After our interview with Ivan Vranetic, he takes us to Jaffa, to the home of his
friend, Mihael Michaelov, who, he explains, lives alone in poor conditions: "He
can't take care of himself very well." On arriving, we can see this is true, but
Mihael's warmth and loving manner soon overpower these impressions. Even
though the interview is difficult because Ivan must translate Mihael's Bulgarian to Hebrew, which is then translated into English for us, we develop a
strong bond with him. When we leave he gives us a bottle of perfume and a
small Bulgarian doll, and during the next two years, he never fails to answer
our letters with a warm note, written in French.*

I was born in 1911 in Sofia. My father was wealthy and very noble: if he
had two pairs of pants he would give one to someone else. My mother
was quiet, she taught school; I loved her very much. I saw her give money
to the poor in a way that they wouldn't know where it came from. We
didn't go to church and pray—we were Eastern Orthodox—but we felt God
in our hearts.

I was a bank clerk during the war, and still living at home. I heard on the
radio that people should turn in Jews and give all their property to the authorities, but instead I decided to hide property for the Jews. About fifty people
left their things with me, and I kept them in the basement, the attic, the
kitchen, wherever there was any room. More and more people found out
about me, that I was a person they could turn to for food or any kind of help
at all. I took food to Jews in the work camps. During the war you could get
only a few coupons but I bought them on the black market so I could get food
for the Jews. During that time people were eating cow's food, anything they
could get their hands on. I had to find food for children because they couldn't
eat that. The Fascists were like animals, or worse: I saw Germans beat the
Jews and break their bones.

If the Germans had known I had Jewish property and didn't turn it in
they'd have sent me to the work camp, too. Soldiers would stop me on the
street at night and tell me to go home because I looked Jewish. But I was
never afraid. My only fear was that if I was sent away my mother would die.

After the war when people came back from the camps, I gave them
clothing and food so they could reestablish themselves. One friend looked
half dead when he came to me; I kept him in my home for a year and nursed
him back to health. I helped during the war—beginning to end—and even
after. I don't know exactly why I helped. It's just the kind of person I am.

When I see someone who needs help I help them, and my whole family is like that. We visit people in old-age homes and hospitals.

My sister married one of the Jews I helped after he came back from the camp. She never converted, but she had children, and one son died. In Bulgaria the children were considered Jewish, so the child was buried in the Jewish cemetery. When my mother died, she had been so attached to this child that she wished to be buried in the Jewish cemetery with him, and she was.

I came to Israel in 1969, probably because I like Jews so much. I think all Jews should live in Israel. All my friends here and in Bulgaria are Jews. But life has been hard here because people in my neighborhood put swastikas on my door and tell me to go back to Bulgaria because I'm not Jewish. They scream at me, "Goy, Goy, Goy!" I think they found out I wasn't Jewish because of the television show about the Righteous. I don't advertise it, but I don't hide it, either, and I do put my cross inside my shirt when I go out, but why should I lie?

I was awarded the Yad Vashem medal in 1972. About twenty people gave the testimony for me. Some of the Jews in Bulgaria still write to me, but many have died. I have some contact with people I rescued who live here. One in particular, Mati Levi, helps me a lot; she gives me things I need. Ivan is like a brother to me, always calling to ask how I am.

All I want now is that the world should have peace and people should learn to love each other, to respect each other, and that children should respect their elders. I want peace because I know how awful war is. And I do think that what I did could serve as an example.

SOVIET UNION/UKRAINE

The systematic attempt to destroy all European Jewry—an attempt now known
as the Holocaust—began in the last week of June 1941, within hours of the Ger-
man invasion of the Soviet Union.

—Martin Gilbert, *The Holocaust*

During World War II, the Soviet Union took any side to protect itself and increase its power. On August 23, 1939, Russia signed a nonaggression pact with Germany, an unlikely alliance that terrified Polish Jews. The pact included a secret agreement between the parties to partition the country, much as Russia, Prussia, and Austria had done to Poland in the eighteenth century. This meant the USSR would not stop Germany from invading Poland. On September 1, Hitler's forces marched into Poland from the west, and the Soviet Union moved in and occupied the eastern half of the country.

In 1939, there were more than 3 million Jews in the Soviet Union, half in the Ukraine. Although the Jews had been given equal status after the October Revolution of 1917, Russia, and especially the Ukraine, had a long, violent history of anti-Semitism, with Jews excluded from every aspect of society. Most Jews spoke only Yiddish, dressed differently, and tried to avoid contact with their feared neighbors.

After the fall of Poland, roughly 300,000 Jews in the German-occupied zone fled into Russian Poland and Lithuania. Because of its neutrality at that time, the USSR became a safe haven to thousands of Jews. In Kovno, Lithuania, the Jews found a Dutch company, Philips, sensitive to their desperate circumstances. Philips offered them travel certificates that allowed them to enter Curaçao in the Dutch West Indies without visas. But getting there involved a complicated process. In the next step, they went to the Japanese vice consul, Sempo Sugihara, who issued transit visas that allowed them to enter Japan. When these Jews from Poland reached Tokyo, they went to the Polish ambassador, who gave them documents to travel to Canada. Sugihara was later honored at Yad Vashem for these rescue efforts.

The Soviet Union also unintentionally saved Jewish lives by sending as many as 10,000 Jewish political prisoners to slave-labor camps in the interior of the country. These included Polish Jews who refused to give up their Polish citizenship.

Germany invaded Russia on June 22, 1941. From the Baltic north to the Ukrainian south, minority nationalities initially cheered Hitler's troops as liberators from their Russian occupiers. Orest Zahajkewycz, his sister, Helena Melnyczuk, and Jean Kowalyk Berger were living in a region of the

Ukraine that was considered part of Poland prior to the Soviet and Nazi occupations. Orest remembered that the Ukrainians thought at first that Hitler would help them achieve their goal of an independent Ukraine. The Nazis regarded the Baltic peoples as racially acceptable, so they allowed them some autonomy. But because they considered the Ukrainians as Slavic inferiors, they quickly instituted an occupation as oppressive as Stalin's had been.

Before the invasion, no Jewish community had lost more than 2 or 3 percent of its population, and Western Europe had not yet lost any Jews. In Eastern Europe, Hitler found eager allies in his plan to exterminate the Jews. This willing population made it possible to carry out what Field Marshal Hermann Goering had called *die Endloesung*, the "Final Solution." Lithuanians and Ukrainians readily collaborated, with many participating in the mass killings: at Babi Yar, 33,000 Jews were shot in two days. Those Jews who escaped the bullets were placed in ghettoes in the larger cities such as Riga, Vilna, and Minsk. Amfian Gerasimov and his family brought food to the Jews in the Riga Ghetto. By the war's end, more than 1 million Russian Jews had been killed, with the Baltic states losing 90 percent of their quarter million Jews.

Unlike the Polish Partisans, who usually excluded and even killed Jews, the Russian Partisans welcomed the thousands who joined the Red Army after the German invasion. To be sure, there were cases of individual Russian soldiers shooting Jews in the forest, but the underground needed fighters and therefore protected Jews within its ranks. By January 1943, with the massive destruction of their forces at Stalingrad, the Germans knew they could not beat the Russians. As the Red Army drove the Nazis from Poland, the Baltic states, Yugoslavia, Hungary, Romania, and Czechoslovakia, Hitler's genocide of Eastern European Jews came to an end.

JEAN KOWALYK BERGER

Jean Kowalyk Berger, 1946.

We meet Jean Berger in a tidy suburban house in New Jersey, where she lives with her nephew and his family. She is treated more like a mother and grand-mother than an aunt. A childhood accident that broke her spine has left her a little over four feet tall and slightly lame, but she looks adorable in the red dress she has made. Her talent with needle and thread has bought this house and she is very proud of it. She smiles when she describes her house in the Ukraine, where she hid fourteen Jewish people in the attic. Proud of her Ukrainian heritage, she tells her story vividly and graphically, pointing out the window to show us where the Nazis walked. It is as though we are watching a movie.

I was born in Cracow in 1909. When I was nine years old my father inherited a farm, so we all moved, seven children along with mother and father, to Czortowiec. Father was a streetcar conductor, and then he was the mayor for three terms. Mother was a midwife; she had a diploma and everything. I was talented in school; I could pick up a mandolin and play and sing with no lessons. One day I heard my father say, "What she would be if she weren't crippled!" I didn't know what crippled meant. When he was dying he called the family together to say, "All of you should take care of poor Jean. The next day he died. I was eighteen years old. My brother sold the farm and moved my mother and the family to Vilna, but I took an apartment and stayed in Czortowiec. I became a seamstress and bought a lot to build a house.

People loved my father so they all helped me. I finished my house, and mother came to live with me. Then one brother moved in with his three children for a while until he rented his own house. When the Germans invaded, they brought young people to our village to build a work camp. I watched the cruelty to these people day after day.

There were two Jewish families in town, and the Germans took them both away. One was named Friedman, and I was friends with Blumka Friedman. I didn't grow up thinking there was any difference between us. One day before they were taken, I went to take Blumka a sandwich and a German shot me in the knee. There was a Jewish doctor who lived nearby and he helped me. Then he asked my mother if something happens to him, will we help save his life. I couldn't imagine how we'd save him. But my brother and my sister's husband came and built a false wall in my house. The only way to get behind it was to go into the attic and come down between the walls.

One night someone knocked on our door and I thought it was for my mother to be a midwife but it was Dr. Berger, on his knees, with his arms around my legs. So now I knew what this false wall was for. Then more people came during that night. In this group was a couple with a three-and-a-half-year-old baby. We knew we couldn't keep the child, so my mother took her to her brother in Cracow. Each month I went to Cracow to take food to her, and she would whisper, "Is my mother still alive?" I'd say, "Yes, she is, but I can't tell you where she is." She cried and cried and said, "I have so many names, but after the war my name will only be Beata Rosenzweig!"

If you could have seen my house you'd wonder how I could save so many people in this tiny little house. Everything was so difficult. For example, the toilet was outside so they couldn't go. They kept a pail in the attic, and every day I had to bring it down. And once when I carried this pail down, I spilled it all over my body. "My God," I cried, "how long will I suffer?" I was crying, my mother was crying. My mother said, "I'm sure I will never die a normal death, I'm sure I'll have to be killed." But God helped us, and we all survived.

You know, we took good care of those people. My mother treated them as if they were babies. At night, we closed the window shades and she bathed them in a big wooden barrel in the kitchen. After their bath, they had to go right back into the attic. Sometimes there were funny things that happened, too. One night Mama was busy and I had to bathe them, and you know, I'm small. I reached over to wash one of them, and I fell in the tub, and only my feet were sticking up.

During the night we had to wash their clothes and dry them right away because they didn't have extra ones. There were seven people hiding, and my mother had to iron them to make them dry. And it wasn't an electric iron, you know. She pressed them, and made them just so. Then the woman said, "Mama," everybody called her "Mama" as long as they were in our house,

"Mama, don't press our clothes. Give it to us like that." They didn't understand that she pressed them to make them dry. We had to keep the shades closed so nobody would see.

Once the Germans stopped at my house. I started playing mandolin to cover up any noise they were making. They sat and listened and then they said, "Thank you very much, little doll." Oh, how I was afraid. You don't know. Many times—every minute, every second—I was in such a dangerous spot. My house was on the main street and cars would go by—you know the expression, "On the thief the hat is burning." I was the one who had to hide my guilt. One time the Germans came to do a security check and one of the women from the hiding place was out helping to peel potatoes. I said, "Please don't go in that room. It's unfinished and the door is nailed shut." Luckily, he didn't go in.

The mother of Beata fell in love with another man who was also hiding in our attic. They fought all the time. They were supposed to be quiet. Once I went upstairs and I saw she had a black eye and the two men were bleeding. After the war she left the husband and the baby and went with the other man. I saw Beata and her mother in Tel Aviv three years ago. They were the only ones who ever tried to find me after the war. I think the others just didn't want to be bothered. But really, I don't mind because it's so awful for me to bring back these memories.

My entire family was involved in helping people. Once we heard about a group which was discovered in a bunker and the Germans threw in a grenade and killed everyone, both the Jews and the Christians. After that someone told me to tell my sister to stop hiding people because it will bring this kind of disaster and shame to them. But my nephew told me, "Auntie, don't listen to them. To save somebody's life is not a shame."

Finally, in 1945, the Germans were pushed out of my village by the Russians. The people had been in my house for almost two years. I was engaged to a nice tailor who finished school in Vienna. One night Dr. Berger—Solomon was his name—came over and told my mother, "That tailor isn't intelligent enough for her. I want to be her husband." So I married Berger, but soon I got an anonymous letter that said since I saved Jews, the same will happen to me as happened to them during the war. So I decided I had to leave.

I left my mother and my little house, and I didn't know where we were going. First we went to Czechoslovakia, and then my sister who lived in Canada sent me papers to come there. I left Berger because he wasn't so nice, but one day I got a letter from him asking me to help him once more. He wanted me to bring him to Canada. I was working in a factory and the boss was Jewish, from Czortowiec also, so he sponsored Berger as a tailor. When he came he got a job in a Toronto hospital and we stayed there for two years. Then Berger wanted to go to America, so I went with him, but it was a miserable life and we had to divorce. I had nowhere to go. I sat on a park bench next to a woman from Poland, a Jewish survivor, and she advised me to go to HIAS [the Hebrew Immigrant Aid Society] and tell them I had no place to live and I needed help. I went to HIAS and the woman interviewed me and I told her the situation. "I don't want to be paid. I never did anything for money, but I'm in such a terrible situation. I wish only to have a roof over my head. Please help me."

So she listened. She went to another room and left me and I waited. She came back and said, "I'm sorry to say, you know you are Christian and we help only Jewish people." This moment I never forgot. I thought I would jump from the window. Not because they didn't help me. But because I heard those words. I said to her, "You have the heart to say to me, when I was expecting to be killed every moment with all my family, when the people during the night came to me and asked me to help them, to save their lives—I didn't tell them, 'Go away because you are Jewish!' "

Finally I got a place to live on 148th Street, and I got a job sewing, on 72nd Street, and I walked every day to save the nickel subway fare. Everything is so different now because I live with my nephew in this nice house, but I help pay for it. I just hope to be strong enough to work to pay off the mortgage. I was so sad to leave my house over there. Now it's nothing, but for me in that time, it was a palace.

People ask me why I helped. When I saw people being molested, my religious heart whispered to me, "Don't kill. Love others as you love yourself." I came from a very religious family and I'm still religious. I believe God exists. I went back to my village in 1985, and my sister was in bed, lying on a bed of straw, paralyzed for two years—so poor, bed sores—and I couldn't give her anything.

I think it's unfair that many Jewish people are against Ukrainians. Many Ukrainians were killed for helping Jews. Blumka's brother survived because he was hidden in the barn of a Ukrainian friend of my brother's.

I was honored by Yad Vashem in 1985. One day a couple of years ago, one of my customers I do some sewing for was saying that her four children weren't in school that day because it was a Jewish holiday. And she told me, "They go to a special school today to learn about the Holocaust." I said, "If you want to know about the Holocaust, ask me. I'll tell you," and I showed her the letter from Yad Vashem. She asked me if she could take the letter and show it to her rabbi, and soon the rabbi came to see me with flowers in his hand from his congregation. They gave me an award. And then I got an award from the ADL. But I hope this is the end. I'm glad you are doing this book because there are many problems still going on today, around the world, and maybe someone will have to know how to help someone else.

Orest Zahajkewycz and Helena Melnyczuk

Orest Zahajkewycz, 1943.   Helena Melnyczuk, 1941.

Orest Zahajkewycz and his older sister, Helena Melnyczuk, sit in her comfortable, book-lined living room in Cranford, New Jersey, and recall their lives in Peremyshl, a town in the Ukraine, during World War II. Their affection and respect for each other is profound but not exclusive. They are part of the intelligentsia but without pretense, and they welcome us as honored guests. When we pull up to their house and begin to remove our photographic equipment from the car, they come out to help us.

HELENA: Orest and I were born in 1921 and 1925—he's younger—in Peremyshl, a town in the western part of the Ukraine.* We had a brother between us, and a little sister born in 1936. Our part of the Ukraine was under Polish occupation, and it was very oppressive. Peremyshl was a town whose population was equally divided into three parts: Polish, Ukrainian, and Jewish, with about 20,000 people living in each part.

We were Greek Catholics and went to church every week, but most of what we learned we learned by just watching our parents and how they were. Father taught Ukrainian and Polish literature in the high school. He was always trying to help somebody, especially his students. I remember he saved all the magazines to give to the students from peasant families. He cared more about knowledge than politics, and he tried to teach his students that only through knowledge could they do something for their country. They spoke of him with great respect.

---

*Peremyshel is in a border region of the Ukraine that has been claimed at different times by Austria-Hungary, Germany, Poland, and the Soviet Union. During the interwar period the town was considered part of Poland, its Polish spelling is Przemysl.

OREST: Our father was always getting invited to go to the synagogue for the main holidays, because he had many Jewish friends. As kids, we always wanted to go, too, to see how it looked.

HELENA: Our mother was also a teacher, but she stayed home with the children. Our brother had a friend who had a miserable stepmother, and Mother asked him to stay with us. He lived with us for some time before the war, and all through the war, too. A Jewish family named Shefler lived in our apartment building. There were four sons, and they all went to the Ukrainian high school, so father knew all of them very well. The Sheflers were very devoted parents; she was a typical Jewish mother, and her four sons were so obedient to her. They were observant Jews; I remember how they buried the silverware every year, and once I saw them kill a goose. Oh, those were happy times. Mr. Shefler would tell us wonderful stories. He gave me jam and taught me how to button my coat. Mrs. Shefler and our mother were very good friends.

In 1939 Peremyshl was divided in half. A part went under German occupation and part under Soviet occupation. On the Soviet side they arrested all the intelligentsia and sent them to Siberia. We were on that list in 1941, but we were saved when Germany took over the whole town. We were hoping the German occupation would be better than any of the others, but of course it wasn't.

OREST: In 1941 I started working in a German military supply factory which was filled with Jewish workers they brought in from the ghetto. I became friendly with many of the Jews, particularly with a doctor, Kuba Reinbach, a lawyer named Landesman, and an engineer named Citron. They all wanted to escape to Warsaw, because at that time it seemed like a safer place. We talked about all this, and they trusted me.

HELENA: The Jewish quarter had always been in the center of town. It was called "Jewish Town." It held about 20,000 people, and when the Germans came they just put barbed wire around it.

OREST: Some people tried to escape, but the people, till the end, somehow they didn't believe that anything could happen like that. So they thought if they would all work, it would end and they'd be spared. But little by little, they first took older people in freight trains and shipped them to wherever, no one knew where.

HELENA: But I don't even think Jews at that time thought about why they were taking people. No one knew anything.

OREST: People began building cement sleeves around the sewer lines and escaping through them. Cement became more precious than gold; they traded their diamonds for cement. They took the sewer lines from the ghetto into the woods where they would be met by the underground and taken to a safe place. Reinbach asked me to make contact for him with the underground, and while we waited for the plans to be made, he threw away his

---

armband and came to live with us. He had no fear. He stayed with us for three weeks and then he went with the underground as a fighter. This is how he survived.

Then I saw Citron walking around town with his two girl friends, without their armbands. Daredevils! They just weren't afraid. Then one day they disappeared, and I heard they had gone to Warsaw. They survived.

HELENA: People who weren't afraid survived more easily. But I don't think anyone could imagine such a horror—that one human being could do this to another.

OREST: See, at that time, people believed that only the Russians could do things like that. In 1933, during Stalin's reign, 7 to 10 million Ukrainians were starved to death. In the Ukraine, the breadbasket of Europe. So we thought when the Germans came it would be better, but then we found out they also wanted to annihilate us because we weren't part of their master race.

HELENA: When the Germans found out that people were escaping, they started asking questions. You know, if you are sinking, even a razor blade is good enough to hold onto. So some of the Jews even started turning in their own people because they thought they'd be spared.

OREST: But I began to find out what was happening. Clothing sent for the Germans working in the factory had a hole and a hard spot in it, so I knew people were being shot. Then Landesman told me he thought they must be killing Jews, and asked if there was any possibility of finding hiding places. This was very hard because Reinbach was already at our house. I don't know what finally happened to Landesman.

HELENA: One night two people came to our house. I woke and I heard strange voices in the room. Father was talking to somebody in Polish. I wondered to whom is he talking in Polish, to Christians, or what? And I saw there were two people sitting beside my father's bed, a man and a woman. I clearly, vividly remember how this man said in Polish, "Professor, I went to every friend's house, I knocked on every door, and asked them to take me and my wife in to hide for a few days. Everybody closed the door and refused. I didn't want to come to your house. I know you have a small child and that you work in the Ukrainian community and you have two other children, but you were our last hope." He was Dr. Koestler and his wife, and he had been my father's pupil. My father said, "Of course, you can stay." Dr. Koestler had friends in Warsaw and he only wanted to stay with us until they could get on the train. We bought the tickets for them and they left. They survived in Warsaw.

Then, one night in September 1943 I answered a knock at the door and Edek Shefler and his wife, Ada, were standing there. He was the Sheflers' youngest son. He asked for the keys to the cellar, and Orest took him down.

OREST: Then they told us what had happened: the Nazis were beginning to liquidate the ghetto. They were killing people and throwing the bodies onto trucks and, at night, they took them to the cemetery. The Sheflers had slipped into the truck with the corpses just after dark and escaped when they dumped the bodies. They had cleaned themselves up as well as they could and then came to our house. They stayed in the cellar for a few days. Since we had rabbits there it looked okay to take food down and bring buckets up. Then we built them a hiding place in our big pantry. They had room enough to sit and lie down.

HELENA: They slept there at night and went there in case of danger, but during the day they moved around freely in our house. Our mother had died in 1942. So it was just Father and us who took care of everything. We did have some fun, though. We danced and played cards every night.

OREST: Yes, but across the street from our house was the Ukrainian police station. The chief of police happened to be Edek's school friend and, of course, also a former student of Father's. One day he said to Father, "What's going on in your house? You'd better tell the kids to pull the shades down." Later he even tried to find another house for the Sheflers to live in, but we decided not to do it because it was too dangerous.

One day I was coming home from work and there were people lined up outside a house just three doors away from ours.

HELENA: What happened was that the Jewish people who were hiding there were careless. They were young, and they went out on the roof to get some air and someone from a nearby building saw them and reported them. The Nazis not only took the Jews but they also took the people who were hiding them. That felt like a close call, but everyone in our house survived.

The Russians came in July 1944, and we had to leave right away. We were afraid of being sent to Siberia since our father had been on the list of intelligentsia in 1941. First we went to Cracow, then to Prague, then to work in Vienna, and then to a DP camp in Germany until 1950.

OREST: The Sheflers stayed a few days after we left, and a priest we had talked to came by to bring them food. First they went to an uncle in Budapest and then they found us in the DP camp in Germany. Unfortunately, only one of Edek's brothers survived the war, and he was killed in a car accident in 1945. The other two had been married and lived in another town, and they did not survive.

HELENA: Edek's wife had a baby, Anna, in the camp, and they wanted us to go to Israel with them. She had a half sister in Tel Aviv. But I had met my husband during the war. He was a friend of Orest's and he stayed in our house for a few months. We married in the camp, and we all decided we wanted to come to the United States, including Father.

OREST: We're so glad to be in America. We went through so much, with the Germans and the Russians. It's a new life here. I wouldn't want to

---

describe the awful sights I saw there every day. You wouldn't want to know about those things. We've had a good life here. Helena's husband and I work in the brewery together.

HELENA: You know, there's a centuries-long feud going on between the Ukrainians and the Jews. We belong to a Ukrainian-Jewish Society, and they wanted to erect a monument in Jerusalem to commemorate the Jewish and Ukrainian victims of the Holocaust. We were asked to go to the ceremony as rescuers, and we did that at the same time we were honored by Yad Vashem in 1986.

OREST: We stayed with Edek and Ada, and their son and daughter and four grandchildren. It was wonderful. I have four children, too, and Helena has two. They're proud of us, and we're proud of them. We've tried to teach them to be human and always help others.

HELENA: I'll tell you, my brother has wonderful children, and, except for our father, I have never met such a good kind man as my brother. He helps everyone. He has a son, Taras, who has long hair and listens to impossible music, but he's also a wonderful human being.

OREST: I just know we have to forget the past and teach the children to be good Christians.

HELENA: Not just Christian, but good human beings. We have to teach our children to love one another, to be their brother's keeper. The truth is that the war didn't change human nature, and if that war didn't change people, what can?

Helena and Orest's father.

Ada and Edek Shefler with their baby in the DP camp, 1947.

AMFIAN GERASIMOV

Amfian Gerasimov is a holy man of his own invention. He was fourteen when the Communists overthrew the tsars in his native Riga, and ever since he has been searching for the God the Communists outlawed. His spare, immaculate apartment in Talpiot, a Jerusalem suburb, with its pictures of King David, could belong to a monk; he possesses the detachment of those who dwell in the life of the spirit. Speaking in Byelorussian, he resists answering questions directly, preferring instead to quote from the well-worn Bible that never leaves his hands. "Judaism and Christianity have one book and I live according to it," he says.

I was born in Riga in 1902. My mother was very religious; my father was a laborer and an alcoholic. Seven of their children before me had died because of him, so everyone was sure I would die, too. When I was fourteen I witnessed the Russian Revolution and I wondered why Communists hated religion, how atheism in the Soviet Union came to be. I was raised in the Russian Orthodox Church, but I soon began studying all faiths. I was searching for a religion that would give me the security I hadn't found in my family.

There were Jews in Riga, but I had no contact with them. The first contact I had was with Judaism, not with Jews. In 1925, when I began studying all religions, I learned about Judaism, too. I learned that both Judaism and Christianity have one book, the Bible, and I live according to it. In 1928 I married and had six children. I didn't really want to marry, but my mother had died and I didn't know how to cook. My wife was also seeking the truth. I read all the books about atheism and I didn't find the truth in them so I turned to religion.

The first Jew I met was my landlady, Mrs. Brill. She was a different class from my family. I was a poor mailman, but in 1941 the "rich" people were suddenly our equals and we had the chance to play a part in their lives. Mrs. Brill had disappeared from our building, which was on an island near Riga, but soon her two daughters, Lela and Dora, who each had a husband and two daughters, took the apartment above ours. So there were two families occupying the same space my family occupied one floor below. Life for me and my family was not easy; however, the lives of our new neighbors were much worse. My wife and I discovered that the Germans had evicted the Brill sisters and their families from the large apartments in which they had lived in the center of town.

In a few months the Germans ordered them to move into the suburb where they had congregated all the city's Jews into a ghetto of only six or seven small streets, an area of two square kilometers. When the families left, they asked us to keep a few suitcases from which they would want us to deliver packages to them from time to time. At first, before the barbed wire went up, my children delivered packages to them. Later I had to make complicated arrangements to meet them, always wearing my postman's uniform and carrying their packages in my pouch. These poor people were moved constantly, and when they could get messages to me, I met them wherever they told me.

For several months we had a plan to meet when they were returning to the ghetto, heavily guarded, after a day of work. One of the armed guards cooperated for a bribe by giving me a hand signal when the time was best. During these meetings we would hand them the packages, listen to the stories of daily experiences, exchange news between us, and determine what to bring in the next package. One tragic night the Nazis did not allow Dora Brill and her two daughters to return to the ghetto, but instead took them outside the city together with the old, the sick, and the children, and murdered them without mercy.

I continued to meet with Lela Brill and her husband, Asak Mizrah, and her two daughters until Asak was deported and executed. On one of these meetings I was stopped by the Germans for questioning. This was a frightening experience, but I managed to convince them that I was simply a postman delivering a package.

One of Lela's daughters, Evta, had married Gary Nis, whom I was soon to meet and hide in my home. By that time, my wife and our children had gone to the country for safety, and I was living at home alone. The front was nearing, and after only a few days, Gary was able to leave and join the approaching Russian army.

A few months after the Germans were expelled, I received a telegram from Evta in Poland, asking me about Gary's fate. When I wrote to say he was alive she quickly came to Riga and told me how she, her mother, Lela, and her sister, Avi, had been liberated from the Germans by the English. A short time later they all left for Haifa. I received letters from them, telling me that Gary had been killed in a work accident and Evta had remarried and moved to Canada. The letters stopped in 1950.

Many years later I started going to synagogue and decided to convert to Judaism. I had myself circumcised at the age of sixty-eight and managed to get an invitation to immigrate to Israel. But the Soviet Union wouldn't allow me to go without my wife, and she didn't want to go. The only way was for us to get a divorce. When I went before the judge, he said, "You already have white hair. It's already time for you to die, not to get divorced. What do you need a divorce for?" I told him, "I don't need a divorce; the government needs a divorce." I finally got it, and in 1975 I came to Israel, accompanied by one of my sons. When I arrived here, I found out that Lela lived in Tel

Aviv. I visited this elderly mother—she's my age— several times, and she was very glad to see me. She was sick and almost blind, but she had maintained herself well and was full of memories of the past. But discussions of a moral or spiritual topic did not interest her. When I told her that the suffering of the Jewish people was a consequence of their deviation from the morals of the Torah, she seemed bored and tended to fall asleep. I find this a typical response of Jews when I mention the cause of their suffering. In this way I think the prophecy of the prophet Jeremiah is being fulfilled [Jeremiah 6:10]: "Behold their ears are closed and they are not able to hear."

I began going to synagogue every day after I arrived in Israel because I wanted to be accepted, but apparently it wasn't enough. Many of the people did not like the ideas I expressed and they started asking me if I was Jewish or Russian, and if I believed in Jesus. I told them that I am Jewish and I do believe in Jesus, and they asked me why. I showed them the Old Testament, where it says that a Messiah will come and die for the sins of all people, and that's what Jesus did. Then I got threats on the telephone for three years, every night, until I finally notified the police and they were able to stop it.

I was awarded the Yad Vashem medal, and many people have asked me why I helped the Jews when the risk was so great. I answer them by quoting the Bible, the New Testament, John, Chapter 15: "There is no greater love than sacrificing your own soul for another's soul." And of course, this passage comes directly from the Old Testament, Proverbs, Chapter 24.

Lela's daughter Evta, with her husband, Gary, in Haifa, 1947.

Amfian Gerasimov with his wife and children, 1940. His son Gabriel (center) now lives in Israel—he helped to save the Jewish family in Riga.

Faces: An Afterword

Rabbi Harold M. Schulweis

M oses sought to see the face of God but he could not. Instead, he was placed on a rock near God and told, "And it shall come to pass while My glory passeth by that I will put thee in a cleft of the rock and I will cover thee with My hand until I have passed by. And I will take away My hand and thou shalt see My back but My face shall not be seen" (Exodus 33). God promised to make "all My goodness pass before you."

Gay Block and Malka Drucker sought to see the faces of the rescuers, the countenance of those who would not turn away from the sites of death pits and crematoria. They had eyes to see and ears to hear and noses to smell the smoke and stench of human slaughterhouses. They did more than observe. They protected the hunted with their lives, within their homes, sheltering the pursued who were not of their faith, neither kith nor kin. Often against a culture of contempt against Jews, against the threat of blackmailing informants, these Christian rescuers formed a clandestine conspiracy of goodness.

Look at their faces. Ordinary features. No radiant glow around their faces marks them off from the others who also saw and heard and smelled but did nothing. These ordinary faces of flesh and bones and lines, however, would not turn themselves into passive pillars of salt. They turned their bodies into hiding places. They unlocked doors, built false rooms, hid the pursued in cellars, sewers, barnyards; stole food for them, lied to the predators, forged passports, visas, baptismal certificates in peril of their lives and those of their children. They bound the wounds of the afflicted, fed them, healed them, disposed of their refuse.

In Hebrew there is no singular term for *face*. A face—*panim*—is always plural. There is more in these faces than meets the eye. Look at their faces and you see the traces of godliness, the lineaments of the likeness of divinity. If we cannot see God face-to-face, we can see the back of God's goodness in the moral courage of those who faced death and refused to cower.

It is my privilege to know Gay and Malka as friends. They were and are deeply committed to the work of the Jewish Foundation for Christian Rescuers of the Anti-Defamation League. That foundation is devoted to raising awareness of the moral heroism of individuals who even in the hell of Auschwitz did not betray their image. The foundation extends its hand to recognize the goodness of these non-Jewish rescuers and, where needed, to help support them with financial and medical aid so that they may live out their waning years with dignity. These tens of thousands of men and women sustain our belief that minorities are not friendless, abandoned, and alone. They teach us to stand with the threatened. They confirm with their bodies our conviction that there were and always are alternatives to passive complicity to evil. We who remember the sinister face of the torturers will not forget the benign countenance of goodness.

EPILOGUE

Malka Drucker

If you keep from rescuing those taken to death and those on the verge of being slain, will you say, "Behold, we did not know this?"

Proverbs 24:11–12

W hen a writer finishes a book, the work is over. We might get a few letters, but we soon move on to another project. Not so with *Rescuers*. Whether we spoke at a museum, college, high school, church, or synagogue, passionate responses told us that just as the rescuers had awakened us, so our work had awakened others. After a talk in Florida where we warned the audience not to make hatred a legacy of the Holocaust, an elderly Jewish man stood with his fists clenched and said to over two hundred people, "I fought in the war and I've always hated Germans. Tonight I feel different." An eleven year-old boy wrote, "The rescuers make me feel like a bystander." *Rescuers* is not only about Jews and the Holocaust, but about how to be better human beings. This new printing is testimony to the yearning we all feel for heroic role models.

The rescuers in this book, however, do more than inspire: they goad us. When they protested that they were not heroes, that they did only what a human being should do, they were not simply demonstrating humility. Rather, they were asking me to probe my definition of humanity. If I view rescuers as extraordinary, then I imply that compassion, empathy, and taking responsibility for each other is exceptional, and that indifference is normal. If I say that the rescuer is someone like Mother Teresa, I let myself off the hook. Who can be a saint? By making the rescuer larger than life as a hero, and by making the Nazi the devil, I exempt myself. I would never be a Nazi, but neither would I ever be a rescuer. This work taught me there were four parts to play in the war: perpetrator, victim, bystander, and rescuer. We still face these four choices. The rescuers not only raise the question: Could I have done what they did? They also force us to ask ourselves: What am I doing now?

There is urgency and fear in that question, because within it is a cry for purpose, for meaning in our lives. The rescuers may have suffered loss for their efforts, but their sacrifice was more than repaid: their youthful deeds transformed them into people they are proud to be. The rescuers made it clear that they did not intend goodness or heroism; the opportunity for rescue presented itself and they were listening. Perhaps our own time doesn't call for radical acts of altruism, and most of us probably don't possess the gift of courage, yet all of us can do more to care for those around us. By listening, watching, and responding to others, we can not only heal our world but help ourselves to understand why we are alive.

We receive letters from teachers who tell us that by including *Rescuers* in their classrooms they are introducing their students to moral courage. Other people tell us that they have begun to give an hour a week to a soup kitchen, a literacy project, or caring for the aged. Some say that the rescuers have made a difference closer to home: they practice patience and generosity as they listen and respond to their children, parents, and friends.

In a time when many believe that happiness comes from getting, the rescuers show us that the deepest joy comes from giving.

Appendix: Righteous Among the Nations
By Country and Ethnic Origin, January 1991*

The Netherlands	3,372	Estonia	1
Poland	3,268	Armenia	1
France	780	Denmark‡	11
Belgium	476	Bulgaria	11
Germany	251	England	10
Italy	142	Sweden	7
Hungary	160	Switzerland	13
Czechoslovakia	117	Norway§	3
Greece	117	Albania	3
Austria	69	Spain	3
Yugoslavia	76	Luxembourg	2
Romania	37	Brazil	1
USSR:		Portugal	1
Byelorussia		Japan	1
and Ukraine†	192	Turkey	1
Lithuania	156		
Latvia	13	**TOTAL**	**9,295**

*These figures represent only the material made available to Yad Vashem and are in no way to be construed as reflecting the number of Jews saved for each particular country; for example, more Jews were rescued in Belgium than in the Netherlands, yet we have seven times as many persons for the Netherlands as we do for Belgium.

† Includes ethnic Ukrainians living in Poland and Lithuania.

‡As a gesture for the rescue of the Jewish community in that country, the entire Danish nation was recognized.

§ In addition, members of the Norwegian underground active in the rescue of Jews were recognized without being named as per their request.

Source: Courtesy of Dr. Mordecai Paldiel, Director of the Department for the Righteous, Yad Vashem, Israel.

Select Bibliography

Bauer, Yehuda. *The Holocaust in Historical Perspective.* Seattle: University of Washington Press, 1982.

Bauer, Yehuda, and Keven, Nili. A *History of the Holocaust.* New York: Franklin Watts, 1982.

Belsie, L. "In the Darkness, Heroes are Found." *The Christian Science Monitor* July 31, 1989): 14-15.

Dawidowicz, Lucy. *The War Against the Jews, 1933-194S.* New York: Holt, Rinehart & Winston, 1975.

Dreisziger, N. F., ed. "Hungary and the Second World War." *Hungarian Studies Review* 10, no. 1 and 2 (1983).

Drucker, Malka. "What Do We Owe the Rescuers?" *Moment* (April 1988): 38-42.

Fein, Helen. *Accounting for Genocide: National Responses and Jewish Victimization During the Holocaust.* Chicago: University of Chicago Press, 1979

Fogelman, Eva. *The Rescuers: A Social/ Psychological Study of Altruistic Behavior During the Nazi Era.* Ph.D. dies., 1986.

Fogelman, Eva, and Wiener, V. L. "The Few, the Brave, the Noble." *Psychology Today* 19, no.8 (August 1985): 60-65.

Friedman, Philip. *Their Brothers' Keepers.* New York: Holocaust Library, 1978.

Gilbert, Martin. *The Holocaust: A History of the Jews of Europe During the Second World War,* I loft, Rinehart & Winston, 1985.

Gross, Leonard. *The Last Jews in Berlin.* New York: Simon & Schuster, 1982.

Hallie, Philip. *Lest Innocent Blood Be Shed: The Story of the Village of Le Chambon and How Goodness Happened There.* New York: Harper & Row, 1979.

Hellman, Peter. *Avenue of the Righteous.* New York: Atheneum Books, 1980.

Hilberg, Raul. *The Destruction of the European Jews.* Rev. ed., 3 vols. New York: Holmes & Meier, 1985.

Karski, Jan. *Story of a Secret State.* Boston: Houghton Mifflin, 1944.

Korczak, Janucz. *Ghetto Diary.* New York: Holocaust Library, 1978.

Langer, Lawrence. *Holocaust Testimonies: The Ruins of Memory.* New Haven: Yale University Press, 1991.

Levi, Primo. *The Drowned and the Saved.* New York: Summit Books, 1988.

von Maltzan, Maria. *Schlage die Trommel und furchte dich nicht* [Beat the Drum and Be Without Fright]. Berlin: Ullstein, 1989.

Mason, Henry. "Testing Human Bonds Within Nations: Jews in Occupied Netherlands." *Political Science Quarterly* 99, no. 2 (Summer 1984): 315-343.

Melnyczuk, Askold. "When Man Was Wolf to Man." *Bostonia* (May/June 1991).

Oliner, Samuel P., and Oliner, Pearl M. *The Altruistic Personality: Rescuers of Jews in Nazi Europe.* New York: The Free Press, 1988.

Paldiel, Mordecai. "The Altruism of the Righteous Gentiles." *Holocaust and Genocide Studies* 3, no. 2 (1988): 187-96.

Rittner, Carol, and Myers, Sandra. *The Courage to Care.* New York: New York University Press, 1986.

Schulweis, Harold M. "They Were Our Brothers' Keepers." *Moment* (May 1986): 47-50.

Schulweis, Harold M. "A Jewish Theology for Post-Holocaust Healing." *Midstream* (August/September 1987): 44-46.

Schulweis, Harold M. "Mastering Jewish Anger." *The Jewish Spectator* (Summer 1987): 34-37.

Stein, Andre. *Quiet Heroes: Dutch-Canadian Rescuers of Jews.* Toronto: Lester & Orpen Dennys, Ltd., 1988.

Tec, Nehama. *When Light Pierced the Darkness: Christian Rescue of Jews in Nazi-Occupied Poland.* New York: Oxford University Press, 1986.

Ten Boom, Corrie. *The Hiding Place.* London: Hodder and Stoughton, 1971.

Weapons of the Spirit. Film directed by Pierre Sauvage. Los Angeles: Friends of Le Chambon, 1989.

A Note from the Photographer

Gay Block

When I began this series of portraits I wasn't sure whether to use black and white or color so I shot both at the first thirty-five sessions. My initial preference had been the black and white, but when I studied the images, only the color seemed to represent what I had seen and felt during the sitting. Only after all the pictures had been made and I was working on selecting and printing did I discover the rationale for the color.

These people had told us stories of unbelievable heroism but they were all unassuming and modest. Therefore I did not need to add drama to their images, which is sometimes the effect of black-and-white portraits. On the contrary, I wanted the photographs to represent the rescuers with as much reality as possible, and black and white, with its qualities of abstraction, moved the images one step further away. Furthermore, although these are stories about the past, I wanted the photographs to be contemporary, to bring viewers into the present, so that they could relate to the rescuers as people living today whose acts of goodness and courage are timeless.

The interview/photo sessions lasted for two to three hours, and making the portrait was the last thing to be done. Often the rescuer could not understand why I wanted to take their picture, and I could understand this confusion: after a powerful and emotionally draining video interview, taking what seemed to them another picture felt superfluous and even frivolous. But they generously cooperated, and I often took no more than ten minutes to make the picture. We had developed a level of trust between us that translated into comfort and openness when they were once again in front of the camera. In their willingness to give me the picture I hoped for, these people collaborated in making the portraits what they are.

Malka wrote all the generated, original text in this book and I edited the interviews. I have learned that I am as fascinated with exactly what people say about themselves and their lives as I am with exactly how they look. To further meld these two interests I made a 54-minute videotape, "They Risked Their Lives: Rescuers of the Holocaust," compiled from the over 200 hours of video interviews.

Technically, in terms of the portraits, my camera was a Pentax 6 x 7, with VPS 220 film. Available natural light was almost always my light source.

About the Authors

As a portrait artist, GAY BLOCK has photographed many different groups of people since 1975. Her photographs have been exhibited internationally, and are owned by public institutions including the Museum of Modern Art, New York, and the Museum of Fine Arts, Houston. She is the recipient of National Endowment for the Arts Grants and other commissions. In 1986 her photographs of artists were published in Chronicle Books' *50 Texas Artists*. Formerly of Houston, she now lives in Santa Fe, New Mexico.

MALKA DRUCKER is the author of over fifteen books for children, including the award-winning Jewish Holiday Series (Holiday House), and *Frida Kahlo: Torment and Triumph in her Life and Art* (Bantam). Her latest titles include *A Family Treasury of Jewish Holidays* (Bantam), and *Jacob's Rescue* (Bantam), a children's novel based on the Roslan family profiled in this book. She is a student of Judaism and frequently speaks before groups of children and adults about the rescuers as role models of moral courage and compassion.